LAST ACTS

Last Acts

The Art of Dying
on the Early Modern Stage

Maggie Vinter

FORDHAM UNIVERSITY PRESS
New York 2019

Fordham University Press gratefully acknowledges financial assistance and support provided for the publication of this book by Case Western Reserve University.

Visit us online at www.fordhampress.com.

Library of Congress Cataloging-in-Publication Data available online at https://catalog.loc.gov.

Printed in the United States of America

21 20 19   5 4 3 2 1

First edition

for my parents,
Donna and Richard

CONTENTS

Introduction: The Art of Dying   1

1. Dying Badly: *Doctor Faustus* and the Parodic Drama
   of Blasphemy   31

2. Dying Politically: *Edward II* and the Ends
   of Dynastic Monarchy   54

3. Dying Representatively: *Richard II* and Mimetic Mortality   87

4. Dying Communally: *Volpone* and How to Get Rich Quick   120

   Epilogue: Afterlife   147

   Acknowledgments   169
   Notes   171
   Index   207

LAST ACTS

The Art of Dying

Dying on stage is an art. Viewed one way, it confirms the essentially illusory nature of dramatic representation; unless something goes horribly wrong, nobody is *actually* killed at the end of the tragedy. Viewed another way, though, it draws attention to the real kinetic efforts that underpin any representational performance. As an audience watches an actor imitate someone sliding from sensibility to insensibility to death, they are brought to consider her activity independently from the inactivity of the figure she is evoking. Even when the dying character stops moving, the actor works to play her, and in consequence the performance of death isolates and showcases dramatic action in its barest manifestation. In the theater, death is not something you suffer but something you do.

This book argues that in many plays from the late sixteenth and early seventeenth centuries, the representational questions raised by theatrical deaths intersect with broader theological, political, and economic debates about the human capacity for action in the face of mortality. Dramatic representations of dying resonate with philosophical and devotional traditions that strive to teach the art of dying well. As homiletic guides to holy death struggle to explain how a comatose or delirious person could make a good end, they offer dramatists powerful models for theorizing constrained and minimal forms of action. Moreover, these models can be extended to contexts beyond the personal crisis of the individual deathbed or the artificial environment of the playhouse. In the hands of Marlowe, Shakespeare, and Jonson (among others), the death scene becomes a productive site for considering problems as various as the nature of human agency under an omnipotent God, the limits to sovereign and parliamentary power, and the possibility of profiting from private bodily labor. Characters strive to assert themselves through their deaths, and as they do so, they reveal the importance of medieval and early modern conceptions of the art of dying to the development of later political institutions and ideas.

Doing More Than Mourning

To say that Elizabethan and Jacobean plays are centrally concerned with death might appear to be stating the obvious. After all, the popular image of early modern drama is Hamlet in a graveyard holding a skull. Yet if we approach the plays in the period primarily through the figure of Shakespeare's melancholic prince, we risk allowing mournful and passive encounters with mortality to overshadow more active approaches. Undoubtedly Hamlet stands for something. Looking backward to lament the murder of his father while simultaneously anticipating his own end, he has become the emblem of early modern tragedy's relationship to mortality for many readers and audiences. His orientation toward death provides two of the most influential twentieth-century theorists of mournfulness and memorialization, Sigmund Freud and Walter Benjamin, with a seemingly perfect instantiation of the phenomena they are describing. For Freud in "Mourning and Melancholia," Hamlet becomes an exemplar of pathological melancholia as he castigates himself for inaction following the death of his father.[1] Walter Benjamin extends Hamlet's pathology to the culture as a whole, diagnosing baroque drama as a melancholic response to modernity.[2] The baroque universe has become disenchanted, and without an eschatology, characters, authors, and audiences find themselves trapped a meaningless and fragmented creaturely world.[3] The Ghost's demand to be remembered and the prince's uncertain responses emblematize a theater that has despaired of producing action and can exhibit only passion. This mournful theater laments individual deaths and through them registers greater losses associated with historical trajectories of disenchantment and social fragmentation. While the best critical work undertaken in this mournful mode illuminates how drama responds to loss, it does so by casting both those who die and those who mourn almost exclusively as passive victims.

Analyzing similar dramatic phenomena from a transhistorical perspective, some contemporary performance theorists have asserted that mortality and performance are constitutively related. The theater enables uncanny and self-shattering encounters with the unknown. Herbert Blau's description of acting as a "ghosting," through which dead and never-living characters possess the performer and haunt the stage, has proven especially influential.[4] Though felt most profoundly by the performer in relation to the character, ghosting affects the total theater experience, since, in Alice Rayner's words, a play becomes an occasion "in which a fully materialized reality, even a representational reality, is haunted by an appearing not-to-be—that is, by its own negation."[5] Onstage actions and characters insistently bring to mind the ghosts that are not, and cannot, be present. For Rayner, "the presence of the ghost acknowledges the reality of death, so that theater's memory must also be somehow engaged with death and a return from the dead."[6] Because of the uncanny potentiality inherent in the phenomenon of ghosting, theater becomes a particularly rich site for exploring and overcoming trauma. As Peggy Phelan puts it, "it may well be that theater and performance respond to a psychic need to rehearse for loss, and especially for death. Billed as a rehearsal, performance and theater have a special relation to art as memorial."[7] In Phelan's work, as in that of critics such as Joseph Roach, Nicole Loraux, and Rebecca Schneider, different types of performance—from Greek tragedy and New Orleans Mardi Gras parades to Civil War reenactments—are revealed as mechanisms that enable the living to confront past trauma through remembrance of the dead.[8] In this critical tradition, which in many cases is heavily influenced by psychoanalytic models, performances function as acts of mourning and memorialization. Although theorists typically stress the risks that performative confrontations with loss entail, they also often conceive repetitive reengagement with trauma as therapy. Theatrical encounters with mortality are redeemed as aids to surviving death.

Of course, a memorial will also serve as a *memento mori*. As Phelan says, a representation of someone else's death can function as "a prompt that enables us to enter an interior cinema that projects our own living and dying."[9] Mourning anticipates future disaster even as it holds onto the past, and it would be misleading to suggest that a drama attentive to mourning necessarily precludes or evades attention to dying. I have no desire to repudiate or deny the value of this mournful tradition. Later, indeed, I argue that the experience of being haunted leads Shakespeare's

Richard II to anticipate and perform death through imitation. I do, however, seek to contextualize mournfulness by contrasting it to affirmative approaches to death. I am concerned with the postures of the self in the face of annihilation rather than with the responses generated by the loss of the other. We recognize situations in which performance mournfully acknowledges the predations of loss and the beloved objects that actors cannot recover. We should also attend to performances that show what, in death, actors can do. The dying may work to align themselves with some transcendent order, or they may pursue detachment. They may resolve their earthly affairs, or they may carry them beyond the grave. They may affirm the communities that form around the deathbed, or they may disrupt them. To illustrate what is at stake in these efforts, I want to contrast briefly the melancholic postures of Hamlet with the acts and experiences of other characters in the play.

Consider Gertrude. Notoriously, she responds to the death of her first husband not with mourning but with remarriage. While Hamlet promises to "wipe away all trivial fond records" from his memory and dedicates himself solely to his father's demand for memorialization, Gertrude does the opposite.[10] And, perhaps surprisingly, the Ghost seems either helpless or disinclined to contest her actions, telling Hamlet to "Leave her to heaven/And to those thorns that in her bosom lodge/To prick and sting her" (1.5.86–88). Under this command, Gertrude's fate will be worked out eschatologically, as a negotiation between divinity and conscience rather than as a response to the demands of the dead who have gone before. Even in her moment of death, the Queen refuses to connect her fate to the mortality of others. Although she will readily acknowledge social and familial obligations, especially to her "dear Hamlet," whom she names in her final speech, she declines to understand those bonds mournfully. When Claudius suggests "She sounds to see them bleed," Gertrude responds, "No, no, the drink, the drink" (5.2.286–87). She turns away from the potential death of the other to focus upon the death of the self. Attending to her perspective might allow us to recognize how dying, perhaps more effectively than mourning, offers individuals who are largely defined in terms of their relationships to others (in this instance, as a wife, a widow, a mother) a way to acknowledge those relationships without transforming them into obligations.

Consider Ophelia. Her drowning occurs at the point of contact between action and passion. The divergent discourses that she evokes—of classical suicide, Christian despair, and insanity—can help us think about how agency, and especially political agency, inheres in dying. Structurally,

Ophelia's death occupies a similar place within the play to that of Lucretia's suicide within the founding myth of the Roman Republic.[11] Laertes, for one, interprets it as a marker of the dysfunction of the Danish court, which has been all too willing to hush up Polonius's murder and smuggle Hamlet out of the country. Like Lucretia, Ophelia is no natural social revolutionary. Even as her death challenges the power of the Danish monarchy, it manifests filial piety. Yet while her protest might appear more palatable to the conservative elements of an Elizabethan audience because it is couched behind submission to patriarchy, Christian condemnations of suicide would make it hard to celebrate. Livy's praise of Lucretia's chastity and republican virtue was challenged by Augustine, who in *City of God* insisted that Christians must view her end either as the culpable murder of an innocent woman or as an admission of adulterous guilt.[12] The Priest's reluctant participation in Ophelia's funeral manifests a similar suspicion. Moreover, Ophelia's acknowledged mental imbalance makes it questionable whether the political statement Laertes derives from her drowning is something she intended. Where Lucretia convenes an audience to witness a performance of suicide intended to inspire revenge, the only account of Ophelia's death we receive is an indirect one, mediated through Gertrude and perhaps shaped for Laertes's hearing.

Yet even as doubts about Ophelia's mental state distinguish her death from Lucretia's public theatrical performance, they foreground the more fundamental question of how agency inheres in mortality. Ophelia's death becomes an interpretive problem for other characters within the play and, through them, for the audience. Onstage deliberations over whether she is entitled to Christian burial turn on the question of when and how will is exerted through death.[13] The Clown's garbled expressions of doubt that a religious funeral is appropriate for someone who "willfully seeks her own salvation" (5.1.1–2) and his attempt to define an act as possessing three branches—"to act, to do, to perform" (11–12)—are, in the usual mode of Shakespearean fools, more intelligent and topical than they purport to be.[14] It is worth taking his pronouncements at least semiseriously. *Can* will be exerted toward salvation without falling into suicidal despair or presumptuous usurpation of divine prerogative? In death—or in its dramatic representation—*are* acting, doing, and performing quite as interchangeable as we might assume? And *do* the religious discourses that teach holy death ever align with secular political ends?

Finally, consider Laertes. His dying attempts to win Hamlet's forgiveness raise questions about whether mortality can be communal. Structurally, Laertes functions as Hamlet's foil, as Hamlet helpfully reminds us in the Folio text when he remarks that "by the image of my cause, I see / The portraiture of his" (5.2.67.10–11). The prince's language of portraiture is accurate but also strikingly disingenuous. The relationship between the two sons' predicaments is as much causal as specular. Since Hamlet has killed Polonius, he bears responsibility for creating the parallel. And certainly it is Hamlet's crime, rather than any similarities between their positions, that appears to occupy Laertes's thoughts for most of the action. Yet Laertes's attitude changes once both have been fatally poisoned by the envenomed blade. Inspired by the imminence of an end he understands as a "just" punishment for his "treachery," he reveals Claudius's role in the plot and seeks to reconcile himself to Hamlet, saying, "Exchange forgiveness with me, noble Hamlet. / Mine and my father's death come not upon thee, / Nor thine on me" (5.2.308–9). According to the stage direction in the Folio, Laertes dies immediately following this line and before Hamlet answers, "Heaven make thee free of it! I follow thee" (310).[15]

In this final exchange, both Laertes and Hamlet assume that the similarities in their positions have generated a connection that will persist through life and into death, though they differ in how they understand this link to function. Their alternative perspectives raise questions about the effect of mortality on interpersonal relationships. Throughout the play, Laertes's model for human interaction has been essentially transactional. Once he discovers his own death to be imminent, he abandons the revenge that would return harms done to his family upon Hamlet, tit for tat, and instead strives to expunge reciprocal wrongs through mutual displays of forgiveness. He looks for salvation in Hamlet's assent to a good bargain (the Prince, after all, gets forgiven two murders for the price of one) and acts in the apparent belief that an exchange between two humans can stimulate a more important forgiveness of debt from Heaven. The quasi-contractual relationship formed with another person offers a way to figure and perhaps control an encounter with the unknown. A skeptical audience member might identify something glib about Laertes's sudden *volte-face*. His earlier response to Hamlet's attempted rapprochement, when he claimed to be "satisfied in nature" but not "in my terms of honor" (5.2.215–17), had demonstrated his skill at manipulating different levels of discourse to participate in an act of reconciliation that was entirely insincere. Here, he seems similarly facile. At the least, his confession illustrates the difficult negotiations between earth and heaven involved in Christian approaches to death. The dying can only manifest their turn toward heaven by attempting to settle their earthly affairs, and as their efforts to do so become more particularized, they find themselves more vulnerable to charges of persistent worldliness or mere social performance.

Yet the fact that Laertes dies in the middle of the bargain, after making his offer but before learning if it will be accepted, complicates such a reading. Whatever he may intend by the exchange—whether it repudiates worldly codes in favor of Christian forgiveness or simply applies them in a different context—his death changes the responses available to Hamlet. Though his bargain starts as one between two humans, it ends as one between this world and the next. Hamlet cannot reply in the terms in which Laertes made his offer, because Laertes is no longer alive to receive his acceptance. Instead, he refers the matter to Heaven before continuing, "I follow thee." One thing that Hamlet's words force us to consider, I think, is how one death relates to another. Laertes has anticipated Hamlet's own entry into mortality. In casting himself as a follower, Hamlet acknowledges the different temporalities of dying that make each death unique. Although Laertes is poisoned second, he dies first, and the manner in which he outpaces Hamlet stands as an index of a fundamental incommensurability between different experiences of dying and so of the truism that every man dies alone. The reciprocity that Laertes had imagined would ground a bargain transcending mortality is thwarted by the absolute isolation of the grave. Hamlet can read his future in Laertes's death, but he cannot, at this moment, share it.

Alternatively, though, to "follow" can mean to imitate. At the same time as he acknowledges a fundamental temporal disjuncture between his death and Laertes's, Hamlet also suggests that they are brought together through similitude. His language echoes a passage in Mark's Gospel where Christ tells his listeners "Whosoever will follow me, let him forsake himself, and take up his cross, and follow me. For whosoever will save his life, shall lose it, but whosoever shall lose his life for my sake and the Gospel's, he shall save it."[16] In the context of devotion, individuals can incorporate themselves into the community of believers, encompassing both the living and the dead, by imitating Christ or another holy figure. Laertes is hardly a saint. Nevertheless, his cause provides a portrait of Hamlet's, in death as well as in life. When Hamlet anticipates following Laertes, he exploits ambiguities within the word "follow" to raise questions not just about the possibility of deathbed sociality but also about the role of similarity in grounding such sociality. Rather than accept Laertes's bargain or repudiate it, he recasts it as an opportunity to overcome isolation in mortality through imitation. Hamlet and Laertes die together and not together, both grasping for interpersonal connections that might survive the grave.

It might be objected that, by suggesting these secondary characters represent early modern understandings of death as a practice better than Hamlet, I misrecognize the intent behind much of the scholarship on the prince. Of course Hamlet is atypical. That is the point. His mournful demeanor manifests his social alienation. His dislocation renders him an untimely anticipation of the modern subject.[17] By contrast, Gertrude's, Ophelia's, and Laertes's approaches to death must appear simple and conventional. But by drawing out the implications of their last acts, I have attempted to demonstrate that even the most banal and routinized death scenes in early modern drama necessarily intersect with vital debates about the possibility of meaningful action under states of duress, about the nature of human will, and about how mortality affects interpersonal relations. Anticipating and practicing the death of the self need not be a nihilistic exercise. Where attention to mourning tends to produce a picture of modernity as fragmented and disenchanted and of human subjectivity as paralyzed and constrained by the influence of the father, affirmative approaches to mortality offer models for the exertion of agency in the face of external constraints.

Active Death

Where do playwrights discover the idea that death can be active? Although many cultures have developed strategies for comforting the sick and dying and rituals surrounding death, the dramas I discuss are most directly influenced by principles popularized in a set of conduct books—collectively known as the *artes moriendi*—that offer guidance to the terminally ill as well as the clergy and laypeople who attend at their sickbeds.[18] The earliest of these texts, the *Tractatus Artis Bene Moriendi*, was probably written by order of the Council of Constance sometime in the first two decades of the fifteenth century. The *Tractatus* was disseminated widely across Europe, initially appearing in English as *The Craft and Knowledge for to Dye Well* around the middle of the century and retranslated and printed by Caxton in 1491. In addition to direct translations, it also spawned a large number of imitations.[19] Although the genre is usually characterized as a medieval phenomenon, English and continental writers produced original *artes moriendi* throughout the sixteenth and seventeenth centuries.[20] These texts are doctrinally diverse, reflecting confessional outlooks from Catholicism to radical puritanism. In important respects, however, the behavior expected from the dying—that they should reconcile themselves to God and confess their sins, assent to a creed, overcome the fear of death, and set their earthly affairs in order—changed little over the period and transcended confession, gender, and socioeconomic status.[21] The art of dying was a transhistorical and cross-confessional devotional project, one attempted unostentatiously in any number of sick chambers and deathbeds across the country over three hundred years, and it would have been broadly familiar to the authors, players, and audiences drawn to Elizabethan and Jacobean playhouses.

To illustrate what this death was imagined to look like around the time that Shakespeare was writing, I want to discuss William Perkins's 1595 tract *A Salve for a Sicke Man: or, a Treatise Containing the Nature, Differences, and Kindes of Death*.[22] While Perkins, a reformist cleric classified by the historian Peter Lake as a "moderate puritan," uses his text to attack some exclusively Catholic practices like priestly confession, most of the obligations he places on the dying individual cleave closely to those outlined in the fifteenth-century *Tractatus*.[23] He prepares his readers for the various temptations they are likely to face on their approaches to death, guides them through strategies for demonstrating their faith, and suggests appropriate prayers for the dying and their attendants. The bare persistence of some pious tropes, though, is not what makes the *ars moriendi* tradition useful for thinking about early modern drama. *A Salve for a Sicke Man* does not only set out the ideal form of a holy death. It also explores what it would mean for a physically or cognitively debilitated person to inhabit that form. In the process, Perkins is forced to theorize how meaningful action could be compatible with bodily and mental failure.

Here, for instance, is Perkins answering an objection that

> in the pangs of death men want their senses & convenience utterance, and therefore that they are unable to pray. Ans. The very sighes, sobs, & grones of a repentant and beleeuing heart are praiers before God, euen as effectuall as if they were uttered by the best voice in the world. Praier stands in the affection of the hart, the voice is but an outward messenger thereof. God lookes not upon the speech but upon the heart.[24]

Rather than reassure his readers that they will be able to surmount the hardships of the deathbed and give voice to a prayer, Perkins lingers over sighs, sobs, and groans. In a different intellectual tradition, exemplified by thinkers such as Elaine Scarry, such sounds would confirm that the dying person has lost the capacity to participate meaningfully in the world; pain brings about "a reversion to a state anterior to language" and so throws the sufferer out of the human sphere.[25] Perkins, though, interprets the sounds of suffering more positively. First, he reminds his readers of the different earthly and heavenly frames of reference through which the deathbed can be viewed and insists that God penetrates worldly appearances to recognize the intent of a believing heart. Death relocates the sphere of action, either inward to the psyche or upward to a supernatural proving field where the forces of good and evil battle over the dying person's soul. Indeed, medieval images associated with the *artes moriendi* often superimpose these two perspectival shifts. Woodcuts printed to accompany a truncated version of the *Tractatus* around 1475 situate a prone figure on a bed at the center of a contention between allegorical figures representing various internal spiritual states as well as angelic and demonic antagonists (see Figure 1).[26]

It would be possible to dismiss such reassurances as pious displacements of the true horrors of death. Yet I do not think the charge is apposite to Perkins or the artist of the woodcut, because neither suggests that their subject has entered entirely into inner communion with God. Through her groans, she also remains part of a worldly community and rests under the continued obligation to respect earthly forms of holy death as far as she is able.[27] *A Salve for a Sicke Man* requires its readers to negotiate between different spheres of action and to recognize both the opportunities and the constraints afforded by death. As devotional readers contemplate the liminal position of the dying, they are brought to acknowledge that what counts as a meaningful activity is a matter of perspective and to consider forms of action that are invisible, even as they are efficacious. The significance of this passage and similar moments in other texts lies in its capacity to shake our confidence that we know how to separate action from suffering or meaningful communication from mere noise. *Artes moriendi* encourage us to look for agential intervention in new or unexpected places.

While Perkins suggests that the postures of the deathbed can sometimes be internalized, he does not assume that death is necessarily a purely isolating experience. Another strategy that can help debilitated people die well is delegation:

> If so be it fall out that the sick party can not himselfe renue his own faith & repentance, he must seek the help of others. When the man that was sicke of the dead palsie could not go to Christ himself, he got others to beare him in his bed:& when they could not come nere for the multitude, they uncovered the roof of the house and let the bed downe before Christ [Mark 2:4–5]: even so, when sick men can not alone by themselves do the good duties to which they are bound, they must borrow help from their fellow members, who are partly by their counsell to put to their helping hand, & partly by their praiers to present them unto God, & to bring them into the presence of Christ.[28]

Figure 1: Anon. *Ars Moriendi*. London, 1506. Sig. AIv. Reproduced by kind permission of the Syndics of Cambridge University Library Sel.5.8.

The community of neighbors surrounding the dying person is placed under a charitable obligation to visit the sick, which, in Perkins's interpretation, amounts almost to an obligation to act on behalf of the sick. The passage just quoted draws striking analogies between the manual (and indeed, acrobatic) assistance offered to the palsy sufferer in Mark's Gospel and the more figurative "helping hands" of counsel and prayer. Physical and mental modes of assistance are conflated, as are the efforts of the dying person and his community. *A Salve for a Sicke Man*, like other *ars moriendi* texts, addresses itself alternatively to those who minister to the sick and those struck down by sickness. Its readers are encouraged to anticipate that over time they will occupy different positions at the deathbed and to recognize the reciprocal structures of care that connect different roles. As the dying person's visitors comfort her and assist her in prayer, they receive from her equally valuable reminders of the fragility of life and examples of the proper approach to death.

Moreover, the local community that forms around a single death stands in microcosmic relation to the universal and transcendent community that draws all Christians together around the example of the Crucifixion. When Perkins labels the sick person's helpers as "fellow members," he alludes to Pauline constructions of the Church in relation to Christ's mortal body. In Philippians, Paul calls on Christians to "know [Christ], and the virtue of his resurrection, and the fellowship of his afflictions, and be made conformable unto his death," while in 1 Corinthians, he characterizes members of the Church as members of a body of which Christ is the head.[29] To be a Christian is to participate in death and to lose oneself within that participation in death. The communities that gather around the deathbed literalize and intensify this dynamic and in the process posit an orientation toward mortality that remains agential even as it relies upon a notion of selfhood at odds with the autonomous modern subject.

The sophistication of the models of action implied within *artes moriendi* becomes apparent when we compare them to other theoretical frameworks that have more often been used by literary critics to analyze dramatic representations of dying. The relentlessly pious tone of most early modern *ars moriendi* texts and the common features they share with medieval forms of devotion may explain why they have been of relatively little interest to scholars of early modern literature—at least before the recent rise of postsecular studies.[30] Michael Neill's otherwise magisterial survey of literary responses to mortality, *Issues of Death*, quickly dismisses the *artes moriendi* as failing "mechanisms that were designed to keep death in its place" and so resist the forces of secularization.[31] As an alternative, Neill argues that the revival and popularization of Stoic ideas, especially through the writings of Seneca, offered the culture a newly theatrical way to approach mortality:

> The ritualized drama of confession and absolution by which the "good end" contained the chaos of death reduced the dying person to a passive sufferer whose only role was willingly to surrender the last frail trappings of selfhood; by contrast, to those who were ready to meet it, the once dreaded *mors improvisa* provided the occasion for the improvisational theatre of defiance in which the power of death was subordinated to self-display.[32]

Neill juxtaposes "surrender" with "defiance" to characterize Senecan death as an occasion for the iconoclastic assertion of secular selfhood against deindividuating religious rituals. Yet this contrast fails to do justice either to Christian or to Stoic understandings of how agency is exerted in relation to mortality. Rather than lining up as opposites, both approaches are in fact intensely concerned with how death forces humans to reconceive the boundaries between activity and passivity.

Stoic philosophy insists that a virtuous ethos can be asserted in the face of duress and discovers in death both its greatest opportunity and greatest challenge. Seneca considers that he will be better equipped to live well if he keeps his mortality in mind: "Death is on my trail, and life is fleeting away; teach me something with which to face these troubles. Bring it to pass that I shall cease trying to escape from death, and that life may cease to escape from me."[33] Death offers a stark reminder that humans cannot control their external circumstances. But when viewed rightly, it inspires the sage to cultivate virtue rather than give way to despair and can become a final opportunity for self-assertion in the face of hardship. And at least this far, the Stoic tradition is compatible with early modern *artes moriendi*. Already in the early fifteenth century, the author of the *Tractatus* had approvingly cited Seneca as "the wyse man that seyeth thus: *Bene mori est libenter mori*. To dye wel is to dye gladly & wylfully."[34] Later texts engaged more deeply with Stoic thought. Amy Appleford shows that some *ars moriendi* tracts by writers working in the humanist tradition, like Petrarch and Thomas Lupset, exploit consonances between Stoic and Christian ideas. Stoic precedents helped these authors present the art of dying as a pragmatic and achievable practice, one that was capable of accommodating shifts in intellectual fashion and, more importantly, that recognized that its readers were embedded in social contexts that constrained how they could express their faith. "Besides its transcendent implications," Appleford argues, death in Petrarch's text "has an explicit, this-worldly ethical function, offering . . . a means of using the ever-present threat of death and the elaborate and laicized culture of dying growing up around it to think about *living*, rationally, in the world."[35]

At the same time, other aspects of the Stoic tradition taken up in early modern philosophy and drama are baldly incompatible with orthodox belief—most prominently the claim by some writers, including Seneca, that suicide is preferable to submission to tyranny or to a prolonged life of pain.[36] Stoic defenses of suicide occupy a special place in the early modern literary imagination. They could only be reconciled with Christian doctrine obliquely or covertly, as in John Donne's *Biathanatos*.[37] And Neill is right to identify them as an important influence on some early modern drama. Plays like *Julius Caesar* and *The Revenge of Bussy D'Ambois* depict characters dying in a particularized Stoic milieu, with little or no reference to Christian practice. More loosely, some revenge dramas like *The Spanish Tragedy* and *The Atheist's Tragedy* contain highly theatrical suicides that exhibit a kind of Stoicism-lite. Insofar as these deaths disregard Christian prohibitions on self-murder, they run counter to the dominant religious culture. But in their very showiness they tend to oversimplify the Stoic ideas they purport to instantiate. I will return to the apparent proximity of discourses of self-murder and holy death in Chapter 3, when I discuss efforts to die in imitation of Christ. But in general, I think that the traditions of Christian Stoicism found in the *artes moriendi* offer more theoretically interesting explanations of how death functions as an act of self-assertion than iconoclastic defenses of suicide can hope to. Rather than perpetuating a fantasy that an act of dying can conclusively counter intolerable forces of oppression, *artes moriendi* must account on a more granular level for the interplay between different manifestations of individual, collective, and divine agency at the moment of death. In the process, they bring us closer to theorizing just what sort of an act dying is.

Mimetic Death

In the *ars moriendi* tradition, death can also be mimetic. Devotional writers often understand the interfaces between suffering and action, or between the death of the self and the death of the other, through theories of embodied mimesis. Drawing on biblical authority, *ars moriendi* authors repeatedly counsel readers to ground their approaches to death in the image of Christ and other exemplary religious figures. Perkins, for instance, urges readers to show obedience to God in times of sickness by imitating the example of Christ, "who in his agonie praied *Father, let this cup passe from me*, yet with a submission, *not my will, but thy will be done:* teaching vs in the very pangs of death to resigne our selues to the good pleasure of God."[38] During the Passion, Christ's suffering is mystically inverted into an assertion of divine power. Though the ordinary mortal cannot hope to match either the depths of Christ's abjection or the heights of his apotheosis, she can mimic Him and through mimicry achieve union with Christ's body in the afterlife.

When devotional writers advocate mimetic approaches to death, they hold out the promise that nobody has to die alone. Attempting to die in Christ's image is not a matter of asserting the primacy of the death of the self over the death of the other or of the other over the self. Nor (given the heterogeneity of human and divine substance) is it a claim that the self and other are ultimately the same. It is the pursuit of a difficult and sustained imitative practice that attempts to draw self and other as closely together as possible while still acknowledging the impossibility of arriving at a simple identity. By dying like Christ, someone can die with Christ and then participate in His resurrection.

These ideas can sound unconvincing in the wake of twentieth-century phenomenological accounts of mortality. Like Seneca, Heidegger has proven attractive to literary theorists in large part because he offers a secular conception of death.[39] For Heidegger, dying alone is not only inevitable. It is the paradigmatic experience that allows us to understand ourselves as individuals. *Being and Time* rejects "the naïve supposition that man is, in the first instance, a spiritual Thing which subsequently gets misplaced 'into' a space."[40] Eschewing metaphysics, Heidegger adopts an ontological approach, which takes as its starting point Dasein's (or consciousness's) everyday experience of Being-in-the-world. Death assumes key significance in Heidegger's thinking because it impinges on the everyday to confront Dasein with the "possibility of absolute impossibility."[41] While most people will seek to evade or deny the possibility of death, an "authentic being-towards-death" involves recognizing its centrality to the construction of Dasein. Death is Dasein's "ownmost possibility—non-relational, certain and as such indefinite, not to be outstripped."[42] That is, it cannot be shared, escaped, or fully apprehended, and for these very reasons, it is the source of individuation, separating individuals from the "they" by revealing to them their own finitude. While being-toward-death necessarily produces anxiety for Dasein, it also offers the only possible avenue for Dasein to possess "an authentic-potentiality-for-being-a-whole."[43] Once alienated from the world by its anticipation of death, Dasein becomes able to understand itself "authentically" as a separate entity and to recognize the potentialities open to it.

When Heidegger claims death is nonrelational, he rejects the Christian salvific promise that Christ's death can redeem the deaths of his followers and thus dismisses the networks of support and care that form around the deathbed. His work implies drama can say nothing meaningful about dying because it can depict only the appearance of the demise of the other. However, alternative perspectives exist within the twentieth-century philosophical tradition. Emmanuel Levinas condemns the privileging of personal death in *Being and Time* as a solipsistic evasion of what is most troubling about theological accounts of mortality. When Heidegger insists on the certainty of the death of the self, he restricts and simplifies the meaning of death to the personal experience of annihilation. While authentic being-toward-death might appear like a posture of intellectual heroism, it actually perpetuates our illusions of individual autonomy and self-sameness.[44] By contrast, Levinas suggests that when we attend to the death of the other, we are drawn into a relation with something unknowable. The other's death generates an affective response through which the self comes to realize its passivity. Not only does it lack the capacity to comprehend the other's being-toward-death, but it must also recognize its ethical responsibility for the other's fate:

> The relation with the death of the other is not a *knowledge* [*savoir*] about the death of the other, nor the experience of that death in its particular way of annihilating being. . . . The rapport or connection we have with death in its exception—and whatever its signification relative to being and to nothingness might be, death is an exception— which confers upon death its depth, is neither a seeing nor even an aiming [*vise*]. . . . It is an emotion, a movement, a disquietude within the *unknown*. . . . In every death is shown the nearness of the neighbor, and the responsibility of the survivor, in the form of a responsibility that the approach of proximity [*proximité*] moves or agitates [*meut ou émeut*].[45]

For Levinas, unlike Heidegger, therefore, death is a relational experience (indeed, it is the paradigm for all relational experiences). The relation that it creates, however, is grounded in the self's awareness of the inadequacy of its responses to the other, and as such it is fundamentally incomprehensible and inexpressible. This encounter constitutes the primal manifestation of alterity; the individual whose death I experience becomes an avatar for all that is other to me and ultimately for the unknowable divine.

Mimetic *artes moriendi*, especially in their dramatic manifestations, offer possible mechanisms for mediating between these two alternatives. The death of the other and the death of the self are not the same. But they can be similar. And devotional and theatrical traditions of imitation can help us theorize this similarity and negotiate between individual and collective experience. As I have already shown in my discussions of *Hamlet* and *A Salve for a Sicke Man*, early modern descriptions of the practice of dying can complicate distinctions between self and other or between activity and passivity. Although they employ a very different conceptual vocabulary, books in the devotional tradition echo Heidegger's assertion that mortality is a uniquely personal ("ownmost") experience when they consider the inevitable gap between onlookers' understanding of the deathbed and the experience of the person lying on it. The demand that the sick individual manifest her faith by dying well reconceives Heideggerian notions of authenticity in religious terms. Conversely, when *ars moriendi* authors describe deathbed communities encompassing the living, the dying, and the dead, they employ conceptions of alterity and affective relationality that have more in common with Levinas. Rather than setting Heidegger and Levinas in opposition, we can turn to early modern devotional writing to appreciate how their ideas can intersect in practice. The theoretical models of dying well found in *artes moriendi* and the concrete examples of good deaths found in martyrologies frequently reinforce each other. Where the genres overlap, revealing the importance of imitation to early modern conceptions of mortality, they suggest that the death of the self and other can be brought into relation through mental and bodily practices of identification, emulation, and witnessing. Attending to these practices reveals connections between the intellectual traditions that Heidegger and Levinas inherit and also helps us understand the importance of devotional practices and theological debates to later notions of individuality and community.

Medieval guides to achieving holy death encourage the dying to recall the example of others. In the Catholic hagiographic tradition, saints (and especially martyrs) are intercessors and mediators between mortals and God. They have achieved an appropriate likeness to Christ by imitating His persecution and sacrifice, and their devotees can choose to follow their example in order to ascend a ladder to the divine. Sometimes intercession is understood in terms of bodily mimicry. The late-fifteenth-century anonymous compilation of the *Miracles of Henry VI*, for example, discusses the miraculous vision of a sailor who, while suffering from gangrenous abdominal wounds, saw that "the holy martyr Erasmus (for whom he chanced to have a special devotion) lay near him, as if with the pain of his sufferings renewed, just as he is often represented in churches, being tortured [with disembowelment] by his executioners."[46] Saint Erasmus becomes an appropriate model and intercessor because of the sailor's prior devotion and analogous physical condition. Rather than striving to attain an impossible resemblance to Christ, the sailor approaches Erasmus as Erasmus is also approaching him. The vigorous growth of local saints' cults around tombs and relics over the course of the Middle Ages demonstrates how similar patterns of saintly intercession and human imitation could harden into more formal ecclesiastical institutions.

However, deathbed performances carried out in the image of Christ sometimes attracted accusations of hypocrisy and drew complaints that ordinary mortals were putting themselves into envious competition with divine models. Sectarian disputes rendered this problem particularly visible after the Reformation. Protestant iconoclasts vigorously condemned Catholic saints' cults as idolatrous misunderstandings of the relationship between God and man. Viewed from a suspicious perspective, the tribulations of Catholic martyrs can look less like intermediate approximations of the Passion through similitude—which might prove easier for individual believers to approach than the Cross itself—and more like blasphemous attempts to emulate or even surpass Christ's example. In 1567, John Jewel, for instance, accused devotees of Thomas Becket (who, as a symbol of ecclesiastical independence from royal authority, became an especially controversial figure after the Henrican revolution) of seeking "*not onely* Intercession, *but also* Salvation *in the Bloude of Thomas*."[47] Becket's own culpable ambition inspires his followers, who idolatrously come to treat him as a substitute for Christ. Jewel inverts the network of godly imitations into an epidemic of contagious blasphemies. Catholic controversialists replied in kind, pushing back against charges of idolatry and launching their own accusations of hypocrisy at iconic Protestant victims of persecution.[48] Both sides continued to insist on the necessity of imitating the Passion and on the value of other holy examples of saints and martyrs for mediating between man and God. But the controversy required religious writers to think hard about precisely how mimetic behavior draws imitator and imitated into relation with each other and to assess the risks involved in bad similitudes. Ultimately, the evaluation of mimetic deaths becomes part of the art of mimetic dying. Texts like John Foxe's *Acts and Monuments* are intensely attuned to the problem of how we know whether a death is good. When Foxe draws on eyewitness accounts to recast state executions of heretics as heroic acts of religious martyrdom in the image of Christ, he makes observers responsible for determining how successfully individual saints have imitated the Passion. These eyewitnesses tell their stories in the knowledge that they may later be called upon to respond with Christlike imitations of their own. The very word "martyr" (derived from the Greek for "witness") conflates observation and performance. The executioners, the dying, and those who merely hope to watch could all find themselves (sometimes unwillingly) drawn backward and forward across the disturbingly thin boundary separating auditor and actor.

As *artes moriendi* evoke exemplary deaths as models, they extend this dynamic to encompass devotional readers. The dramatic public violence of martyrdom only intensifies and renders more visible phenomena that are equally present at the ordinary death. When *ars moriendi* authors ask readers to recall holy martyrs, they treat the scaffold and the sickbed as homologous. In devotional manuals, the acts of reading about an exemplary death or of visiting a dying neighbor form part of a practice of anticipating and preparing for mortality. The death of the other informs the death of the self through postures of similitude that may be assumed deliberately or accidentally. As they explore mimetic death, devotional texts challenge philosophical assumptions about individuality and alterity. In the process, they sometimes posit imitation as an intervention that brings self and other into new relations, achieving redemption or confirming damnation, creating communities or breaking them.

The Politics of Dying Well

The communities and energies created by dying are not exclusively spiritual. Although I have lingered over the devotional origins of deathbed practices in the previous two sections, this book is less concerned with explicating nuances of early modern religious culture than with demonstrating how devotional models of action are detached from purely religious contexts and redeployed to assert agency in situations of worldly constraint. In Chapter 1, I consider how this detachment can occur. I argue that Marlowe's Faustus inverts the art of dying well into a perverse art of dying badly and so encourages watchers to consider how the human will could manifest in the absence or displeasure of God. In the process, Marlowe offers us models for thinking about the migration of theological concepts and devotional practices into more secular contexts. Subsequent chapters then explore how similarly active approaches to death might be used to exert political power within regimes of dynastic sovereignty, representative governance, or protocapitalist markets. Although in some instances the playwrights I discuss draw on devotional culture explicitly, their (and my) interest is less in how this culture functions in its own terms than in how it can be reappropriated for other purposes.

The many theorists who assert that the political treatment of life and death changed in important ways at the advent of modernity tend to associate greater attention to biological life and death with disempowerment. Hannah Arendt, for instance, argues that the modes of action that citizens employed in the classical public realm were gradually displaced, first by the work of the *homo faber* and subsequently by forms of bodily labor that merely aspire to support the metabolic existence of the human animal.[49] Michel Foucault, adopting a different and historically later frame of reference, contrasts the medieval sovereign's right to put subjects to death with the modern government's disciplinary concern over the management of life.[50] In either case, modern power is exercised by those best placed to redescribe diverse individuals as homogenous populations. While this newfound attention to life may be characterized positively as a concern for the health of the people, it is often accompanied by what Foucault terms a "formidable power of death" that ensures "Wars are no longer waged in the name of a sovereign who must be defended; they are waged on behalf of the existence of everyone; entire populations are mobilized for the purpose of wholesale slaughter in the name of life necessity: massacres have become vital."[51] Killing is far easier once dying can be reduced to a matter of demographics. For Giorgio Agamben, this power of death is not merely the occasional corollary of power over life but its essence.[52] Distinguishing between Greek concepts of *bios* (a "qualified form of life") and *zoe* ("natural reproductive life"), he suggests that biopolitics is characterized by "the production of bare life as originary political element and as threshold of articulation between nature and culture, *zoe* and *bios*."[53] "Bare life," emblematized by the Roman figure of the *homo sacer*—a man who can be killed by anyone but who cannot be sacrificed—can be understood as the simultaneous evacuation of *bios* to the point where it becomes no richer than *zoe* and the incorporation of *zoe* into the realm of the political as the primary site over which power should be exercised.

Although Arendt and Foucault situate the origin of biopolitical modes of governance in the eighteenth century or later,[54] many early modern literary critics have found their ideas useful for explaining changing political institutions in Tudor and Stuart England. I am heavily indebted to scholars such as Eric Santner, Patricia Cahill, and Paul Kottman for their accounts of how biological understandings of life may be deployed to repressive effect or come to inhibit meaningful political action.[55] But I want to shift my focus of inquiry to consider how political agency could reemerge from positions of bare life. Rather than ascribing agency only to the enactors of sovereign violence (or taking a liberal perspective and focusing on those institutions that seek to constrict violence within secular legal and normative structures), I consider what those who are generally cast as the victims of biopower do to take control of their fates, if only by inhabiting their own approaches to death.

In making this shift, I am inspired in part by Agamben's more recent work on forms of life as well as by Roberto Esposito's investigation of *communitas*. In *The Highest Poverty*, Agamben explicates the Franciscan concept of *forma vitae* (form of life), insisting that this genitive phrase needs to be understood both objectively and subjectively. It does not only imply the subjection of human existence to a disciplinary rule, as is the case in the popular understanding of monastic orders. For Francis and his followers, it also suggests that holy life can be raised to "the paradigm of the rule."[56] Controversially, the Franciscans claimed that their form of life exempted them from the reach of the law as well as from normative codes. As mendicants without personal property, their use of the things of the world is governed not by human regulations or Church codes but by necessity:

> Necessity, which gives the Friars Minor a dispensation from the rule, restores (natural) law to them; outside the state of necessity they have no relationship with the law. What for others is normal thus becomes an exception for them; what for others is an exception becomes for them a form of life.[57]

My inversion of a form of life into a practice of death is less perverse than it initially seems. In part, this is a matter of intellectual history; *artes moriendi* were one of the key avenues through which ascetic models were disseminated into lay culture in the late Middle Ages.[58] They can help us see how medieval monastic modes of living persist in modified form in later, and worldlier, contexts. But I also take Agamben's investigation of monasticism as a more general encouragement to look at how postures of obedience or bodily constraint can function as acts of resistance. And in this instance, arts of dying supply an important limit case. The practice of dying well does not merely take life as a rule. It takes the most debilitated and abject form of life as a rule. What would it mean for our conception of biopolitics if extreme suffering could be reconceived as action in some of the ways that the *artes moriendi* suggest? Would we discover the forms of political engagement discussed by Agamben to be not peculiar to the Franciscans but far more widespread?

While Agamben and the Franciscans are useful for analyzing how dying might function as a practice, Esposito can help explain its communal dimensions. In *Communitas*, he begins his investigation of community with the root element "*munus*," a word that in Latin means both a gift and a duty. Constructed around the *munus*, the community is the opposite of the *res publica*. It is not a shared common thing but instead "the hole into which the common thing continually risks falling"—an open-ended obligation owed by all members to the collective that threatens to consume them completely.[59] Rather than providing a benefit, the community demands everything from its members, including death. In his genealogy, Esposito suggests that Roman notions of *communitas* persist into the modern era through the Pauline conception of the Church. Christ's sacrifice stands as the "originary *munus*" of the Christian community, which in turn is rendered secular in postmedieval political institutions. Yet modern individuals "can no longer bear the gratitude that the gift demands," and in consequence political philosophy develops as a series of "immunitarian" attempts to limit the reach of the community.[60] The *artes moriendi* can help us track this interplay between *communitas* and *immunitas*. When devotional manuals explore how dying persons' actions might simultaneously assist their incorporation into a Christian community and enable them to resolve their earthly affairs, they help us see how the concept of community can become secularized. Moreover, the peculiar and tentative forms of agency that *artes moriendi* ascribe to the dying encourage us to consider what consequences might result if the gift of death inherent in community is freely given rather than withheld.

My reliance on later Agamben and Esposito can also help explain why I am interested in looking at political action primarily through the paradigm of the ordinary deathbed rather than through the executions and martyrdoms that are more often read as sites of political resistance. As theorists, historians, and critics from Foucault onward have acknowledged, public executions (especially of traitors and heretics) are volatile occasions of political theater.[61] John Foxe's transformation of the disparate victims of Marian persecution into a pantheon of Protestant martyrs illustrates how effectively state displays of terror could be claimed by dissenters as scenes of ideological resistance. As I discussed earlier, *artes moriendi* and martyrologies are in many cases mutually supporting. Both Protestant and Catholic guides to holy death encourage the dying to recall the example of others—and most Catholic tracts assume that martyred saints will be present at the deathbed as intercessors. I will consider martyrological traditions more extensively in my discussions of *Edward II* and *Richard II* and argue that the protagonists in both plays exploit parallels between sovereignty and sanctity as they confront their ends. However, I worry that the very theatricality of executions makes them—rather paradoxically—an unhelpful site through which to explore the deeper relationships between dying, playing, and political action.

In part, the problem is that the final acts of the condemned can be understood too easily as merely instrumental performances. Some readers, for example Stephen Greenblatt, explicate the strategies that executioners and the executed use to acquire political and cultural capital or assert a particular performative identity but largely discount the religious motives of the various participants.[62] In the wake of the religious turn, other more recent critical work illustrates what can be gained by complicating this picture. Julia Lupton's *Citizen-Saints* gestures toward a middle ground between the occasion of martyrdom and the ordinary deathbed that might enrich such ideological readings of public death. Lupton uses the label of "citizen-saint" to denote persons whose actions take place on the boundary between charismatic messianism and the civic obligations of the citizen. Historical figures like Saint Paul and literary characters like Shakespeare's Isabella undergo symbolic or real sacrificial deaths into citizenship, which infuse civic institutions with reformist energies or inaugurate new political orders.[63] Lupton's model suggests we can position martyrs and traitors on the scaffold at an interface between bureaucratic institutions designed to promote the ordinary functioning of society and exceptional forces that do not acknowledge the rules through which those institutions operate. Whether or not it makes sense to ascribe the messianic charge of a particular citizen-saint to an actual encounter with the divine, such figures channel energies and desires that are not capable of legalistic or normative description but that may nevertheless be necessary for human communities to flourish. Moreover, Lupton encourages her readers to look for something more than a zero-sum conflict between executioner and executed. The neologism citizen-saint "implies not only the opposition but also the yoking of the terms, an incomplete passage from one to the other that marks their once and future union as a site of bridging as well as division and separation."[64] Public executions need not only be seen as binary disputes between the totalizing disciplines of the state on the one hand and the radical resistance of martyrs on the other. We do not need to refight the battle between containment and subversion. This language of yoking additionally suggests we can read dying as a site of political intervention without thereby assuming that it must lack a spiritual dimension. Public martyrdoms are significant precisely because they combine spiritual and earthly forms of action in unstable, paradigm-shattering ways.

That said, I think Lupton understates the importance of certain practices of dying because she ties sainthood to the political concept of the exception. To focus on the exceptional is not necessarily elitist. Exceptions, by definition, cannot be localized or anticipated by general laws and rules, and as a result they are liable to pop up anywhere.[65] However, such an approach tends (if only rhetorically) to denigrate the ordinary and the everyday by comparison. When we associate power in the face of death primarily with a condemned person's capacity to adopt iconic and legible postures of martyrdom, we risk dismissing more ordinary approaches to mortality as passive or powerless when in fact their political significance can be substantial. A textual lacuna at the end of *Edward II* illustrates the problem. Because there are no stage directions describing the king's death, editors disagree about precisely what Marlowe had in mind.[66] Readers attentive to the play's depiction of sexual dissidence have often imported from Holinshed the tradition that Edward is anally raped with a red-hot poker. The king has proven easy to read as a martyr, sacrificed to the demands of dynastic sovereignty or normative heterosexuality, as he suffers a sodomical death that recalls the torture narratives of the *Golden Legend* in its luridness.[67] Yet, as I show in Chapter 3, not only is this possible violent end enfolded in the banal and normalized insensibility of sleep, but approaches to dying modeled on sleep may actually grant Edward more political agency than postures of martyrdom. The citizen-saint can do little to help clarify situations where the exception is rendered normative by the successional mechanisms of sovereignty or otherwise evaded. By contrast, *ars moriendi* authors, who instead stress the banality and omnipresence of mortality and ask their readers to treat every day as if it were their last, may help us see political resistance in new postures and new places.

Finally, when I draw attention to the experiences of the dying, I align myself with a number of significant recent discussions of the politics of weakness in early modern literature and philosophy. James Kuzner has explored the role of vulnerability in civic participation as well as the possibility that epistemological skepticism might constitute a valuable mode of existence precisely because of its fragility.[68] Joseph Campana has analyzed the vulnerable male bodies of Spenser's *Faerie Queene* and the place of the child within the sphere of early modern sovereignty.[69] By arguing the ordinary deathbed is a site of political engagement—and moreover one that often prefigures modern political ideas and institutions—I join in this attempt to account for the political lives of the constrained.

Yet I am not persuaded that weakness can easily be isolated on the deathbed. By troubling distinctions between activity and passivity, the *artes moriendi* make it almost impossible to identify and locate vulnerability as a meaningful category. Kuzner, for instance, distinguishes between responses to constraint where "we seek to convert weakness into pragmatic strength" and those where "we accept epistemological weakness," arguing that, while Shakespeare flirts with both possibilities, "only the second kind of response, the embrace of epistemological weakness, leads anywhere near redemption."[70] The binary, while helpful for understanding Shakespeare's engagement with skeptical philosophy, fails to do justice to some of the most interesting features of devotional approaches to death because it discounts strains of early modern religious thought that refuse the distinction between the pragmatic and the redemptive. In one sense, the *artes moriendi* are intensely pragmatic. As we have seen, they acknowledge the existence of physical hardships, cognitive limitations, and uncongenial social contexts, all of which will affect a dying person's ability to achieve a holy end, and then suggest modifications to prescribed practice in order to accommodate these contingencies. Onlookers, too, are advised to suit their interventions to the contingencies of the hour, meeting the various temptations to which the dying person is exposed (overconfidence, despair, impatience, worldliness) with countervailing and shifting words of advice. These will sometimes work against one another, at least in tone, if perhaps not in doctrinal content. However, the whole point of these pragmatic maneuverings is to achieve redemption.

More fundamentally, the deathbed can never escape a certain form of skepticism, since all earthly judgments on who has died well and who has died badly are provisional. From a heavenly perspective, what looks like a good death may in fact be a bad one, and vice versa. In consequence, the epistemological uncertainties that emerge around the deathbed mean that any attempt to separate pragmatism from faith would itself be entirely contingent and subject to doubt. A binary between weakness and strength just does not apply. Rather than focusing on vulnerability as such, then, I stress activity in the face of uncertainty and agency asserted despite constraints that render its significance unclear. To die well becomes a political act and a possible means to regain a degree of power from a position of bare life. Alongside the actions of heretics and traitors on the scaffold, we should appreciate the arts of dying for their capacity to suggest new forms of life and new ways to enter into or detach from political communities. Let us gather round the deathbed not to pity or romanticize the suffering that we see there but to attend to what the dying are doing and to learn how to replicate their practices in our own lives and deaths.

Skeleton

The main chapters in this book form a loosely chronological narrative that starts with the religious drama of the 1570s and 1580s and ends with Ben Jonson's *Volpone*, first published in 1607. I show how dramatists appropriate concepts from the *artes moriendi* to understand social, political, and economic change, and in the process I note many instances where later playwrights rework the writings of earlier ones to new ends. Nevertheless, *Last Acts* does not aspire to offer a comprehensive history of devotional writings about death or an exhaustive survey of the influence of religious conceptions of mortality on drama. Instead, I have chosen to focus intensively on a small number of texts that grapple in a sustained manner with the problem of how to die: Marlowe's *Doctor Faustus* and *Edward II*, Shakespeare's *Richard II*, and Jonson's *Volpone*. These plays use performances of dying to engage with sectarian religious debates over the nature of grace and the capacity of humans to act well, political disputes over the location of sovereignty, cultural anxieties about the emergence of an increasingly market-driven economy, and metatheatrical questions about the nature and effect of dramatic actions. By adopting this approach, I readily admit that I have pursued death at the expense of breadth. But *artes moriendi* are conceived as sustained practices that unfold gradually over time, and the best way to see how they are adapted for the theater is to track carefully how specific characters oriented toward death comport themselves over the course of a play as a whole. The art of dying is embedded in the fabric of Elizabethan and Jacobean drama. To understand it, we must attend closely to the warp and weft of that fabric and tease out the interactions between devotional practices and the contexts in which they are embedded.

Chapter 1 traces how arts of dying migrate from devotional texts into homiletic dramas and finally to the commercial playhouse between 1570 and 1590, around the same time that antitheatrical condemnations of the stage as inherently blasphemous come to cultural prominence. Facing a growing suspicion of religious drama, the playwrights I discuss avoid direct depictions of holy dying. Instead, their representations of bad deaths imply that theater constitutes an important site of religious instruction and theological investigation not despite but rather because of its blasphemous potential. William Wager's *Enough Is as Good as a Feast*, Nathaniel Woodes's *The Conflict of Conscience*, and Marlowe's *Doctor Faustus* all employ parodies of the *artes moriendi* to represent evil action. Parodic arts of dying help dramatize a predestinarian cosmos where distinctions between the elect and the reprobate are foundational yet invisible from a human perspective. The bad deaths in these plays function like negative theologies, manifesting and explicating divine will through attempted departures from it. In *Doctor Faustus*, Marlowe additionally brings the reprobate parodist into focus alongside the divine parodied and makes the magician's vicious death a site for analyzing human agency. As practices of dying well become detached from the *artes moriendi* and inverted into theatrical arts of dying badly, Elizabethan dramatists discover occasions to explore the nature of action and the forms of agency available in situations of extreme constraint or privation.

Subsequent chapters then investigate how these models of active death are further removed from their devotional origins and employed in new political, social, economic, and aesthetic contexts. Most readers of Marlowe's *Edward II* locate the play's radicalism in the sexualized challenge that Edward's homoerotic relations with Gaveston and the Spensers pose to dynastic monarchy and aristocratic governance. In Chapter 2, I shift my focus from erotics to necrotics to argue that royal sodomy and homoerotic friendship can be accommodated by the play's political order with relative ease; royal death, by contrast, exposes fundamental weaknesses within dominant conceptions of sovereign power. While recent queer theory, especially the work of Leo Bersani and Lee Edelman, has aligned queerness with mortality, *Edward II* detaches sexuality from death, offering Edward political opportunities in dying that are unavailable through queer eroticism. Once he is imprisoned, Edward, like Faustus, seeks out arts of dying that will allow him to act from a position of abjection. By choosing to sleep through his murder rather than participate in a scene of martyrdom, he subsumes regimes of dynastic sovereignty within the biological existence of the body. Moreover, the end of the play associates the continued political potential of Edward's death with the conditions of dramatic performance. Though dead, Edward is not superseded, because the theater suggests he may still be minimally present—in the slippage between bodies and props, in the presence of an actor offstage, and in the violence carried out in his name. Rather than supporting a particular structure of power, Edward's death indicates the range of political potentialities inherent in exposure to mortality, which might alternatively support republican, absolutist, bureaucratic, or tyrannical regimes.

Chapter 3 investigates a different form of sovereignty. Shakespeare in *Richard II* shares Marlowe's interest in the forms of political power enabled by sovereign mortality, but where Marlowe's Edward discovers power in an obscured, bloodless end that evades tragic and saintly precedents, Richard courts immediate legibility. As he confronts usurpation, he evokes the iconic postures of martyrs and the example of the Passion and so ties his anticipated death to the devotional practices of *ars moriendi* and *imitatio Christi*. By relying on a tradition that links dying like Christ to dying with Christ— and so asserts that imitation can rise to identity—Richard seeks to affirm his divine right to the throne and presage a political second coming. While he attempts to recruit mimetic death as a support for absolutism, the play as a whole develops a more complex politics around exemplary mortality. Richard's alignment with holy martyrs is disrupted by his repeated, and often unwitting, evocation of negative examples of dying badly. Judas, Faustus, and disavowed saints like Thomas Becket flicker behind his persona, indicating his limited control over the politics of resemblance. Moreover, the audiences who witness and adjudicate Richard's performance are also implicated in political mimesis. When Richard abdicates, he draws members of Parliament into his performance of the Passion as representatives in a double sense: Already witnesses standing for the interests of the country, they become Pilates and Judases authorizing his self-presentation as Christ. Richard seeks political purchase in the slippages between devotional, aesthetic, and political representation. His efforts align sovereign mortality, dramatic imitation, and political surrogacy to anticipate ideas underpinning both Hobbes's conception of absolute sovereignty in terms of personation and modern notions of representative governance.

In Chapter 4, I shift my focus away from sovereign and parliamentary politics to consider the power of performances of death within local communities and institutions. I argue that Ben Jonson's *Volpone* uses the situation of the deathbed to explore how communal obligations are created and broken. To account for Volpone's fraud, I contrast the value-creating spiritual and material economies that *artes moriendi* imagine to operate at the good communal deathbed with Roberto Esposito's account of the *munus*, the unending, life-threatening obligation to give embedded in community. Gatherings of onlookers at Volpone's couch superficially resemble the traditional deathbed communities supposed to offer comfort and spiritual support to the dying. But in fact, divergent economic interests separate Volpone and his visitors. The play investigates how natural, biological processes and traditional understandings of interpersonal relations can be refigured as willed actions that entitle their performers to profit. In the process, it uncovers affinities between dying and theatrical playing and asks what kind of value-creating or value-destroying community the commercial theater might be.

Finally, in my Epilogue, I ask what continued relevance the *artes moriendi* have for artistic, political, and social practice. Following Philippe Ariès's history of Western approaches to mortality, *The Hour of Our Death*, the notion that we no longer know how to die has become a commonplace.[71] In this view, the end of life has medicalized, sanitized, and (especially in the United States) monetized to the point where it can no longer be understood as a practice. Rather, it marks the ultimate site where individual humans are fully subsumed into a biopolitical and capitalist state. To complicate this narrative, I discuss a number of disparate efforts to sustain an art of dying from the seventeenth to the twenty-first centuries, including Elizabeth Jocelin's *The Mothers Legacie to Her Unborn Childe*, Samuel Richardson's *Clarissa*, and "Lazarus," the final music video David Bowie released before his death. As they echo earlier devotional tracts and dramas, these texts and artworks encourage us to consider how we might continue to appreciate, and even practice, the art of dying today.

CHAPTER I

Dying Badly

Doctor Faustus and the Parodic
Drama of Blasphemy

FAUSTUS: Lucifer and Mephastophilis! Ah, gentlemen, I gave them my soul for my cunning.

ALL: God forbid!

FAUSTUS: God forbade it indeed, but Faustus hath done it.[1]

What, exactly, has Faustus done? How has he come to act against the command of God? The moral and theological framework of Marlowe's *Doctor Faustus* has proven notoriously hard to pin down. Critics have plausibly viewed the play through a variety of religious and philosophical lenses, from Calvinist predestinarianism to freethinking iconoclasm.[2] And turning to the text scarcely clarifies Faustus's theological context and devotional milieu. Heaven is never represented on stage, and characters describing it tend to demonstrate the distorting effects of human perception more effectively than they invoke the divine. Faustus jostles against Catholics and Protestants, the godly and the godless, social superiors and inferiors, and angels and devils, all of whom offer different and sometimes shifting interpretations of the cosmos. These voices agree on almost nothing. Nothing, that is, except that Faustus's bad actions will end in damnation.

That Marlowe should emphasize the bald fact of Faustus's badness over the religious context from which it emerges is all the more surprising because badness has traditionally been conceived in terms of privation or distortion. Augustine influentially defined evil as a departure from God.[3] The Good is a unitary, positive attribute of divinity, which stands as both the source and the model for all goodness on earth. The Bad, as such, is nothing. Rather, different badnesses represent different, ever-multiplying perversions of the Good. This negative characterization of evil found new expression in the sixteenth century through the theology of Luther and Calvin, who offer broadly similar accounts of agency after the fall. The human will is at once entirely derivative and, when not illuminated by grace, irredeemably vicious.[4] When Marlowe emphasizes Faustus's depravity while obscuring the divinity it rejects, he perversely presents the consequence without the cause, the flawed reflection without the object it mirrors.

Perhaps, though, representational perversity is the point. In this chapter I argue that theories of parody can help us comprehend such free-floating badness and that the parodic bad death becomes a key site for understanding the nature and limits of human agency. From Scaliger's definition of parody as *ridicula* in 1560 through to Mikhail Bakhtin's analysis of carnival, parodic techniques have generally been understood as derogatory in intent.[5] However, Giorgio Agamben suggests a fruitful alternative approach when he argues that parody might not simply deflate its target but could also function as a strategy for representing mysteries obliquely.[6] To assess the value of Agamben's ideas, I analyze Marlowe's *Doctor Faustus* alongside two other sixteenth-century dramatizations of dying badly, William Wager's *Enough Is as Good as a Feast* (1570) and Nathaniel Woodes's *The Conflict of Conscience* (1581). All three of these plays certainly use derogatory parody to ridicule characters who, at the last, are unable to relinquish worldly things. But they also suggest that parody can function as an investigative and representational tool, akin to a negative theology, that helps us explicate obscured divinity through avowedly imperfect imitations. Marlowe, Woodes, and Wager share Calvin's interest in depravity, but they reverse his emphasis.[7] Instead of simply asserting that human will is irredeemably vicious, they ask what viciousness can reveal about the scope and limits of human agency or about the gap between fallen perception and divine truth. In particular, parody in their plays becomes a tool for analyzing and representing the approach to death, when the disjuncture between a person's earthly and spiritual state can appear especially stark and in need of resolution.

Furthermore, a focus on the affinities between parodic techniques and privative understandings of bad action can clarify the changing fortunes of religious theater in the sixteenth century. Between the publication of *Enough Is as Good as a Feast* around 1570, the writing of *Doctor Faustus* in the late 1580s or early 1590s, and the virtual prohibition on religious language onstage under the Act to Restrain the Abuses of Players in 1606, a growing group of religious thinkers came to understand dramatic representation as an inherently blasphemous practice.[8] While there is no necessary link between antitheatricality and predestinarian accounts of the will, both discourses share a common concern with how imperfect human imitations approach an unseen, perfect original. Moreover, many of the same Protestant thinkers who elaborated Augustine's account of evil to deny the possibility of good works independent of God's grace also engaged in polemics against drama.[9] *Enough Is as Good as a Feast* can help explain this slippage because it indicates how hard it is to inoculate any representation of a religious subject from charges of profanation. By the end of the play, the derogatory potential of parody subsumes its use as an investigative strategy, and all forms of mimesis risk being revealed as blasphemous. Wager himself seems to have become disenchanted with religious theater: He abandoned dramatic writing toward the end of the 1570s even as he remained "active in the Anglican ministry well into the 1580s."[10]

This context suggests that Marlowe, in writing *Doctor Faustus*, was engaged not so much in secularizing religious forms as in reviving a dead genre abandoned by its original practitioners as unsatisfactory. His play, I argue, offers an implicit rejoinder to antitheatrical condemnations of drama. Marlowe appears to agree with the polemicists that dramatic mimesis necessarily offers a distorted, deficient version of what it imitates. But the theater's representational badness reflects the ingrained badness of human performances generally, each of which are necessarily failed imitations of an inaccessible model. We are all doing what Faustus is doing. By foregrounding the validity of parody as a representational strategy for figuring otherwise unapproachable mysteries and by attending to the forms of human agency that make such representation possible, Marlowe implies drama is compatible with theological investigation precisely because of its blasphemous potential. The play encourages us to expand Scaliger's, Bakhtin's, and Agamben's understandings of parody to theorize performances in the Elizabethan theater and beyond and to see dramatic arts of dying badly as powerful models for human action onstage and off.

Parody, Beside and Below

The impulse to parody is ancient. The word derives from the Greek term *parodos*, which was probably initially used to describe any variant poem or song written beside an older work but took on particular connotations of comedy by the time Aristotle used it in the *Poetics*.[11] Although the term (transliterated into Latin as *parodia*) and the concept disappeared from rhetorical manuals by the fifth century, a vigorous European tradition of adapting privileged genres or subjects for new ends persisted through the Middle Ages.[12] The *Coena Cypriani*, celebrations of feasts of the fool, and drunkards' and gamblers' masses all manifest an appetite for burlesque revision, especially of sacred models. While modern critics have disagreed over the significance of these texts, Martha Bayless is persuasive when she emphasizes their diversity and cautions against any grand theory of medieval parody as prima facie orthodox or heterodox.[13] The technique was everywhere and capable of advancing many ends.

By the early modern period, though, parodies (especially of religious subjects) were attracting more controversy. Sixteenth-century discussions of parody focalized broader debates about the aesthetic and moral value of imitative art. Humanists revived *parodia* as a rhetorical term but altered its connotations to imply that comic imitation of a serious subject necessarily derogates that subject. In 1560, Scaliger influentially defined the word as "*Rhapsodia inversa mutatis vocibus ad ridicula sensum retrahens* [rhapsody turned upside down, redirecting the sense toward amusing things with altered words]."[14] Where the Greek prefix *para-* had suggested juxtaposition, Scaliger describes inversion and institutes a hierarchy between serious literature and comic travesty. Though *ridicula* may neutrally signify an amusing subject in Latin, Margaret Rose suggests Scaliger's sixteenth-century English readers largely understood parody as derogatory.[15] The folio text of Ben Jonson's *Every Man in His Humour* (1616), for instance, describes parody as what would make something "absurder than it was."[16]

And this revaluation of parody was not confined to rhetorical theory. Over the same period that Scaliger's construction of parody started to gain more widespread acceptance in literary contexts, religious reformers came increasingly to reject comic adaptations and inversions of religious motifs as blasphemous by definition. The Henrican state suppressed festivals of boy bishops in 1541, objecting that "boys do sing mass and preach in the pulpit . . . rather to the derision than any true glory of god, or honour of His saints."[17] In 1583, Philip Stubbes's *Anatomy of Abuses* condemned surviving festivals of the Lord of Misrule in similar terms as "horrible prophanation[s] of the Sabboth."[18] Significantly, Stubbes's objection to misrule immediately follows his more famous condemnation of theater on the grounds that "the blessed word of God, is to be handled reverently, gravely, and sagely with veneration to the glorious Majesty of God, which shineth therein, and not scoffingly, floutingly, and jybingly as it is upon Stages in Playes and Enterludes."[19] Stubbes's direct intellectual inspirations are the antitheatrical Church Fathers, including Augustine, whom he cites in his own support.[20] However, when he denies the possibility of any genuinely sacred theater, he evokes an older, Platonic logic that sees all imitation as inherently duplicitous. Plato's *Republic* depicts Socrates condemning the tragic poet as "in his nature three removes from the king [i.e., God] and the truth, as are all other imitators."[21] For Stubbes, the problem is not that playwrights sometimes choose to mock God. Rather, he suggests that it is impossible to talk about God on stage without mockery. Any attempt to represent a religious truth dramatically, no matter what the motive, will necessarily fall into blasphemy. Imitation is parody.

Modern critics trying to account for the character of parody in the early modern era or to explain the hostility it increasingly inspired have most often drawn on the ideas of Mikhail Bakhtin.[22] Bakhtin essentially accepts Scaliger's definition of parody as ridiculing inversion, but he revalues ridicule as a folk challenge to elite monoculture and spur to social and aesthetic change. Parody provides "the corrective of laughter and criticism to all existing straightforward genres, languages, styles, voices; to force men to experience beneath these categories a different and contradictory reality that is otherwise not captured in them."[23] It defamiliarizes the object of representation and anticipates the development of novelistic heteroglossia by revealing the power of language as language.[24] Applied to Elizabethan theater, Bakhtin's account would align dramatic parody of religious models with subversive and secularizing impulses. Though elements of Bakhtin's historiography have been questioned, the theoretical framework he proposes has remained powerfully influential, and it (superficially, at least) feels consonant with the iconoclastic, scoffing Marlovian persona evoked by documents like the Baines note.[25]

Descriptions of parody as inversion, however, are by themselves inadequate to explain texts like *Enough Is as Good as a Feast* and *Doctor Faustus*. These plays sometimes exploit the deflationary capacity of imperfect imitation. But at other points they employ dramatic parody in a more speculative manner, to explore theological problems or even to model orthodox behavior. As a corrective to Scalinger and Bakhtin, we might consider Agamben's strikingly different claim that "parody does not call into question the reality of its object; indeed, this object is so intolerably real for parody that it becomes necessary to keep it at a distance . . . parody holds itself, so to speak, on the threshold of literature, stubbornly suspended between reality and fiction, between word and thing."[26] Departing from Scaliger—and effectively dismissing the dialogical play celebrated by Bakhtin as mere "fiction"—Agamben instead follows Plato in focusing upon the relationship between the representation and the distanced reality it purports to stand for. However, he crucially revalues Platonic concepts. Where Plato asserts the hierarchical inferiority of representations, Agamben notes that the prefix *para-* implies a horizontal arrangement of original and copy. And where Plato rejects mimesis on the grounds of its imperfection, Agamben argues that avowed distortion has a sacralizing effect. When parody draws attention to its inability to display an object directly, it reverently casts that object as a mystery. Viewed in this light, the "liturgy of the mass, the representation par excellence of the modern mystery, [is] parodic," and medieval scatological reworkings are respectful elaborations, rather than profanations, of liturgical form.[27] Agamben rejects Bakhtin's suggestion that parodies contest privileged forms and ideas from below and claims instead that they offer esoteric avenues to otherwise inaccessible truths.[28] Reworking the terms Stubbes uses to condemn the theater, we might say that the scoffing, flouting, and jibing of players does not misappropriate or dampen the light of God's majesty shining within his word so much as it veils that light so that it can be looked on indirectly, without the risk of being blinded.

Although Bakhtin and Agamben's accounts of parody are markedly different, I do not think we need to choose between them in all cases. Parody is capable of being deployed for many purposes and of appearing in many forms and many locations. It can emerge reverently beside or profanely below the object it mimics.[29] Superimposing these two theoretical models, moreover, might be particularly helpful for understanding sixteenth-century texts. During this period, the reemergence of *parodia* as a topic of explicit consideration in rhetorical studies and the increased religious scrutiny of representation combined to render parody's true position especially uncertain. Moreover, this uncertainty seems to have been recognized by at least some Elizabethan writers, who responded to it in markedly different ways. The ambiguous place of parody contributes to Stubbes's distrust of scoffing mimesis. But to other writers struggling to depict ambiguous or dangerous subjects, the very instability of parodic forms might prove useful. To see just how useful, I now turn to representations of the bad death.

Dying Like a Protestant

As I discussed in the introduction, popular *ars moriendi* texts present death not just as a misfortune to be suffered but also as a discipline to be studied or an action to be performed. From its inception in the fifteenth century, homiletic literature of the good death troubled easy distinctions between activity and passivity and considered complex interactions between divine and human will. However, questions of how to die well became charged in new ways after the Reformation. The art of dying, like other devotional practices, served as a site of sectarian controversy. Some of these arguments focused on the outward forms of death. Protestant reformers challenged many Catholic rituals, such as the anointing of the sick and intercessory prayers.[30] Polemicists from both confessions politicized the moment of death through highly publicized accounts of victorious martyrdoms[31] and propagandistic accusations that dying leaders of rival sects had despaired or recanted.[32] Doctrinal disputes could pose more foundational challenges to *artes moriendi*. When influential predestinarian theologies denied the importance for works and stressed the necessity of grace, they threatened the conceptual basis of conduct books. The deathbed renders this theoretical challenge especially pressing, for two reasons. First, the dying person's diminished mental and physical capacity can render the limitations of the human will more apparent. Second, the moment of death was commonly understood to unmask the true distribution of agency between the human and the divine. Death reveals whether a person was always already saved or damned, and this revelation has two effects that are somewhat in tension with each other.[33] On the one hand, it demonstrates the importance of grace to salvation and the insufficiency of human endeavor. On the other hand, it encourages onlookers to reconceive an individual's earthly actions as direct expressions of her ultimate spiritual status. Her earlier moral vacillations must be retroactively reclassified either as true expressions of her election (or depravity) or as temporary and misleading departures from her essential nature. Sectarian disputes and doctrinal innovations did not destroy the genre of *ars moriendi*; indeed, more, and more varied, examples were produced by both Catholics and Protestants over the sixteenth and seventeenth centuries than ever before.[34] But controversy altered the nature of the genre. *Ars moriendi* developed from a broadly applicable template for the final good work of a Christian to a site of contention over what both a Christian and a work could be.

Doctrinal disputes about mortality also had consequences for the form of religious theater. The longstanding link between deathbed conduct books and drama is evident in the 1528 printed edition of *Everyman*, which advertises itself as a "treatyse how ye hye fader of heuen sendeth dethe to somon euery creature . . . in maner of a morall playe."[35] Medieval moral interludes dramatizing the approach to death typically illustrated the practices outlined in *ars moriendi* texts by depicting morally malleable, universalized protagonists who oscillate between good and bad impulses. Elizabethan Protestant dramatists sought to reorient this theatrical tradition to better account for the belief that spiritual status is predetermined. William Wager's *Enough Is as Good as a Feast* illustrates how an alteration of this sort works. The play is a fairly representative example of a subgenre labeled "homiletic tragedies" by David Bevington.[36] Whereas earlier medieval moralities had emphasized forgiveness and ended hopefully, Bevington claims that in the 1570s and 1580s, predestinarian doctrines shifted some dramatists' focus "from forgiveness to retribution." These new tragedies discover "the materials for a tragic resolution" within the episodes of moral degeneracy typical of the earlier morality tradition. Transforming a comedy into tragedy merely requires "terminating its usual progression of spiritual downfall and recovery before the final phase."[37] Bevington's demonstration that there are significant structural continuities between homiletic tragedies and earlier plays is convincing. Yet in focusing on historical persistence, he understates the extent to which these plays redirect or even subvert the forms they inherit as they accommodate new doctrinal positions.

Enough Is as Good as a Feast centers on a protagonist named Worldly Man, who is torn between the moderation advocated by the virtuous figure of Heavenly Man and the avarice promoted by the vice Covetousness. Though initially attracted to Heavenly Man's words, he eventually aligns himself with Covetousness and with his help is shown extorting a tenant and cheating a hireling. As the pair conspires to evict the tenant, Worldly Man is suddenly struck down by God's Plague. Covetousness ministers to him, along with Ignorance (an ineffective priest) and a Physician, but he continues to sicken. On his deathbed he attempts to dictate a will but dies before he finishes speaking the opening sentence "In the name . . ." and is finally claimed by Satan.[38]

Wager dramatizes a distinction between the saved and the damned that is absolute but obscured for much of the action. Worldly Man's initial motions toward repentance appear sincere. Embracing moderation, he offers thanks

to God the father of all might,
Which will not the death of sinners as Scripture doth say,
It hath pleased him to open unto me the true light
Whereby I perceive the right path from the broad way;
Therefore, I am content myself for to stay
With Enough which bringeth me to quiet in body and mind
Yea, and all other commodities therewith I do find. (658–64)

Worldly Man is a reprobate—and marked as such by his name—but in this speech he scarcely sounds like one. He claims to feel internal, affective satisfaction with "Enough," and his statement that God has "open[ed] unto me the true light" implies a genuine change in position and perspective brought about through grace. Arguably, the speech is ironized by the term "commodities," which implies that Worldly Man understands godly rewards through analogy to material ones.[39] Yet the word by itself does not prove Worldly Man is speaking in bad faith. Such comingling of worldly and spiritual language is common, especially in texts focusing on last things. Sixteenth-century wills, for example, performed dual religious and economic functions. Ostensibly secular testamentary documents typically had devotional preambles, and sample testaments sometimes show up in religious texts.[40] Thomas Becon's devotional dialogue *The Sycke Mans Salve*, published in 1561, offers an instructive counterpoint to Wager's play. Epaphroditus, the godly man at the center of Becon's text, manifests his religious charity by dictating a will containing specific bequests to his dependents and friends and even offering forty pounds for the upkeep of public highways.[41] The need for the godly to engage with the world in material terms, if only in order to provide analogies for heavenly action, mirrors the tendency of the fallen to express themselves with spiritual language. A reprobate character such as Worldly Man held in the grip of a virtuous impulse looks the same as someone exhibiting genuine virtue. And the convergence raises questions about whether the two can ever be distinguished.

The end of the play insists they can—in death. Wager uses a parody of the traditional postures of the good death to overwrite the apparent convergence between saved and damned with a radical differentiation. Superficial similarity is significant only because it reveals a far more profound distinction. The dying Worldly Man exhibits his degeneracy through perverted approximations of correct godly behavior. Like Becon's Epaphroditus, he is surrounded by friends and advisors. However, most of them are vices; only the Physician shows even a formulaic concern for his spiritual well-being. Also like Epaphroditus, he is explicitly concerned with settling his affairs before death. However, Worldly Man envisages a will that would help his wife "(as near as she can) forgo nought" (1392) rather than support acts of charity. The process reaches its climax as Worldly Man is prevented from using a spiritual formula simply as a formula once he finds himself physically incapable of speaking God's name. Whereas initially Worldly Man's mimicry of Heavenly Man had made him look like one of the saved, by the end of the play, his close approximation of godly behavior is itself a marker of his fallenness.

Ultimately, *Enough Is as Good as a Feast* rejects the apparent convergence of godly and reprobate behavior in will making to affirm a clear hierarchy between them. The worldly death is conclusively marked as a failed imitation of the godly death. This second convergence of worldly and godly, in which the sinner parodies the saved, counters the first, where the reprobate temporarily displays repentance. Elements separated sequentially in the earlier part of the play (so that Worldly Man is wicked, then good, then wicked again) are here compressed (so that wickedness and goodness attach simultaneously to the same postures and become available to the audience together). For Wager, the ostensibly poor fit of inherited dramatic models centered on a malleable everyman with a predestinarian outlook becomes dramatically advantageous. Worldly Man's apparently perfect and sincere mimicry of godliness acknowledges epistemological difficulties inherent to predestinarian beliefs.[42] His moral oscillation indicates how earthly uncertainty of election obscures the distinction between the saved and the damned, and his fall into explicit parody reaffirms the primacy of that distinction.

Over the course of the action, the play's implicit understanding of parody evolves. Wager increasingly codes variant imitations as not merely comic but also morally inferior; he then encourages the audience to apply retroactively an assessment of inferiority to earlier episodes. An implicit understanding of parody resembling Agamben's is replaced by one more like Scaliger's. At first, Worldly Man's approving reference to commodities accrued through godliness seems a handy material analogy for intangible heavenly rewards. Later, it appears like a telling departure from true Christian practice. Once the ridicule evoked by Worldly Man's behavior during death is belatedly extended to encompass his earlier actions, what had first emerged beside becomes refigured below. What remains unclear is if there is any necessary endpoint to this process or if *Enough Is as Good as a Feast* wants to suggest that all imitations are parodic and derogatory. If even

Worldly Man's repentant motions can be redefined as reprobate inversions, it is hard to imagine what imitation could conclusively avoid accusations of inappropriateness and failure. Such doubts seem to have underpinned a turn by religious writers away from the stage, a turn in which Wager seems to have participated.

To illustrate that the approach taken by Wager in *Enough Is as Good as a Feast* is not unique, we can look at Nathaniel Woodes's *The Conflict of Conscience*, which pushes the confusion of parody with other forms of imitation still further. Woodes's play was inspired by the life and death of the Italian Protestant apostate Francesco Spiera, who was held up by writers from Calvin to John Foxe and Thomas Beard as a monitory example of the dangers of equivocation.[43] Structurally, Woodes's plot resembles Wager's. His Spiera analogue, called Philologus, is a Protestant who is convinced to convert to Catholicism by a vision of worldly joys. After a brief period of pleasure, during which Philologus rejects Conscience's calls to renew his faith, he is abruptly arrested by Horror and informed that he has "extinguished the holy Spirit of God," so that grace is no longer available to him.[44] Immediately, he falls into despair. Friends and family members gather around him and attempt to redeem him through collective prayer. He speaks the words of prayers but insists that they are ineffective because they are not matched by any inner feeling, since "all grace [is] gone."[45] Philologus leaves his friends, still unconsoled, and in the final scene a messenger appears to announce that he has hanged himself.

The Conflict of Conscience and *Enough Is as Good as a Feast* both employ a psychomachic structure centered around an everyman figure to make evident the close resemblance of the behavior of the potentially saved to that of the inevitably damned. But Woodes goes further than Wager in dramatizing this closeness and in showing how the use of parody to signal reprobation can undermine the integrity of mimesis more generally. The godly Philologus of the first half of the play performs his part more successfully, for longer, and with less prompting than does the briefly reformed Worldly Man. And while Worldly Man could not name God on his deathbed, Philologus names him repeatedly, performing acts of prayer well enough to convince his auditors that he is actually praying. In its first printed iteration, the play offers its readers explicit signs to distinguish Philologus's near approach to godliness from actual godliness; in the final scene, Philologus makes the point that he is without grace repeatedly, and his assessment is ratified by the pronouncements of the character Horror. Yet the subsequent textual history of *The Conflict of Conscience* makes parody still harder to locate. While the original version of the play ended

with Philologus's death, a later revision was printed with a happy ending.[46] The only changes Woodes makes to transform tragedy into comedy
are to remove references to the historical Spiera from the paratext and to
rewrite the final messenger's speech from an announcement of Philologus's death to an announcement of the restoration of his faith. Together,
the two versions of the text signal the impossibility of distinguishing true
godliness from its depraved simulacrum without additional contextual
information. Although in this particular instance Woodes's revision aspires
retroactively to transform parodic imitation into a sincere and eventually
successful motion toward repentance, his move is easy to reverse. Every
representation of faith has the potential to be revealed as parody, especially
given that in the dubious context of the commercial theater the performer
is always distinguishable from the parts he performs.

   Doctor Faustus confronts these difficulties. Marlowe, like Wager and
Woodes, adapts older forms to fit new doctrinal contexts and deploys parody
to adjudicate between godliness and depravity. However, his play differs
from *Enough Is as Good as a Feast* in several important respects. First, it is less
clear that there are alternatives to parody. Where *Enough* counterbalances
the vices with unambiguous virtues, *Doctor Faustus* refers to heaven in terms
of privation that foreground the distorting effects of human perception.
Ruth Lunney notes, for example, how the Good Angel is usually misheard
or misunderstood by Faustus and starts to appear more like a manifestation
of psychological uncertainty than a clear link to the divine.[47] The B text,
though often described as the Arminian version of the play, stresses structural impediments to Faustus's perception of Christian teachings through
Mephastophilis's boast that "when thou took'st the book / To view the scriptures, then I turn'd the leaves / And led thine eye" (B text, 5.2.992–94). In
the context of heaven's occlusion, Faustus's behavior can be read as a practice of negative theology that engages the divine through demonstrating
what it is not. Second, any attempt to characterize Faustus's downfall simply
as a blasphemous inversion is complicated by the sheer variety of ways that
he perverts divine truth. Worldly Man undergoes a single, conclusive bad
death; Faustus stages multiple arts of dying badly. His imitations of religious
postures never disavow their dependence on a divine original. They constitute alternative approaches to inevitable damnation rather than challenges
that could evade it. But in their diversity and their refusal to explicate their
precise relation to that original, they focus attention toward what constitutes fallen human action.[48] Faustus may even discover a limited degree of
freedom, not to avoid hell but to choose between different paths to hell.

Third, parodic approaches to death in *Doctor Faustus* ground a metatheatrical investigation of the ethics and aesthetics of theater. If Wager's equation of parody with depravity risks expanding (maybe unwittingly) into a condemnation of all mimesis, Marlowe's depiction of shifting relationships between parodic religious and artistic practices explores what case can be made for embodied imitation despite, or even because of, its inevitable distortion of its object.

Heaven or Helen?

Doctor Faustus moves in the opposite direction to *Enough Is as Good as a Feast*, from parody as inversion to parody as juxtaposition. Marlowe begins the play by establishing blasphemy as the normative mode of dramatic representation and then investigates whether mimesis can be recuperated either as a secular practice or as a tool for representing religious truths. The first scene introduces Faustus as an intellectual iconoclast, dismantling and rejecting the disciplines of the sixteenth-century university.[49] As Edward A. Snow demonstrates, Marlowe's protagonist proceeds by strategically confusing two definitions of the word "end" and by misunderstanding the goals of the various disciplines as their termini.[50] The fact that Faustus has learned to dispute well, for instance, means he has achieved logic's "chiefest end" and can now abandon its study (1.1.8). Magic alone survives because Faustus considers it to lack any positive content. While he glories that the scope of its study is limited only by "the mind of man" (1.1.62), his conception seems circumscribed by the disciplines he already knows and defines magic against. His practice does not strike out into new territory but perverts other modes of thought and behavior—most notably the religious ceremonies he parodies in the black mass that summons Mephastophilis and his exclamation "*consumatus est*" (2.1.74) as he finalizes his contract with Lucifer. Significantly, Faustus's distorted performances initially stand alone and unchallenged. The play initially lacks positive examples of *imitatio Christi*—let alone manifestations of heaven—to act as counterweights. Even Faustus's Bible appears to contain no promise of salvation. In the absence of divine grace or revelation (and in *Doctor Faustus* both can be presumed absent), it scarcely seems possible to secure faith or mimesis from falling into parody. Religious concepts can only be expressed in a blasphemous register, and imitation and damnation are knotted together. The final two scenes of the play—containing Faustus's encounter with the Old Man who urges repentance, his vision of a spirit representing Helen, and his soliloquy in the face of death—represent a series of attempts to untangle this knot.

The project starts with Marlowe's nearest analogue to one of the virtues from the morality tradition. The Old Man, the one unambiguously godly figure in the play, attempts to inspire Faustus to repent. Yet his words conspicuously fail to produce the divine intercession he invokes. When he tells Faustus he sees "an angel hovers o'er thy head, / And with a vial full of precious grace / Offers to pour the same into thy soul" (5.1.53–55), we, the audience, do not see anything. Perhaps his vision descries an interrupted but realizable offer of salvation. Or perhaps a gesture of offering is the most that Faustus can hope for. Heaven is a suspended and uncertain possibility, hidden from both the human characters and the audience. The nonappearance of grace onstage has led some critics to question the Old Man's motives. For John Stachniewski, the character's Calvinist perspective undercuts his words, which constitute cynical imitations of a call to repentance, less concerned with inspiring spiritual regeneration than with demonstrating Faustus's depravity.[51] Under the cover of holding out grace to Faustus, the Old Man anticipates an inevitable rejection that will then justify the magician's damnation.

Precisely because heaven is banished from the stage, I am wary of attempts to fix the theology of *Doctor Faustus* or its characters with any precision. I do, however, want to consider why the Old Man's words feel insincere to so many readers. Whatever his ultimate intentions toward Faustus, the difficulties the character experiences in making a persuasive case for repentance reflect the more general difficulty of rescuing religious mimesis from debasing parody once parody is established as the default mode of expression. Some examples will show how this works. The Old Man intervenes against the baseline set by Faustus's blasphemy. He repeatedly refigures images and concepts from Faustus's speeches in an orthodox guise. When he encourages Faustus to "guide thy steps unto the way of life, / By which sweet path thy may'st attain the goal / That shall conduct thee to celestial rest" (5.1.36–38), he overwrites Faustus's earlier confusion of different forms of endings with a Christian approach to death that unites a linear movement along a path with teleological striving toward "the goal." And when he exhorts Faustus's heart to "Break . . . , drop blood, and mingle it with tears" (5.1.39), he envisions reversing the coagulation that accompanied Faustus's diabolical deal.

However, Faustus is able to counter the Old Man in exactly the same manner. While renewing his vow to Lucifer, he makes a request,

To glut the longing of my heart's desire:
That I might have unto my paramour
That heavenly Helen which I saw of late
Whose sweet embracings may extinguish clean
These thoughts that do dissuade me from my vow. (5.1.81–87)

He replaces the Old Man's gradualist "sweet path" with a sudden, "clean" extinguishing. His hope that Helen will "glut the longing of my heart's desire" echoes the Old Man's earlier address to his heart but aligns the organ with lust rather than repentance. This pattern of oscillation between godly and worldly versions of the same image is confirmed when Faustus's response to Helen is again matched by a godly revision. Faustus demands that Helen make him "immortal with a kiss" that will "suck forth my soul" and fantasizes about engaging in "combat with weak Menelaus" (5.1.92–93, 99). The Old Man—who comes onstage to overhear Faustus and is then attacked by devils as punishment for his interference—responds in kind, again reworking elements of Faustus's language. As devils enter, he taunts them, insisting

My faith, vile hell, shall triumph over thee!
Ambitious fiends, see how the heaven smiles
At your repulse, and laughs your state to scorn:
Hence, hell, for hence I fly unto my God. (5.1.113–18)

This challenge to the devils appropriates images of flying souls and combat from Faustus's address to remind listeners that Helen, also, is a (disguised) spirit and to counter Faustus's hedonism with morality.

The risk, though, is that the Old Man's orthodox revisions will never appear conclusive. *Enough Is as Good as a Feast* establishes a divinely sanctioned hierarchy that situates authentic heavenly approaches to death above devalued worldly ones. By contrast, *Doctor Faustus* produces a sequence of distorted revisions, which can be extended indefinitely, since parody, like magic, lacks a natural end. While it might be tempting to attribute the equivalent weight given to the Old Man and to Faustus to a peculiarly Marlovian perversity, John Parker traces a long patristic and medieval tradition of similar convergences between Christ and Antichrist.[52] Orthodoxy will never make a statement that heterodoxy cannot respond to.

In the absence of any revelation clearly privileging the Old Man's perspective over Faustus's, other criteria for judgment must emerge. One possible candidate is beauty. Faustus's conversation with the scholars, which had established Helen as "the admirablest lady that ever lived" (5.1.12), primes us to consider the aesthetic. And here Faustus would seem to win out. In comparison to his poetically inspired praise of Helen, the Old Man's steadfast assertion of faith can seem banal by virtue of its very orthodoxy. Faustus's speech almost seems to announce the emergence of a secular, classically inspired theater from a religious medieval past.[53] Yet his words, far from simply celebrating Helen's beauty, test the limits of what imitation can accomplish when it is conceived in aesthetic terms. As Richard Halpern observes, Faustus's opening question, "Was this the face that launch'd a thousand ships?" (5.1.90), can be taken to express a real skepticism as to whether this magical (and theatrical) vision represents Helen adequately.[54] Conversely, the magician's attempt to insert himself into the drama of the Trojan War by promising to "be Paris" and sack Wittenberg instead of Troy (5.1.97) risks absurdity in its superimposition of Helen's aestheticized domain onto the everyday milieu of sixteenth-century Germany. The speech maps out a continuum from artistic representations that fail because they are too distanced from their underlying models to those that fail because they refuse to acknowledge distinctions between representation and reality. Faustus's journey from doubt to overidentification implies that secular mimesis and religious mimesis encounter the same problems. It is no easier to identify an accurate imitation of Helen than an accurate imitation of Christ. The Trojan War, like the Passion, can be parodied.

Moreover, one of the classical models underlying Faustus's speech suggests a very different criterion for judgment: *memento mori*. The question "Was it then for this that the thousand ships were manned from all Greece, for this that so many Greeks and barbarians fell, and so many cities were devastated?" was first posed by a character in Lucian's *Dialogues of the Dead*.[55] However, "this" is not Helen's face but her skull, now fleshless and indistinguishable from the other human bones that surround it. Lucian's reminder of the inescapable fact of death shifts the balance between the Old Man and Faustus. As he embraces Helen, Faustus aestheticizes and eroticizes mortality, while missing or ignoring Lucian's admonition. By contrast, the Old Man faces death squarely, though his conception of the afterlife is Christian rather than Hellenic. His final words to the devils, "hence I fly unto my God" (5.1.118), anticipate that their torment will be fatal.[56] And this acceptance of death hands the Old Man a sort of victory. He ends the inconclusive series of mutual revisions and variations by walking off the earthly stage. He leaves Faustus confronting a void that cannot be parodied because it has no substantive content.

Now I Die Eternally

Or can it? Perhaps we can read Faustus's praise of Helen not as a doomed attempt to substitute artistic achievement for religious truth or the harsh reality of death but as a serious parody that investigates how art, religion, and death inform one another.[57] In Helen—as face, skull, and succubus—death manifests as a problem that is simultaneously representational, material, and theological. As Faustus's soul is lost to and received from her embrace, so dramatic representation might aspire to illuminate mortality by circling around, becoming absorbed in and reemerging from it. Intimations of blasphemy, skepticism, or naïve identification do not hamper this movement. Rather, they drive it. The same dynamic also governs Faustus's final soliloquy, as the unavailability of an orthodox approach to death again propels the magician toward parody. In this last speech, moreover, parallels emerge between parodic practices of dying badly and the mimetic theatrical performances that Marlowe, like Wager, uses to dramatize bad deaths. Compounding allusions to dramatic form encourage audiences to question whether any form of embodied or textual imitation can escape association with blasphemy and failure.

Throughout the final two scenes of *Doctor Faustus*, Christian models of death are invoked and then revealed as unsatisfactory. The Old Man is succeeded by the scholars, who also ineffectively exhort Faustus to repent. Once they exit the stage, conventional arts of dying appear to have failed. Faustus is left alone to inhabit or invent new genres. His last speech threatens to associate practices of dying with mere performance and so to condemn both. Like a prisoner on a scaffold, Faustus theatrically acknowledges his crimes. But his confession is arrested before it moves toward wholehearted repentance and then salvation. He admits sin but, rather than turn to God for forgiveness, only produces more perverse departures from the established art of dying well. Instead of adopting a single system of belief (even a blasphemous one), Faustus ventriloquizes Hermetic, Pythagorean, and Epicurean cosmologies alongside heretical fantasies of a hell of limited duration (5.2.85–104). He entertains multiple conceptions of what death should look like. However, at no time does he alight upon a mode of dying that appears sustainable. If anything, the pattern of parodic variation on established discourses becomes more emphatic, as a panicked Faustus cycles through different philosophies, in each case acknowledging their falsity or irrelevance.

From a purely characterological perspective, Faustus's various death fantasies, like his responses to the Old Man, indicate despair and sinfulness.

None of the alternative cosmologies enable him to die better in a religious or even an aesthetic sense. The vacuum left by the failure of the Old Man and other representatives of orthodoxy does not give Faustus an opportunity to approach his death in an affirmative manner; it simply clears a space in which he can die badly without any outside interference. Yet if the soliloquy offers no coherent approach to death, it does not reject *ars moriendi* as a genre. As Faustus abandons each individual alternative model of death, he moves on to a new one, suggesting that he might find some value simply in rehearsing different practices of dying. To take one example:

> Why wert thou not a creature wanting soul?
> Or why is it immortal that thou hast?
> Ah, Pythagoras' metempsychosis, were that true
> This soul should fly from me, and I be chang'd
> Unto some brutish beast,
> All beasts are happy, for when they die
> Their souls are soon dissolv'd in elements; (5.2.97–103)

Faustus scarcely attempts to sustain his Pythagorean fantasies. He admits he has an immortal soul and acknowledges metempsychosis as untrue. His logic is associative, and his terms are muddled. When he talks about his soul "fly[ing] from me," "me" is presumably the body. But in the second half of the line, "I" is described as something to be transformed into a beast, presumably through transmigration, so that "I" has to be the soul. Then the Pythagorean framework is silently dropped, as the happiness of beasts is linked to the mortality of their souls—an idea Pythagoras rejects. What the speech dramatizes, then, is not a viable or consistent art of dying but the art of generating arts of dying. Faustus's existence has become the continuous production of approaches to death. He embarks on a search for a narrative of dying that would harmonize his subjective experience with a metaphysical order.

Since Faustus never arrives at a viable philosophy of how to die, his speech marks how human experience (even as it remains a fallen derivative of divine truth) resists absorption into any particular metaphysical context. This resistance emerges precisely through the acts by which it tries to efface itself. And it is here, in these patterns of failed self-effacement, that the practice of dying starts to emerge as a meaningful exercise of human agency. As Faustus continuously narrates alternative futures for himself while simultaneously denying the reality of his own narrations, he comes into focus as the exemplar of the bad death. In *The Highest Poverty*, Agamben discusses the Franciscan ideal of *forma vitae*, a holy life that is not constrained by monastic rules but that causes those rules (along with other disciplinary and legal codes) to bend to the strength of its example.[58] Ever the parodist, Faustus supplies a mirror image of this framework. As he struggles and fails to bring himself into conformity with either the heavenly order that condemns him or the heterodox philosophies that would allow him to escape, his bad death emerges as the only unifying principle, distorting and drawing together divergent metaphysical frameworks. Faustus in this moment can do no more than register the bare existence of something like a *forma mortis*. Caught in despair, he in no way matches the claims made by the Franciscans to evade legal codes by virtue of the form of their lives. But as he illustrates how practices of dying can emerge in distinction to the metaphysical principles that purport to govern them, Faustus suggests new possibilities for human agency in death. He offers an example that other playwrights will extend in more affirmative directions.

Already in *Doctor Faustus* there are intimations that Faustus's practice will persist into new contexts. As Michael Neill notes, the play suggests that Faustus never dies as such but rather becomes caught up in an endless process of dying, which might continue even after he is taken to hell.[59] *Doctor Faustus* never fully clarifies what the devils receive in their bargain. While the deed of gift purports to grant them "body and soul, flesh, blood, or goods," this clause cannot be parsed so it is certain which elements are cumulative and which alternative (2.1.109–10). Confusion persists in Faustus's fear that his soul "must live still to be plagu'd in hell" (5.2.104) and in his claim that Lucifer will bear him "quick to hell" (5.2.109). Faustus's own ambiguous words could simply indicate his state of denial—except they are echoed by the Chorus, which describes Faustus as "gone" rather than as "dead" (Epilogue, 4).[60] When Faustus tells the scholars "now I die eternally" (5.2.4), he most obviously evokes Paul's characterization of damnation as spiritual death. Yet the statement also suggests that Faustus's subsequent existence will be an eternity of dying.[61] The play asserts a heavenly order that has determined Faustus's fall. But even after this fall, something of Faustus persists as a continually failing yet never ceasing performance of dying badly. Rather than the conclusive, parodic inversion of the good death that Wager used to mark Worldly Man's end as bad, *Doctor Faustus* adopts a form of parody grounded in juxtaposition, producing variant arts of dying that may never cease.

Other aspects of the final soliloquy, however, anticipate a more definitive conclusion. Something very peculiar happens with the time scheme of Faustus's final speech. Faustus makes a bid for temporal dilation when he asks

That time may cease, and midnight never come!
Fair nature's eye, rise, rise again, and make
Perpetual day, or let this hour be but a year,
A month, a week, a natural day,
That Faustus may repent, and save his soul. (5.2.62–66)[62]

While Faustus wants time to slow, his words formally enact compression, substituting increasingly short time periods for perpetuity. In consequence, the speech gestures toward extension and contraction simultaneously. Faustus's evocation of contradictory temporal movements finds an analogue in the mismatch between stage time and real time. Faustus's final hour, as marked by the striking of the clock, obviously passes far faster than the time that would elapse in any actor's feasible performance of the speech. The final soliloquy implies three incompatible time schemes: the extended one of Faustus's fantasies, the compressed one marked by the clock, and the real one experienced by the audience and players.

What reconciles these different temporalities is midnight, which at once marks the end of the period Faustus hopes to extend, the end of the compressed hour, and, if not the end of time itself, then the end of the time depicted within the play. The structural importance of midnight is emphasized for readers (as opposed to viewers) by Marlowe's ending tag "*Terminat hora diem, terminat Author opus* [the hour ends the day, the author ends the work]." This line reaches backward to the play's composition and forward to its textual afterlife, impossibly asserting that the narrative, the writing of the play, its performance, and its reading all end in a single terminus.

Because it reconciles inconsistent time schemes at the moment of Faustus's damnation, midnight has a role in Faustus somewhat analogous to that of death in *Enough Is as Good as a Feast*. Dramatic time schemes that cannot be synchronized coincide at a moment of ending. Importantly, however, midnight imposes a less hierarchical resolution in *Doctor Faustus* than death does in *Enough*. The two clauses of "*Terminat hora diem, terminat Author opus*" are arranged paratactically, not causally. The author determines the end of the day just as much as the hour determines the end of the play. Faustus's inability to slow time as he desires perhaps derogates his perspective, but the control asserted by the author means that the subordination of Faustus does not necessarily imply the subordination of human experience.

There are, then, two distinct models of ending in Faustus's final soliloquy: Faustus's continuous production of failing *artes moriendi* and the depersonalized assertion of midnight as a terminus in which all time schemes are reconciled. The former is obviously closer to worldly experience; the latter resembles an imposition of cosmic order. Faustus, the bad performer of unsustainable, ineffective arts of dying, is subsumed by a Latin tag that allows authorial participation in a transcendent conclusion. However, midnight only brings about nominal resolution. The ending tag asserts a purely formal control that bears no relation to the panicked, despairing content that fills up Faustus's final hour. A dramatized art of dying that could be aesthetically pleasing or spiritually effective is an aspiration beyond the stage and the text rather than something visible in the play.

Theater and the Art of Dying

"I think hell's a fable," Faustus tells Mephastophilis as he signs the deed giving the devils his soul (2.1.128). In the moment, his comment exposes his hubris and self-deception. By the end of the play, it has assumed a new metatheatrical significance and greater accuracy. Faustus's dying and after-life are characterized by the ceaseless production of imaginative narratives of death. The only hell that can be shown onstage is a fictional one, and Faustus's remarks on its fabulous nature tie his production of arts of dying to the dramatic production of death within Marlowe's tragedy.

If hell's a fable, does it follow that fables are hellish? I have traced how Elizabethan dramas of damnation associate parodic inversion with blas-phemy and have argued that this association might justify broader suspi-cion of mimesis because parody is hard to separate from other forms of imitation. This context should caution us against reading Marlowe's play as an iconoclastic demystification exemplifying an emergent, secular theater, as Graham Hammill does when he argues that the play dramatizes move-ment from a theological framework to "the world of the literary."[63] The precedent of the homiletic tragedies and *artes moriendi* suggests that the theology and the literature offer different approaches to the same problems of representation. *Doctor Faustus* implicitly rejects the easily gained, hierar-chizing separations of heavenly original and reprobate parody that we see at the end of *Enough Is as Good as a Feast*. But in this rejection, Marlowe only mirrors widespread dissatisfactions expressed by many Protestant thinkers (possibly including earlier playwrights like Wager) with the whole notion of religious drama.

Doctor Faustus suggests two possible responses to such suspicion of mimesis. The first is to follow authors like Wager, who abandoned embod-ied dramatic performance for other media, such as the prose treatise. The substitution of prose for performance is already implicit, though marked as diabolical, in Faustus's pact with the devils. The bloody deed of gift counters the recalcitrance of Faustus's congealing blood. Then, during the final act of the play, traditional communal *ars moriendi* models embodied by the Old Man and the Scholars give way first to Faustus's solo performance of dying badly in the last soliloquy and then, second, to the figure of the author, invoked by a Latin tag that exists only on the page. The masterful author, capable of terminating the day and the drama in the same stroke, replaces ineffective and inconclusive performers and observers.

Yet *Doctor Faustus* also offers reasons to be skeptical of a turn from performance to text and philosophy. Faustus puts faith in books, but he does not move beyond distortion and appearance, as Plato and the antitheatrical polemicists might seem to promise. In his final soliloquy, his fantasies of alternative cosmologies showcase his learning. But the products of this learning are impossible counterfactuals, and any hope they supply is predicated on an ability to confuse or evade unitary divine truth rather than reveal it. Faustus's offer to "burn [his] books" (5.2.115) suggests he sees prose rather than performance as the source of his damnation. His panicked cycle through different philosophical approaches to death, seemingly without end, offers devotional writers a monitory example. In hunting for a genre that avoids the pitfalls of mimetic performance, they risk embarking on a similarly indefinite pattern of recursion and substitution. Rather than accept the antitheatrical conclusion that treatises must replace drama in order to produce a true art of dying, Marlowe implies that the distortions of performance could be equally present in prose.

Perhaps, then, similarities between blasphemy, parody, and mimesis are not reasons to abandon drama but reminders that certainty is always absent from mundane experience. The other response *Doctor Faustus* suggests is to affirm the failed and distorting nature of theatrical mimesis and to base a theory of performance on the parodic art of dying badly. In his depiction of Faustus, Marlowe understands parody not only, like Scaliger, as a strategy of travestying debasement nor, like Bakhtin, as a folk challenge to elite monoculture. Rather, like Agamben, his work openly acknowledges distortion as inevitably present in mimesis. Parody functions almost as a negative theology that uses failure to represent relations between the human and the divine. Marlowe accepts the antitheatrical accusations that dramatic representations are at a double remove from the truth. But he implies, counterintuitively, that this makes tragedy a better avenue to truth than the writings of philosophers or theologians who purport to represent it directly. The proliferation of alternative failed approaches to death becomes a strategy for exploring the eschatological event that acts as their center of gravity.

Viewed one way, *Doctor Faustus* represents the endpoint of a particular strand of Tudor religious theater; it is the bad death of the drama of dying badly. Extending the techniques that earlier dramatists had used to explore reprobation, Marlowe produces a play in the model of a homiletic tragedy from which God is entirely absent and where the parodic forms of the bad death totally overwhelm authentic representations of goodness. In the process, he suggests that such a slantwise approach to religious mystery might prove more productive than direct analysis. Only through practices like Faustus's can we hope to consider the interactions between human and divine will. Even as it implicitly justifies parodic approaches to theological questions, *Doctor Faustus* makes it easy to understand why overtly religious drama became increasingly rare toward the end of the sixteenth century. The play refuses to acknowledge a meaningful difference between orthodox homiletic plays and their heterodox perversions. If in some respects Marlowe appears to solve the difficulties Wager and Woodes encountered in representing reprobate protagonists who occasionally felt repentant impulses, his solutions require acknowledging that parody and perversion taint all mimesis.

But even as the play signals the conclusion of one dramatic tradition of representing death, it opens the way to new alternatives. Marlowe allows us to see how practices of dying can be detached from purely devotional contexts. Faustus's approach to death will find analogues in other plays with secular settings, which put the art of dying to new political, social, economic, and aesthetic uses. The remainder of this book tracks the consequences of this transposition.

CHAPTER 2

Dying Politically

Edward II and the Ends
of Dynastic Monarchy

Faustus dies alone but not singularly. Marlowe dramatizes a similarly extended death for the protagonist of *Edward II*. Once pressured to give up his crown, Edward is surprised to discover that abdication does not result in annihilation but instead leaves him, like Faustus, caught up in an indefinite experience of dying. Tortures designed to weaken him merely draw attention to his continued vitality. Marlowe's dramatization of Edward's end poses a challenge to the most influential early modern accounts of sovereignty, which employ concepts of perpetuity to minimize the political importance of biological finitude. In common understanding, the periodic deaths of monarchs pose no threat to the institution of monarchy—on the contrary, they serve to confirm that the crown persists beyond the life of any individual king. But the depiction in *Edward II* of a king enduring after his abdication in an indeterminate space between the juridical concept of royal demise and the biological fact of bodily death raises questions about whether a king's death could ever function as more than a comma in a series. The play suggests that rather than simply perpetuating the institution of sovereignty within its established form, active practices of sovereign dying could afford both Edward and his enemies opportunities to alter the relationship between the king's legal identity, body, and dominion and so to pursue any number of alternative political futures.

Like many readers, then, I discover political radicalism in *Edward II*. But I dispute where that radicalism usually is located. Since Alan Bray drew attention to sodomy's function as a label for socially destabilizing sexual acts, most scholarship on *Edward II* has assumed the play engages with politics primarily through eroticism.[1] Edward's ambiguously sodomical relationships with Gaveston and the Spensers, just like Isabella and Mortimer Jr.'s adulterous alliance, challenge normative matrimony and governance simultaneously. While the coimplication of politics and sex within the play is impossible to deny, death should be recognized as an important third term.[2] Legitimate sexuality and paternal mortality function as twin supports to monarchical succession, and attending exclusively to the conditions that promote or threaten the former risks displacing or even denying the latter. In fact, the challenges presented to sovereign perpetuity by Edward's idiosyncratic practice of dying strike me as more fundamental and more persistent than those implied by his homoerotic relationships. Within the play, efforts to manage the monarchy through sexuality rely on established discourses of legitimate and illegitimate relations. By contrast, characters involved in accomplishing Edward's death generally eschew precedents like saintly martyrdom, tragic murder, and *ars moriendi* in favor of unspeakable actions and contingent performances. Though their efforts to render Edward's death a transformative political action sometimes do have analogues in contemporary cultures of dying, they strive to disavow these antecedents. The silences and lacunae that result enable unexpected political affiliations to emerge that challenge the fiction of the perpetual, corporate crown more effectively than sodomy or adultery could.

By reading the politics of *Edward II* primarily through death rather than sex, I seek not only to refocus critical attention on an underappreciated dimension of the play but also to raise broader questions about the capacity of deaths to function as political events within the early modern era and beyond. As they develop strategies to control the king's vitality and mortality, characters in *Edward II* are forced to acknowledge the political potentialities contained within biological life. In response, they often turn to ephemeral performances of dying in order to resist established notions of institutional perpetuity and royal dynasty in favor of tentative and provisional political affiliation. Their actions reveal genealogical links between early modern practices of dying and later political philosophies.

The King Who Never Dies or the King Who Never Grows Up

Edward's practice of dying emerges as a potent political action, and a compelling subject for drama, against the background of assertions that sovereign mortality is impossible or—what paradoxically amounts to the same thing—irrelevant. In *Les six livres de la République*, Jean Bodin influentially insists upon perpetuity as a necessary property of sovereignty, which "ought to be perpetuall, for that it may bee, that that absolute power ouer the subiects may be giuen to one or many, for a short or certaine time, which expired, they are no more than subiects themselues."[3] Echoing him, sixteenth- and seventeenth-century English jurists and political philosophers with otherwise radically different outlooks speak in surprising agreement. The king never dies. And if (or rather when) he does, his death does not matter because the institution he has embodied is perpetual. The crown is a corporation, and its temporal existence transcends the lifetime of any individual monarch. It functions as the locus of sovereign power despite changes in regime—including changes that might radically alter the national or religious makeup of the country or that might supplement or perhaps entirely displace the notional monarch with multiple representatives. Disputes about the line of succession following Elizabeth, the unification of England and Scotland under James, the assertion of the royal prerogative by Charles I, the legality of the Civil War, and arguably even the regicide were carried out under the assumption that Bodin, in this respect at least, was right.[4] Sovereignty is eternal and the institution of the crown, in an important sense, undying. Even writers who explore republican alternatives to monarchy start with the assumption that to be valid, political formations must persist indefinitely.[5]

This assumption still feels remarkably natural today. Historians have often taken the time to explain why, for instance, Elizabeth might seek to control the marriages of potential successors or suppress discussion of heirs. But that her death would not threaten sovereignty per se because some successor would be able to perpetuate the institution is too obvious to mention. Yet, although the conceit of the undying monarch seems intuitive—perhaps because it largely accords with how we still understand political institutions—the doctrines that were used to justify it during the early modern era were often conflicting and internally incoherent. In different accounts, the perpetual aspect of the sovereign might constitute an eruption of the sacred into the mundane world, a convenient legal fiction, or some hybrid of the two. The crown might redeem the infirmities of individual monarchs or itself be in need of protection from their predations.

Analyzing overlaps and inconsistencies between these various justifications reveals how central notions of perpetuity were to constructions of power and also the difficulty with which that perpetuity is defined or sustained.

Today, thanks to the work of Ernst Kantorowicz, the best-known account of corporate sovereignty is the theory of the king's two bodies. Edmund Plowden's *Commentaries* indicate that many jurists understood a monarch to have two separate aspects, akin to the two persons of Christ: a "body natural" subject to human impairments such as age and sickness and a corporate "body politic" in possession of the royal dignity.[6] Since this second body is eternal and incorruptible, it guarantees the persistence of the institution of the crown in perpetuity and the continuing potency of royal acts beyond the reign of any individual monarch. This doctrine appears in both mystical and pragmatic manifestations and could be deployed to enhance or limit sovereign autonomy. On occasion, the notion of the body politic certainly bolstered absolutist understandings of divine right.[7] But jurists sometimes also restricted the free action of individual monarchs in the name of the rights of the monarchy as a corporation.[8] This uncertain position of the body politic inside and outside of the legal system arguably constitutes an essential aspect of the doctrine rather than an area of incoherence. Agamben, for one, reads Kantorowicz alongside Carl Schmitt's notion of the exception and the Roman legal figure of the *homo sacer* (the person who can be killed but not sacrificed) to argue that legal systems depend on mutually constitutive forms of power and vulnerability that resist codification; "the body of the sovereign and the body of the *homo sacer* enter into a zone of indistinction in which they can no longer be told apart."[9] The contested status of the body politic within Elizabethan thought is a local manifestation of a more fundamental confusion of the exceptional with the normative in any understanding of sovereignty.

Though modern critics sometimes present the theory of the king's two bodies as an Elizabethan orthodoxy, it was in fact only one of a number of available accounts of the corporate crown that were deployed inconsistently across the culture and sometimes even within the course of the same argument.[10] Another option, for instance, was to view the crown as a perpetual minor, as had been more common in medieval jurisprudence.[11] Kantorowicz notes that "from the same corporational premises there could originate two diametrically opposed opinions: a king *ever* under age versus a king *never* under age. In either case, of course, the intention was to emphasize the exceptional position of the king and his rights, that is, the perpetuity which he shared with the crown."[12] Perpetual minority, like the king's two bodies, aims to shield the institution of sovereignty from the effects of human infirmity. A sequence of individual kings each serve as guardians to a crown that is an eternal minor and consequently legally protected from disinheritance. The future of regal maturity is always to come, never to be achieved by any individual king, and as a result the fiction (like that of the king's two bodies) could be used to constrain royal power in certain circumstances. Individual kings found themselves barred from alienating the royal dominion, and rebels against the governments of both Edward II and Richard II complained of "disherison of the Crown."[13]

Kantorowicz constructs a developmental narrative in which the less sophisticated model of minority was gradually superseded by the more sophisticated, and more stable, model of the two bodies. He notes how jurists wavered between describing the crown as a minor and describing the king as a minor in a way that reflected a confusion of institution and person and that risked absurdly implying either that all of the king's actions were void on account of incapacity or that there should be "some other king to be the guardian of the fictitious nonage king, and so forth in eternal regress."[14] The king's two bodies more successfully distinguish office and individual; the ever-mature body politic may even have emerged as a counter to the ever-underage crown. As a result, this theory became increasingly influential by the sixteenth century, while the model of minority withered away.

In reality, however, the supersession of perpetual minority occurred less conclusively than Kantorowicz claims. John Cowell's 1607 legal dictionary *The Interpreter* follows Plowden in asserting that the king "is alwaies supposed to be of full age, though he be in yeares neuer so young."[15] Yet it makes frequent recourse to the concept of "disherison of the crown" when defining the scope of the powers of the king's agents.[16] Cowell demonstrates that at different moments even within the same text, the Crown might be considered always of age or never of age, according to the exigencies of different contexts. Disherison remains a potent constitutional concept well into the Civil War years, when it was used to define the geographical limits of the realm and to argue for the respective powers of King and Parliament.[17] Perhaps it remains important. The image of the innocent child, as Lee Edelman demonstrates, is still a staple of political rhetoric and is often deployed to restrict the rights of existing adults in the name of an imagined, unblemished future.[18] Perpetual minority continues to function as a governmental organizing principle, though now generally attached to the populace rather than the sovereign. This persistence through and beyond the early modern era suggests that the fiction of the king's two bodies could coexist with other contradictory fictions so long as neither of them challenged the fundamental principle of perpetuity.

Furthermore, both these models implicitly draw justification from a third—that of family dynasty. Admittedly, most Tudor theorists seem reluctant to say so explicitly, perhaps because of the tenuous nature of Henry VII's claim to inherit from the Plantagenets and the uncertainties about who would succeed Elizabeth.[19] Although it would be possible to ground a defense of absolutist perpetual monarchy in the naturalized principles of primogeniture and to claim that sovereign power passes between generations exactly as biological substance does, such an argument gained little public traction until after Robert Filmer's *Patriarcha*, written in the 1630s or 1640s but not published until 1680.[20] Nevertheless, even in the sixteenth century, familial inheritance offered a useful analogy for sovereign succession. Margreta de Grazia and Katherine Eisaman Maus have demonstrated how Shakespeare's plays often register crises in sovereignty and in the intergenerational transfer of property through analogy to each other.[21] Social and economic changes that put pressure on traditional models of inheritance around the end of the sixteenth century also affected how the transmission of royal power was understood.

My immediate aim in laying out these possible accounts of sovereign perpetuity is not to argue that one is superior to the others. Quite the contrary, I want to stress, first, their complementary coexistence, despite the ostensibly incompatible premises from which they start, and, second, the parallel mechanisms through which they manage mortality using fictions of perpetuity. In each case, the pious assertion that the king never dies conveniently anticipates the king's death and renders it politically insignificant. Of course, interested parties might care intensely when particular kings or queens were likely to die and which particular heirs would succeed them. But in most cases, the bare fact that monarchs do die was something the constitution was designed to accommodate easily. Mechanisms existed at once to deny sovereign mortality and then exploit sovereign mortality in that very moment of denial as the means of transferring power from one person to another. The king is dead. Long live the king.

Against this background, Marlowe's *Edward II* encourages audiences to ask what would happen if the king's death actually mattered, not because it confirmed the transfer of sovereign power to the next office holder but because it undermined or altered the basis upon which that transfer took place. In what circumstances would dying function as a political intervention? And what would a politics that emphasized the destabilizing potential of sovereign mortality, instead of repressing it, look like? The play evokes the conceits of the two bodies, perpetual minority, and dynasty almost indiscriminately as supports for the corporate crown and then demonstrates how performances of dying might offer challenges to all of them. The action opens immediately following the transfer of power to Edward II on the death of his father, Edward I. However, the naturalized understanding of royal dynasty implied by this succession soon comes under pressure, initially because Edward's relationship with Gaveston threatens to replace the intergenerational transfer of dominion with an eroticized, homosocial sharing of power but then more fundamentally because Edward abdicates but, to everyone's surprise, remains alive. His unexpected existence in the fissure between demise and death creates a political crisis, since it threatens to expose the incoherence of the theories used to account for the corporate character of the crown. Finally, through the various performances surrounding Edward's murder, Marlowe suggests a range of political futures that could be grounded in a project of sovereign mortality, from absolutism to republicanism, quiescence to revolution, and indiscriminate terror to utopian community.

From Erotics to Necrotics

Edward II initially evokes a naturalized ideology of dynastic succession and then dismantles it by revealing it to be founded on an unstable relationship between demise and death. The play opens with Gaveston reading a letter from Edward, stating, "My father is deceased; come, Gaveston, / And share the kingdom with thy dearest friend."[22] Edward comes into being as both king and character through his father's death. His domain and his dramatic existence are coterminous with the mechanisms of succession. Yet already this opening invitation raises questions about how those mechanisms function. Edward, having inherited the kingdom dynastically, celebrates that he is able to share it with someone to whom he has no genealogical affiliation. He has gained the kingdom through the death of his father, but he seeks to inaugurate a new mode of sovereignty, one exercised through homosocial friendship rather than patriarchy. This political project becomes the principal object of contention between him and the magnates.

As critics have generally recognized, Edward's attempt to bypass patrilineal and social hierarchies precipitates a political crisis, which both Edward and his enemies navigate with continual recourse to competing discourses of eroticized friendship and sodomy. An interchange between

the Mortimers makes the coimplication of politics and sex explicit. When
Mortimer Senior counsels acceptance of Gaveston, since "The mightiest
kings have had their minions" (4.390), his nephew replies:

Uncle, his wanton humour grieves not me;
But this I scorn, that one so basely-born
Should by his sovereign's favour grow so pert,
And riot it with the treasure of the realm,
While soldiers mutiny for want of pay. (4.401–5)

In neither of the two Mortimers' accounts is it possible to extricate assessments of Edward's political and economic sway from judgments on the
propriety of his relationship to Gaveston. Both nobles use political and
sexual insinuations as covers for the other. As Jonathan Goldberg and
Mario DiGangi have demonstrated, politics and sex are similarly conflated
in the representation of Isabella and Mortimer Jr.'s uprising.[23] Their affair
is not easily separable from their insurrection, and both characters become
coded as sodomical through their involvement in Edward's overthrow.
Although critics have disagreed about whether Edward and Gaveston's
relationship ultimately falls on the side of friendship or sodomy—and about
whether, if it is sodomy, this is something Marlowe wishes to disavow or
subversively celebrate—there is a striking consensus that the political and
sexual subtexts of the play are intertwined.[24] While I generally accept this
claim, I believe that to understand fully the crisis at the center of the play,
we need to bring a third term—mortality—into consideration alongside
politics and sex. Natural death and the production of legitimate heirs
through marriage function together as twin supports for dynastic monarchy, justifying the transmission of sovereignty through a biological line of
succession. If the king or his enemies choose to contest the terms on which
that transmission takes place by altering how sovereign sexuality is understood and practiced, they may also transform how sovereign mortality can
manifest.[25]

The interrelation of these terms becomes evident when Isabella and
Mortimer Jr. demand Edward II resign the crown to his young son, in
whose name they will rule as protectors. When Mortimer Jr. protests that
the king is overturning established social hierarchies by sharing the kingdom with "one so basely-born" (4.402), he presents his rebellion as a conservative reaction to Edward's innovations.[26] His complaints about
Edward's ennoblement of Gaveston and the Spensers do not contest
Edward's legitimate right to hold the kingdom on his father's death. Indeed,
his distrust of Gaveston's obscure origins ostensibly commits him to a

defense of the principles of heredity that support Edward's dominion.[27] In this context, he understandably seeks to maintain (or simulate the maintenance of) the line of succession by presenting Edward's son and heir as the true beneficiary of rebellion. When Mortimer's supporters Trussel and the Bishop of Winchester are sent to Edward's prison to demand his crown, they insinuate that his abdication is necessary to maintain the principles of heredity. Responding to Edward's complaint about Mortimer's usurpation, Winchester insists, "Your grace mistakes. It is for England's good / And princely Edward's right we crave the crown" (20.38–39). By stressing the shared name of Edward, proper to both father and son, Winchester presents heredity as a support for perpetuity. Edward must pass the crown on and lose his own identity entirely within his successor. If he does not, the rebels will be forced to consider a more radical regime change, under which "the prince shall lose his right" (20.92). Edward is asked to sacrifice his own interests to the hereditary movement of the crown and to become complicit in his supersession into a lineage.

In resisting abdication, Edward does not contest Winchester's characterization of the mechanisms of succession but makes explicit their proximity to mortality. He questions Mortimer's motives and so reminds his listeners of the mortal threats that are just as important to effecting regime change as principles of dynastic inheritance. Edward insists the crown is

> for Mortimer, not Edward's head,
> For he's a lamb encompassed by wolves
> Which in a moment will abridge his life;
> But if proud Mortimer do wear this crown,
> Heavens turn it to a blaze of quenchless fire,
> Or, like the snaky wreath of Tisiphon,
> Engirt the temples of his hateful head;
> So shall not England's vines be perished,
> But Edward's name survives, though Edward dies. (5.1.40–48)

Edward, understandably, doubts that his son's safety will be ensured by his own abdication. At first, he anticipates bequeathing mortal vulnerability to his son rather than kingly authority. And in keeping with the play's earlier conflation of discourses of erotics and politics, that danger is sexualized as a predatory threat to the Prince's childlike innocence.[28] Both Edward and his enemies project disputes over the future of the crown and the kingdom onto the idealized figure of the legitimate child, whose interests can be used to justify divergent political projects.

But as Edward's speech continues, mortality starts to seem less like the converse of sovereignty or a marker of the weakness of Edward and his line and more like its essence. In his prayer that Mortimer will be consumed by the act of wearing the crown, Edward casts his enemy as both a righteously punished traitor and a vulnerable, mortal sovereign. The image suggests that as Mortimer becomes more kinglike, he will become more exposed to death. Then, with his final reference to the survival of "England's vines," Edward ties this mortal potential inherent in sovereignty to divine favor and dynastic persistence. Death (whether Edward's or Mortimer's) enables the continuation of both the nation and Edward's name. As W. Moelwyn Merchant notes, the conventional symbol of the royal vine reworks the image of the vine of Israel in Psalm 80, where the psalmist prays, "Return, we beseech thee, O God of hosts: look down from heaven, and behold, and visit this vine / And the vineyard which thy right hand hath planted, and the branch [that] thou madest strong for thyself."[29] The Geneva Commentator emphasizes God's role in cultivating the "young bud [He] raised up again as out of the burnt ashes" and so presents the vine's biological vulnerability as a marker of the divine favor without which it, and the nation it represents, would not survive.[30] Equally, its branching shape recalls the branching dynastic line through which Edward's name may survive, even after his death, in the person of his son. Divine right and dynastic succession are united in an image of biological growth and death. Over the course of the speech, Edward develops a political outlook that places dying at the heart of sovereignty, as a fact that must be reckoned with by all monarchs. The latter part of the play reveals that death might become a source of royal power instead of a limitation. Edward moves from challenging Mortimer's representatives to acknowledge the rebels' true motives to hinting at a more constitutive link between kingship and death that his successors may be able to exploit even if his own annihilation is inevitable.

Between Demise and Death

Edward is right to think that sovereign death is important but wrong about why. He is so confident that kingship and mortality are coimplicated that the possibility he might physically survive the handover of the crown does not seem to occur to him. Edward repeatedly insists that forced abdication is an act equivalent to regicide and invites those asking for the crown to kill him and render death visible as the inevitable corollary to his dispossession.

Taking the crown is equivalent to taking "the life of Edward too," since "Two kings in England cannot reign at once" (20.57–58). Edward expresses vacillating desires for procrastination and violent extinction—to be allowed to "be king till night" and to be subjected to a violent murder that will absolve him of "so foul a crime" as abdication (20.59, 99)—that closely resemble the final soliloquy in *Doctor Faustus*.[31] As I discussed in the previous chapter, when Faustus imagines impossible counterfactual cosmoses that simultaneously fantasize about escape from hell and acknowledge its inevitability, he both draws out and anticipates an approach to death. Similarly, Edward views relinquishing the crown as a cataclysm, equivalent to the striking of midnight that ends Faustus's earthly existence.

Edward's assumption that the king's crown and his life are coterminous reflects influential juridical explications of royal demise, a concept that is paradigmatically defined in relation to the king's death even as it is distinguished from it. Plowden's *Commentaries* state that "the Death of him who is the King is in Law called the Demise of the King, and not the Death of the King, because thereby he demises the Kingdom to another, and lets another enjoy the Function, so that the Dignity always continues."[32] The term "demise" allows Plowden to acknowledge the inevitability of the monarch's death in a way that minimizes its disruption by emphasizing the institutional perpetuity achieved by the conveyance of the body politic over the annihilation of the body natural. But it is worth asking whether the separation between death and demise is entirely complete. Even if demise occurs within the lifetime of a king—something that Plowden notes in the succession treatise is possible "when the kinge hath been deposed" or chooses to abdicate—does it nevertheless entail a kind of mortality?[33]

This question becomes urgent in Marlowe's play because Edward gets trapped a space between demise and death. As Trussel and Winchester leave with their prize, Edward informs them that "I know the next news that they bring / Will be my death, and welcome shall it be. / To wretched men death is felicity" (20.125–27). Yet felicity is denied to him for a significant while, and his continued existence reveals the connection between sovereignty and mortality to be more flexible than he had anticipated. Where *Doctor Faustus* merely hints that Faustus would be condemned to "die eternally" in a hell made up of an endless succession of failing *artes moriendi* continuing beyond of the space of the play, *Edward II* dramatizes an earthly version of such a torment. To the "wonder" of his jailor Matrevis, Edward fails to sicken, despite being confined

> in a vault up to the knees in water,
> To which the channels of the castle run,
> From whence a damp continually ariseth
> That were enough to poison any man,
> Much more a king brought up so tenderly. (24.1–6)

Edward persists in a hellish, subterranean dungeon, where he survives by inhaling the noxious "savors" of the channels (that is, the sewers) that leave his captors "almost stifled" (24.9). David Stymeist, focusing on sexuality in the play, aligns these channels with the anus and so with Edward's earlier sodomical actions.[34] Without denying the sexual connotations of the setting, I wish to note that it also places Edward at odds with natural biological processes and so traps him in an uncanny half-life.[35] Waste products expelled by other creatures, which should be enough to poison any man, do him no apparent harm but rather draw attention to his continued physical existence, in a manner that pointedly disrupts the natural progression of nourishment and decay. The aura of invulnerability that might be expected to attach to the royal dignity instead emerges as a property of Edward's mortal flesh. Matrevis concludes that "He hath a body able to endure / More than we can inflict" (24.10–11). Edward in the dungeon is perversely more physically present than he was as king, and that presence manifests through a continual approach to death that never quite arrives at its terminus.

As a number of readers have recognized, Marlowe repeatedly describes Edward's predicament in language that evokes common conceptions of sovereignty, encouraging audiences to consider the relationship between Edward's personal torments and England's constitutional crisis.[36] When Edward, for instance, complains to Lightborn that "My mind's distempered and my body's numbed, / And whether I have limbs or no, I know not" (24.62–63), he suggests not just his own enfeeblement but also the commonplace analogy between the commonwealth and the human body, with the king as the head and the subjects as the limbs. Rather than aligning the play with a single, coherent model of corporate sovereignty, these allusions, I think, demonstrate the overlaps and inconsistencies between different figures of perpetual, embodied kingship.

It is tempting to link Edward's bodily persistence after abdication with the survival of the body natural, which reveals itself in distinction to the body politic not only through its potential impairment by age or injury but also through its exhibition of inconvenient vitality. However, this vitality also manifests the porousness of the boundary between body politic and body natural, each continually transforming into the other. Edward reconfigures and confuses the respective roles of sovereign and animal man when he expostulates, "O would my blood dropped out from every vein, / As doth this water from my tattered robes" (24.64–65). The decay of the sumptuary symbols of Edward's royal status and the exposure of the naked body underneath seem to mark Edward's former kingship as illusory in comparison to the abject, creaturely presence of his *physis*. Yet I think it would be a mistake to assume that sovereignty is simply contained within the robes. Edward's complaint also registers a complex ecology through which different liquids pass and mutate into one another, confusing growth and decay. The deterioration of the fabric is caused by the watery "mire and puddle" to which it is exposed—the same water that Edward complains of being given to drink (24.57). While water degrades the outward signifiers of his rule, it also nourishes his blood—the marker of his inherited claim to kingliness, which, despite Edward's plea, will not drop "out from every vein." Even in his reduced state, Edward is capable of the weak imitation of transubstantiation common to every animal, turning water into blood. His watery torture points in two directions, at once destroying an outward sign of his kingship, which can be presented as a merely epiphenomenal cover to his vulnerable body, and strengthening the kingly blood proper both to the individual body natural and the dynastically conceived body politic.

Agamben suggests a way to theorize Edward's condition when he draws attention to the two different Greek words that correspond to what most modern European languages understand as life: "*zoe*, which expressed the simple fact of living common to all living beings . . . and *bios*, which indicated the form or way of living proper to an individual or a group."[37] Though the Greeks founded Western politics on the exclusion of *zoe*, biological life can be brought back into political consideration when it is subjected to sovereign violence. Lives that exist under this threat are denied their own political autonomy and so denied the status of *bios*; nevertheless, they are not merely animal. Agamben gives the label "bare life" to the "zone of indistinction and continuous transition between man and beast, nature and culture."[38] Agamben's model accords with Edward's existence in the dungeon, which emblematizes a state in which *bios* and *zoe* have become indistinguishable and equally present—since every merely biological phenomenon experienced by his body has a sovereign resonance, and every sovereign act is expressed somatically. However, the play also seems to demand further consideration of how this "continuous transition" is effected and whether the mechanisms that propel it can ever be redirected as forms of resistance. Although in the dungeon Edward's apparent bare life is cause for despair, I will suggest later that if Edward can discover any agency for himself, it will be in performances that merge *zoe* and *bios*.

Beyond the personal suffering it entails for Edward, this confusion of kingly dignity with kingly *physis* also generates constitutional uncertainties that threaten to render political action inefficacious, or even impossible, through the nation as a whole. Isabella and Mortimer wish they could do away with an enemy who is a source of political instability and an increasingly sympathetic figure to the commons, but they are reluctant to be directly implicated in the crime of regicide and seek for a way to bring about Edward's death "not by [their] means" (21.45). They encourage Matrevis and his fellow jailor Gurney to subject Edward to psychological and physical hardships, which they hope will break him down physically to the point where he deliberately or accidently kills himself. But as we have seen, Edward's body has a greater capacity to absorb life-ending treatment than Matrevis has to inflict it, leaving the wish that Edward would die without a decisive act of regicide seemingly incapable of fulfillment.

Though Mortimer worries about rebellion, Edward's continued minimal life after demise in fact does nothing to empower those who would rescue him and arguably harms them just as much as it does his usurper. Edward's son complains about many of Mortimer's actions but is unable to command him to alter their course. Edward's brother Kent also suffers from the old king's persistence. Facing execution for a failed attempt to rescue Edward from the dungeon, Kent seeks salvation in the incomplete conveyance of royal power, reminding Mortimer that "Either my brother or his son is king/And none of both them thirst for Edmund's blood" (23.103–4). Kent's inability to identify the true monarch and his vacillation between Mortimer's party and Edward's have left him exposed to charges of treason, but he hopes that this uncertainty will also shelter him from the effects of those charges. Since neither candidate for kingship actually desires his death, he argues it would constitute an extralegal murder, not a legally sanctioned execution. While Kent here is solely concerned with the illegality of his own execution, his objections have wider implications. He suggests that the failure of Edward to die has introduced a crisis in the political distribution of power and justice within the nation as a whole. His complaint partially anticipates Thomas Hobbes's argument that the sovereign's right to inflict death is justified by his or her own assumption of a general exposure to death.[39] The breakdown of sovereign mortality places the right and ability of the state to deal death to its enemies under question. Kent is unable to save himself and is carried off to a beheading by Mortimer's soldiers, but the crisis he discovers in the absence of sovereign bloodthirstiness is real. The persistence of Edward's body after the demise of his regal person, then, is not only a problem for those who have usurped him but threatens to destabilize the whole realm by evacuating the ultimate basis for royal justice. The failure of royal death to occur, despite demise, throws the nation into chaos.

Spits, Tables, and Featherbeds

The obvious solution is recognized by all, including the king: If Edward's biological death will not occur naturally, it must be precipitated. Cultural taboos make it virtually impossible for characters to acknowledge regicidal or suicidal impulses openly, but the play suggests that such desires are compatible with or even necessary to the proper functioning of dynastic monarchy. That Edward's death is a secret but shared communal project becomes evident when Mortimer Jr. encodes an order for his killing in an ambiguously unpunctuated Latin sentence. Mortimer claims the document

> Contains his death yet bids them save his life:
> "*Edwardum occidere nolite timere, bonum est,*"
> "Fear not to kill the king, 'tis good he die."
> But read it thus, and there's another sense:
> "*Edwardum occidere nolite, timere bonum est,*"
> "Kill not the king, 'tis good to fear the worst."
> Unpointed as it is, thus shall it go
> That, being dead, if it chance to be found,
> Matrevis and the rest may bear the blame,
> And we be quit that caused it to be done. (23.7–16)

As Marjorie Garber notes, the letter's semantic ambiguity does not prevent its meaning from being immediately apparent to most of its readers.[40] While Gurney admittedly appears unsure how to understand the sentence, Matrevis is easily able to infer that it has been "left unpointed for the nonce," in an attempt to cover Mortimer's murderous intent with a degree of plausible deniability (24.16), and Edward III is equally certain that it can stand as "proof" of Mortimer's complicity (25.43). While irreducibly ambiguous in form, the Latin phrase in fact conveys meaning transparently. This is because it registers not a hidden irresolvability but the open secret that Edward's death (and the death of the king more generally within a regime of corporate sovereignty) is not just feared but also needed. Even as the sentence instigates a treasonous act of regicide, it recapitulates the double logic of sovereign demise, which at once constitutes a rejection of royal mortality and the legal mechanism that marks its inevitability. The letter's general legibility indicates that this perpetuating logic and this regicidal desire are not Mortimer's alone but are widely shared among the characters of the play.

Modern critics often fall back on assumptions similar to those of Mortimer Jr.'s onstage readers and generate narratives of legitimate succession out of the obscurity of Edward's death. Like Mortimer's sentence, Edward's murder takes an indeterminate form in the printed text of the play. The 1594 quarto, generally recognized as the most authoritative text of *Edward II*, lacks stage directions for the regicide. This lacuna may be a historical accident, yet its reception offers evidence of the potency and persistence of the constructions of royal demise I have been discussing. Critics assume that Edward is killed in one of two possible ways.[41] The first is the method given in the *Chronicle*, Marlowe's primary source. Holinshed notoriously describes how Edward's murderers

> kept him down and withall put into his fundament an horne, and through the same they thrust vp into his bodie an hot spit, or (as other haue) through the pipe of a trumpet a plumbers instrument of iron made verie hot, the which passing vp into his intrailes, and being rolled to and fro, burnt the same, but so as no appearance of any wound or hurt outwardlie might be once perceiued.[42]

Because Lightborn requests that Matrevis "get me a spit and let it be red hot" (24.30) when he first enters the dungeon, most critics and editors have assumed that Marlowe also envisages a violent anal penetration. However, the spit is not mentioned again, and later Lightborn explicitly requests help from his assistants with crushing Edward under a table. Consequently, Stephen Orgel and Andrew Hadfield suggest Marlowe's company would more likely have staged the death as a suffocation.[43] And while one or another staging must be chosen in each individual instance, the play text encourages the audience to remain aware of alternative murderous possibilities. When Lightborn first meets Mortimer Jr., he boasts of his past assassinations and promises to kill Edward in "a braver way" than anything he has yet attempted. The suspense he creates before he puts his plan into action and his allusions to various possible props (table, spit, and featherbed) encourage the audience to imagine different possible alternatives, which can then exist as counterfactuals even if they are not realized onstage.

Rather than attempt to adjudicate definitively between the various staging possibilities, I want to emphasize how different critics' justifications of different interpretive choices inevitably tie the act of killing to regimes of sexuality and theories of succession. If we assume a spit is used, then Edward is sodomized to death in what might either be read as a brutal *contrapasso* recapitulating his earlier sodomical relations with his favorites or as confirmation that the taint of sodomy has conclusively passed from Edward to his enemies.[44] In either case, sodomical murder can be disavowed by Edward III, who ultimately inherits the throne, as outside of and antagonistic to the principles of legitimate succession that his rule restores. Conversely, Hadfield aligns Edward's possible suffocation with the punishment of *peine fort et dure* (pressing to death), which was administered to defendants who refused to enter a plea in a criminal case and so could not be tried by a jury of their peers. Though pressing was a form of execution, it did not imply a successful conviction for the crime charged, which would have entailed the confiscation of the criminal's property by the crown. The fatal act of refusing to plead, therefore, allowed defendants to retain control of their estates and the lines of succession that enabled those estates' transmission between generations. By submitting to pressing, Hadfield suggests, Edward enables the legitimate succession of his son to the Crown.[45]

These critical accounts, though opposed not just in how they see Edward's death occurring but frequently also in the value judgments they offer of the characters involved, all end up in roughly the same place. Edward III's rule is legitimated as an authentic example of succession either because his father's death was sodomical or because it was not sodomical. However Edward's death occurs, and whatever symbolic resonances we attach to the actors and objects involved, it seemingly affirms dynastic monarchy.[46] Critics, like Mortimer's readers, effortlessly read the ambiguity surrounding the death back into established models of sovereignty. Patrilineal ideologies of succession that treat all monarchs as interchangeable are so powerful that they still draw in methodologically opposed critics today.

The cultural dominance of accounts of corporate sovereignty that both need and disavow the king's death may explain why Edward's murder has an aporetic structure. But perhaps characters and audiences can still form alternative political relations through and around that aporia. Rather than seeing the radicalism of the play in Edward's relationship to Gaveston, we might look for new political possibilities in the interactions between otherwise antagonistic figures—including Mortimer Jr., Isabella, Prince Edward, Lightborn, and Edward—at Edward's deathbed. Because Edward's death is an open secret, something widely anticipated but only discussed in oblique terms, it can support unexpected and scarcely acknowledged political communities, which seek to discover new political potentials in mortality. In the remainder of the chapter, I will discuss two of these: the partnership created between Lightborn and Edward immediately before the murder occurs and the unexpected identifications generated between Edward's corpse and other characters in the final scene.

Marlowe departs from Holinshed, his primary source, by inventing the character of Lightborn and staging an extended conversation between him and Edward before the murder, during which both characters imagine a series of alternative endings for the king. Neither character seriously disputes that Edward's death is inevitable. Instead they use counterfactuals to contest how it should be read. Their negotiation reveals that recognizing Edward's death as an open secret is merely a starting point for a deeper investigation of the relationship between politics and epistemology. Both plainness and obscurity afford certain types of power to the participants. By contesting what balance should be struck between them, Lightborn and Edward evoke alternative political formations that rely on the overt or implicit acknowledgment of sovereign mortality, rather than its denial.

When he first sees Lightborn, Edward expresses an instinctive fear of his future murderer by saying

> These looks of thine can harbor naught but death
> I see my tragedy written in thy brows.
> Yet stay awhile. Forbear thy bloody hand
> And let me see the stroke before it comes,
> That even then when I shall lose my life,
> My mind may be more steadfast on my God. (24.71–76)

Edward's speech juxtaposes two distinct conventional narratives of violent death: tragedy and martyrdom. The first emphasizes the actions and intentions of the murderer; the second highlights the mental steadfastness of the innocent victim, who wrenches a form of agency out of abjection by transforming dying into an act of devotion. While these narratives emphasize different elements of the scene, they are not strictly speaking incompatible. Indeed, the murderer and the martyr each need the other. Though at other points in the scene Edward pleads for the chance to avoid death altogether, in this instance he negotiates with Lightborn to assume a share of responsibility for his own end, a responsibility that may have political as well as spiritual consequences. Practicing a devotional art of dying in the image of a saint will not just offer him the best chance of reaching Heaven; it could also afford him a posthumous political recuperation. No longer the weak king whose deposition was the virtually inevitable consequence of his failings, he might become the iconic victim of treason in whose name political resistance could be launched.[47]

Many early modern dramatists recognized the political potency of postures of martyrdom. In the next chapter, I will show how Shakespeare's *Richard II* connects royal death to the Crucifixion and in the process suggests that saintly postures underpin different forms of political organization, from absolutist monarchy to republicanism. But this option is not available in *Edward II*. Lightborn's response to Edward indicates that the question is not what conventional narrative (tragedy or martyrdom) will govern Edward's death, or what political implications that narrative will have, but whether any conventional narrative will be allowed to apply. Denying that he intends violence toward the king, Lightborn insists, "These hands were never stained with innocent blood,/Nor shall they now be tainted with a king's" (24.80–81). For the audience, already primed to recognize Lightborn as a secret assassin by his earlier commission from Mortimer Jr., the double meaning here is obvious: Lightborn will not stain his hands, because his murder will leave no visible trace. It is possible, and initially tempting, to read Lightborn's demurral here in generic or strategic terms. His hypocrisy aligns him with other Marlovian Machiavel-villains like Barabas and, behind them, a longer line of dramatic vice figures. Perhaps he also hopes to make the act of killing easier by reassuring Edward of his benign intentions.

However, if Lightborn is attempting to act strategically here, he is singularly ineffective, since Edward never appears truly reassured. As an alternative, I want to consider if Lightborn's speech constitutes a serious riposte to Edward. Rather than the two conventional narratives of death Edward evokes, Lightborn offers silence. Without denying murder is imminent, he alters the terms under which it will be inflicted. Death will occur in the absence of tragedy or martyrdom because the blood that would mark both murderer and victim will not be shed. Instead, Edward and Lightborn will interact bloodlessly. Lightborn's emphasis on blood is significant given its privileged status not just as a sign of violence but also as a symbol of royalty founded upon a principle of heredity. The anticipated bloodlessness of Edward's murder enables unexpected alliances and energies, which bear no relation to dynastic lines, to emerge across the dying body of the king. Lightborn proffers less an ironic denial of murderous intent than an oblique invitation to Edward to participate in his own death in a way that will not be fully legible within extant scripts of regicide.

And how will Edward participate? By using Lightborn's third murder weapon, which critics focusing on the table and the spit have largely ignored: the featherbed. Through an agreement that Edward should sleep, Edward and Lightborn finally reach an accommodation, one that gives Edward some agency within his own death, while sidestepping narratives that would clearly announce Lightborn as a murderer and Edward as a martyr. Benjamin Parris draws intention to the importance of sleep as a site for figuring the nature of sovereignty in Shakespeare's plays.[48] Sleep is one of the regular events of royal incapacity that fictions of perpetuity are required to account for, and its resemblance to death anticipates the end of the sovereign. Sovereign postures of vigilant wakefulness, insomnia, fatigue, or insensibility become metaphors for different possible relationships between monarchs' dominion, their embodied selves, and the commonwealth. When sleeping kings are murdered, as in *Hamlet* and *Macbeth*, the ensuing political crises often anticipate the modern condition of indistinction between political action and procedures designed to regulate biological life.

Although Parris does not discuss *Edward II*, I would argue that the play uses sovereign sleep as a similarly potent signifier of the political challenges occasioned by the king's bare life. The primary difference is that while in Shakespeare sleep generally advertises the king's vulnerability, for Marlowe it becomes an occasion for negotiating power between different actors. The whole exchange between Edward and Lightborn is worth quoting because it indicates how Edward's sleep functions not just as an accidental anticipation of death but also as an opportunity to practice dying and to further political agendas through that practice.

> EDWARD: I feel a hell of grief. Where is my crown?
> Gone, gone. And do I remain alive?
> LIGHTBORN: You're overwatched, my lord; lie down and rest.
> EDWARD: But that grief keeps me waking, I should sleep
> For not these ten days have these eyes' lids closed.
> Now as I speak they fall, and yet with fear
> Open again. O wherefore sits thou here?
> LIGHTBORN: If you mistrust me, I'll be gone, my lord.
> EDWARD: No, no, for if thou mean'st to murder me,
> Thou wilt return again, and therefore stay. [*He falls asleep*]
> LIGHTBORN: He sleeps. (24.89–99)

Edward's complaint aligns the gap between demise and death with the experience of insomnia. After the loss of his crown, he experiences fluctuating emotions of grief and fear that cause him to hover between wakefulness and sleep. As an insomniac, he simultaneously evokes the unsleeping vigilance of the body politic and the stupefying physical demands of the body natural. However, his dynamic emotional constitution undoes any stable opposition between the two bodies. Fear and grief, through which Edward attempts to understand his past demise and anticipated death, bring him alternately closer to sleeping and waking. Grief throws him into a "hell" from which bodily death appears like an insignificant or even desirable change. Fear marks his instinct for self-preservation because it is directed at the man he believes will become his murderer. Though the emotions are conceptually separable, they each pass unexpectedly into the other when grief turns into fear, and they seem unpredictably to inspire sleep and sleeplessness. Overall, these complaints, like Edward's earlier ones, allude to conventional bodily metaphors and legal fictions through which royal power is understood, but they then suggest that the breakdown of a link between death and demise has rendered the forms of power these metaphors support unstable and ineffective.

In this context, Edward's agreement with Lightborn's suggestion that he should sleep can be read as an effort to reconfigure the relationship between his sovereignty and his body by adopting an affirmative relationship to dying. Lightborn asks Edward, as near as possible, to kill himself by voluntarily becoming a mere *physis* and entering into a simulacrum of death, so that he can be murdered without impediment. This request for Edward to perform an imitation of death (by falling asleep) seems to respond to and perhaps counteract Winchester's earlier request for Edward to perform an imitation of death (by giving up the crown). Abdication, as I demonstrated earlier, did not function effectively as a dynastic passage of sovereignty but instead threw king and country into an uncanny half-life between death and demise. Sleep might resolve the uncertainty or increase it. Fear has been keeping Edward wakeful. When he consents to try to sleep in Lightborn's presence, he does so not because his fears are removed but because he assumes that Lightborn would easily be able to carry out the murder at a later time. It would certainly be possible to interpret Edward's behavior as a fatalistic acknowledgment of his impotence. But given the earlier negotiations between Edward and Lightborn about how the regicide will occur, he could also be understood to assume an active and consenting part in the murder that remains at its heart opaque. Edward will not "see the stroke" that Lightborn inflicts on his body so that he can perform martyrdom according to a conventional narrative (24.74). However, he will nevertheless be able to claim a relationship to death that allows him to exert some control over his end.

What degree of control that might be emerges in the contrast between two opposed moments in Edward's sleep, which together map out the range of political actions that might be grounded in a project of sovereign dying. In the first moment, the sleeping Edward, insensible and inert, imitates a corpse in anticipation of becoming a corpse. By rendering himself in appearance dead already, Edward blurs the boundary between his own assumed lifelessness and Lightborn's murderous action. He thus alters the field upon which political action might take place. By deciding to sleep, Edward transforms his existence from *bios* to *zoe*. Regicide, as an event through which an agent like Lightborn might wish to effect substantial political change, becomes subsumed within natural, cyclical processes of wake and sleep, life and death.

By contrast, the second moment in which Edward's sleep anticipates his death suggests that such biological passivity can always be reconfigured as politically significant activity. Immediately after Lightborn remarks that Edward has fallen asleep, the king exclaims, "Something still buzzeth in mine ears/And tells me if I sleep I never wake" (24.101–2). Crucially, this buzzing is reported rather than enacted. The moment of renewed vigilance occurs invisibly within the appearance of sleep; insensibility can mask awareness of an incipient attack. Like his earlier somnolence, Edward's reawakening exploits similarities between sleeping and dying to political effect. It serves as a reminder that sleep is never merely somatic but in fact engages consciousness unpredictably through dreams—something that, as Hamlet remarks, might be equally true of death. The particular form that Edward's monitory dream takes—a buzzing guardian voice opposing the devilish figure of Lightborn to warn him of danger—is also significant. As it brings to mind swarming insects, the sound evokes forms of political organization or vigilance that are not products of reason but rather emerge at the level of biological existence.[49] Simultaneously, this buzzing also recalls the psychomachic deathbed dramas common to many morality plays and *artes moriendi*. As I discussed in the Introduction, these texts often strive to support sick individuals by redistributing agency among members of a deathbed community, some of whom, such as angels or intercessors, may be invisible to outside observers. In certain circumstances, the actions of those around the deathbed may be allowed to count for the sick person on the deathbed so that his or her apparent torpor can be understood as theologically significant activity. In its evocation of psychomachic conventions,

Edward's warning dream suggests that quiescence may be illusory and perhaps also marshals supernatural supports to his cause. Therefore, though Edward's outburst superficially takes the form of a final desperate plea for continued life, it also hints at the range of political actions that might be founded upon sovereign mortality. Even if Edward may not fully realize its potential, the form his sleep takes suggests that his murder is not just a regrettable necessity that will rejoin demise and death in the service of dynastic sovereignty but an opportunity to reconceive what the political impact of mortality can be.

Playing with Hearses and Heads

Both moments of Edward's sleep leverage the conditions of their dramatic performance to extend their political implications into the theater. The resemblance between sleep and death is compounded onstage, since the postures of inactivity actors use to represent sleepers and bloodless bodies are identical. Once the threat that the murder will shed visible blood is removed, audience members will be left unable to adjudicate whether a performer represents a sleeper or a dead body without some additional contextual information. Conversely, the presence of the actor, whose body advertises its own vitality and skill through the very effort involved in remaining impassive, renders the possibility that renewed political action will emerge unexpectedly from torpor more plausible. And the onstage and offstage members of the theater company, who collectively help sustain the illusion, mirror the psychomachic deathbed communities that form around the *moriens*. This association between death, dramatic imitation, and political activity only intensifies in the final scene. Though dead, Edward persists spectrally through the capacity of other persons and objects to evoke his dying body. Rather than ending the challenge to sovereign perpetuity occasioned by his existence between demise and death, regicide in fact enables such challenges to become more widely available.

The surviving beneficiaries of Edward's death do not want him to stick around. They seek to deny their complicity in his murder in two ways: by affirming the minority rule of Edward's son, the new Edward III, and by identifying and then killing scapegoats who can be made to bear responsibility for the regicide. They celebrate the figure of the child as a token of the perfected, perpetual corporate monarch in whose name all acts of killing are justified. Simultaneously, they seek to obfuscate that this justification encompasses Edward's murder by overwriting it with other deaths. That these scapegoats' transgressions are presented as forms of sodomy or adultery supports the public narrative that emphasizes legitimate sexuality as the mainstay of dynastic sovereignty and downplays the equal necessity of death. In Mortimer Jr.'s hands, the strategy is a patently disingenuous attempt to hijack the lines of succession for his own personal ambitions. Mortimer disposes of Lightborn to conceal that he has ordered the murder of Edward II and is interested in Edward III only as a puppet. Yet when Edward III repeats the same acts of scapegoating sexual transgressors and affirming perfected minority rule, the play suggests that the traitorous protector and the legitimate heir are in fact doubles of each other or two opposite but essential moments within dynastic corporate sovereignty. Edward III is able to assume the full powers of the monarchy after his father's death because he is able to take on both roles, stepping into the place of the sinister usurper of royal power while remaining the innocent minor whose inheritance must be protected.[50]

This pattern might suggest the play reverts to an understanding of sovereign perpetuity grounded in dynasty. But in Mortimer's and Edward III's efforts to identify scapegoats, unexpected challenges emerge that disrupt linear successional narratives. The gap Edward II opened up between demise and death cannot simply be closed through the simultaneous announcement of a new undying king and the execution of a scapegoat. Instead, after Edward's murder, mimetic resemblances between half-alive and half-dead bodies proliferate that blur distinctions not just between different characters but even between actor and object and that seem to distribute the political potential of mortality widely and unpredictably among sovereign and subjects. Sovereign mortality may underpin dynastic order, but dynastic order cannot contain it, because Edward's practice of dying continues to have political potency even after his death as it is evoked in the postures of others. Rather than a linear progression of kings, the final scene of the play takes the form of a shell game—played with hearses, corpses, and heads—in which dying and living sovereigns are never quite where you expect them to be.

The first intimation that regicide has not curtailed Edward's uncanny existence in a space between life and death but will instead induct others into his position occurs while his body is still warm. Edward's jailors kill Lightborn on Mortimer Jr.'s orders. Lightborn's very name (an Anglicization of Lucifer) marks him as a traitor, making him the obvious choice for a fall guy, the morality devil who will counterbalance any aura of saintliness Edward might accrue through martyrdom. The stage directions in this case are explicit. Gurney stabs Lightborn, producing something avoided in the case of Edward: visible blood signaling both violence and lineage.

He then prescribes different, morally weighted, treatments for the two corpses intended to sustain the distinction between sovereign and murderer: "Come, let us cast the body in the moat / And bear the king's to Mortimer our lord" (24.116–17). Lightborn's final resting place signals the disavowal of the killer and also seems designed to counteract the uncanny qualities of Edward's existence between demise and death. Since in many castles the moat was connected to the sewage system, Gurney's command returns the assassin to the same channels that had run through Edward's dungeon.[51] Decomposing in the muck, his body will absorb the pollution that had come to mark Edward's perversely persistent vitality. Meanwhile, the corpse of the king will be returned in state to the center of power, supposedly reflecting his privileged position even in death but in reality showing the control Gurney's lord Mortimer has over the mechanisms of sovereignty.

The problem is that Gurney does not link "the body" to be cast in the moat to a proper name. Listening to the command unfold, it is possible to imagine that he wishes Edward simply to disappear into the liquid pollution that for so long has been surrounding him. His second clause ("And bear the king's to Mortimer our lord") eliminates the confusion on a practical level. But grammatically, it makes the king's body appear parasitic on the murderer's. Lightborn's body is "*the* body," universalized by the definite article. Edward's is particularized as "the king's." The subjection of dual bodies to separate treatment reinstates the twinning at the heart of the fiction of the king's two bodies but threatens to reverse its significance. Plowden imagines a universal, undying sovereign, temporarily impersonated by a succession of different kings. In Gurney's speech, by contrast, "the body" evokes a general mortality that subsumes identities by rendering them interchangeable, while "the king" is a mere individual subjected to death.

The capacity death has to generate similitudes by removing individuating features becomes still more evident on Edward III's assumption of power, despite the new king's efforts to align his regime with the restoration of proper dynastic rule. Edward III condemns Mortimer to execution, insisting, "Traitor, in me my loving father speaks / And plainly saith, 'twas thou that murd'redst him" (25.41–42). With these words, he asserts his abhorrence of patricide and his newfound power to wield death in the name of the father. The new king identifies a scapegoat, who can be made to absorb all responsibility for the murder of Edward II. Mortimer is summarily executed following Edward III's command "Bring him unto a hurdle, drag him forth;/Hang him, I say, and set his quarters up!/But bring his head back presently to me" (25.52–54). Edward III here invokes the standard punishment afforded to traitors—hanging, then drawing and quartering. This ritualized torture and desecration asserts an opposition between sovereign and criminal, countering the secret and bloodless murder of the old king with a public demonstration of the new king's right to inflict open violence upon those who threaten his line. Where Edward's cause of death is obscure, quartering and beheading transform Mortimer into an instantly recognizable, spectacular display of the mechanisms of execution.[52] Simultaneously, Edward III presents his political ascension as a rejection of sexual deviance (here, Mortimer and Isabella's adultery) and an affirmation of legitimate patrilineal succession.

Yet Edward's funeral hearse and Mortimer's severed head complicate the triumphant assertion of dynastic sovereignty by supplementing it with contrary intimations of less centralized forms of political power. Patrick Cheney and Thomas P. Anderson have both located nascent republicanism within the final scene of the play.[53] Cheney argues that when Edward III calls for Parliament to try his mother, he circumscribes the sovereign power he asserted by executing Mortimer.[54] Anderson notes that royal funerals typically displayed an idealized effigy of the monarch, signifying the persistence of the royal dignity, on top of the coffin. The effigy functions as a prosthetic, supplementing but also exposing the lack within the natural body of the king. Consequently, it reveals the artificial structures needed to sustain a fiction of sovereign perpetuity. When the effigy is performed by a living actor, Marlowe evokes an "ambivalent republicanism that rules *through* the sovereign body."[55] The royal dignity is revealed to rely on the common player who stands in for it.

Though Cheney and Anderson's arguments are highly suggestive, I hesitate to read too rigid a political symbolics into a funeral tableau that (like Edward's death) affords various different dramatic realizations.[56] Instead, I propose that *Edward II*'s insistent metatheatricality highlights the contingency of any politics grounded on the dying and the dead. If republicanism is implicit in the final scene, it is of a precarious sort, which distributes power unexpectedly by creating resemblances between one dying body and another and undoes itself as quickly as it emerges. The scene therefore notably fails to dramatize the perpetuity that was held to be essential to political institutions within the different accounts of the corporate crown. Since resemblances between bodies are created through stagecraft, their success is tenuously predicated on representational decisions that will vary from production to production or even from occasion to occasion, as well as on the skills and efforts of the actors who produce them and the perceptiveness of the audiences who view them. To demonstrate how contingent performances of dying can challenge conceptions of perpetuity, I offer two quite different readings of two different hypothetical dramatic realizations of Edward's funeral. As a counter to my earlier discussion of the susceptibility of different interpretations of Edward's murder to the same critical narrative legitimating Edward III, I want to show how different possible enactments of Edward's funeral might employ mimetic resemblance to death to different political ends.

Original stage directions for the funeral are missing, so possible performances must be hypothesized from limited textual and contextual information. Marlowe's dialogue implies that a "hearse" is present on stage, a property that Alan Dessen and Leslie Thomson define as "a means for carrying the dead comparable to a coffin or a bier . . . perhaps . . . distinguished from a simpler coffin by objects lying/hanging on it."[57] In this instance, much turns on the word "perhaps." Depending on whether Edward's hearse is particularized by the presence of the actor playing Edward upon it, as Anderson assumes, or whether it is a generic coffin, the tableau becomes open to strikingly different readings.

If the staged hearse is essentially a mobile coffin, the audience encounters the inverse of Edward's unbruised body. Where Edward's mortal injuries were concealed, leaving no marker of the differences between death and sleep, his coffin attests to the fact of death while obscuring the particulars of the person who died. In performance, this deindividuation is compounded because nobody will be inside the hearse, which as an inanimate prop bears only a metonymic relationship to mortality. Reviving Gurney's language, we might say the lack of a body stands in for "the body" rather than for "the king." The hearse, therefore, signals the unknowability of mortality and also delocalizes it, representing death as a generic phenomenon while suggesting that the specific remains of Edward's performance of dying may in fact be elsewhere. The play hints at a number of different possible locations for those remains: Edward III, who claims his father speaks in him; Isabella, who echoes Edward's suicidal language on her way to prison; Mortimer Jr., whose head is dedicated to Edward's ghost; and somewhere offstage, when an audience member detaches herself from the illusion and recalls the actor who had been playing Edward.

Evoking Edward as a dying or dead figure offers characters opportunities to appropriate some of the political energies inherent in his existence between death and demise. Importantly, the mere act of evocation does not commit them to any particular politics. The very different performances given by Edward III, Isabella, and Mortimer Jr. go some way to illustrating the range of potential political effects that can be achieved through the mimicry of sovereign mortality. The death of Edward II offers Edward III, for one, a pretext for deemphasizing the bond between husband and wife and between mother and child in favor of that between father and son and so for sustaining a fantasy of succession as the parthenogenetic reproduction of patriarchal males. He tells Isabella she is "suspected for [Edward's] death" (25.78) and bars her from her husband's funeral. From Edward III's perspective, the settlement at the end of the play anticipates *Hamlet*, only with a happy ending. The son overcomes his father's killer and sublimates the psychosexual drama of his family romance into an authentic appropriation of patriarchal power. In this context, every associative link that Edward III can sustain between his father's death and his own reign—from his insistence that his father speaks in him to his description of the execution of Mortimer as a propitiation of his father's ghost—serves to affirm the primacy of a purely masculine line of succession.

Isabella, by contrast, demands that Edward III recognize her central place within the family. She asserts a right to "mourn for my belovèd lord" (25.87) and attempts to win her son's pardon by reminding listeners "I am his mother" (25.90). By this point in the play, this tactic should seem both familiar and cynical. Throughout *Edward II*, Isabella has been defined almost exclusively through marriage and motherhood. Yet, as Jonathan Goldberg notes, her participation in these institutions becomes increasingly perverse after she begins her affair with Mortimer. By using adultery to gain political power, she does not merely set herself at odds with her husband but reconceives the privileges inherent in matrimony on an illicit basis.[58] For her subsequently to claim the privilege of legitimate familial relations in order to win mercy must appear hypocritical.

Yet Isabella's evocations of Edward II might help us envisage a new sort of bond between husband and wife that can complicate this picture. Where Edward III's claim to channel the words of his dead father is overt, Isabella's ventriloquism is unacknowledged and unwitting. When she describes her journey to prison as a procession "to my death, for too long have I lived/When as my son thinks to abridge my days" (25.83–84), she recalls Edward's anticipation of death as the inevitable sequel to abdication. Precisely because this echo is accidental, it enables her to assert her familial claims in a new way. The queen does not simply perform a knowingly illicit inversion of the institutions of legitimacy or make a belated and cynical attempt to reclaim the benefits of the interpersonal relationships she has

disrespected. Like Edward, Isabella here situates herself in a state of temporal dislocation, at once regretting a life that feels too long and one that
is being cut unnaturally short by her son's desires. She therefore sets up a
parallel between the political opportunities available to a king between
demise and death and those that might be available to a woman constrained
to understand herself through matrimony and maternity while simultaneously being alienated from those institutions. In the moment, Isabella's words
do little more than mark this resemblance. They clearly have some effect
on her son, who fears that he will be driven to pity if he continues to listen
to her, but they do not prevent her trial. However, her words hint that
female characters can exert agency through connecting mimetic death to
marriage and motherhood, and as I will discuss later, Shakespeare and
Webster both find ways to exploit this possibility.

Like Isabella, Mortimer—the final and most significant impersonator
of a dying monarch—does not evoke the old king deliberately. After his
execution, Mortimer's head is brought back to Edward III, who presents
it to the ghost of his dead father, presumably by placing it on or near the
hearse. This act effectively creates a chimera out of two dead bodies. If
Edward is only notionally present within the coffin, the audience encounters Mortimer as the visible face of this hidden representation of death.
Where the play began by positing homosocial friendship as the utopian
alternative to a politics predicated on the dual supports of legitimacy
and sovereign mortality, it ends by presenting a monstrous aggregation
of killer and victim. Notably, both men could be said to occupy both
positions, since Edward III insists that his father speaks in him to order
Mortimer's death. Here, sovereign power is recognizable through its
simultaneous capacity to kill and to survive being killed, and it is evoked
wherever death is. Juxtaposing a coffin and Mortimer's head, Edward's
hearse suggests that subjects have the capacity to become the face of a
dying king. Yet since it is a product of execution, this wider distribution of
sovereignty might not only anticipate republican devolution but could also
function as a mechanism to distribute vulnerability and an origin point for
a regime of terror.

The other staging possibility is that the actor who has played Edward
lies on top of the hearse. In this instance, I think there would be no obvious
way for audience members to tell whether what they were looking at was
supposed to represent an effigy of the king or the king's actual corpse,
especially given Lightborn's concern to leave the body outwardly inviolate.
Even Anderson implicitly registers this indeterminacy because he relies on

Susan Zimmerman's account of dramatizations of corpses to describe the effects of staging an effigy.[59] Zimmerman notes that in playing a corpse,

> a material, sentient body was supposed to signify an insentient one, severed from "its real materiality"—a *dis*embodied body. Further, because death was outside the experience of actor and theatre-goer alike, the illusion of death could not be evoked through the prism of memory: "corpseness" itself was unsignifiable.[60]

Anderson wants to suggest that this failure of signification attaches to the effigy, which is revealed as a prosthetic consolation for loss rather than a transparent evocation of sovereign perpetuity. All this may be true, but Zimmerman's reading also serves as a reminder that the appearance of a prone body on the hearse creates not only a conceptual confusion between avatars of the body politic and body natural but also a more fundamental one between person and object.[61] Moreover, Marlowe dramatizes the killing of Mortimer so as to compound this indistinction. The different rituals performed around Mortimer's traitorous and Edward's royal corpses ostensibly reveal the differences between sovereign and criminal. But they inadvertently demonstrate how the political identities of both sovereign and traitor are predicated on the capacity of living and nonliving things to take on resemblances to each other. Dragged off to his execution on a hurdle that barely raises his body above the ground, the still-living Mortimer is forcibly objectified, made to take on the characteristics of a vehicle and so to echo Edward II's hearse.[62] Then, when Mortimer's "head" is brought back and shown to the audience, that head is necessarily an inanimate prop.[63] As this prop head is juxtaposed to the prone body of the actor playing Edward, death is evoked simultaneously in two contrary ways—through the prop that has never been alive and the living person pretending to be dead. These two instantiations each become supplements for the other, each providing the missing component of the other representation of death but also demonstrating the inadequacy of that representation. The tableau unites questions about the nature of mortality with questions about the nature of representation and performance.

The same juxtaposition of living body and prop head then generates questions about whether sovereignty is a natural or artificial phenomenon and whether it is exercised primarily through the bodies of the king and his subjects or through symbolic systems. The king's effigy and the traitor's head each represent the capacity of sovereign power to manage and overcome death. Yet they rely on different assumptions—that the king is mystically invulnerable or that he must continually protect his mortal self from very real enemies. If the effigy is performed by a body while the body part is performed by an effigy, the two ways of understanding sovereignty in relation to mortality are brought together unstably in the slippage between human and object.

It would certainly be possible to claim that Marlowe demystifies sovereignty by unmasking the theatrical strategies upon which it depends. The play might be taken to reveal sovereignty not as the assumption of power over death by a corporate perpetuity but rather as a strategic use of props and performance. Royal power, as the new historicists suggest, can be seen as a theatrical technique rather than transcendent divinely sanctioned right or genuine political action.[64] Alternatively, one could draw on Walter Benjamin to argue that the revelation that sovereign power is mere theater reflects baroque artists' perception of the disintegration of the medieval cosmic order. Such readings, however, fail to do justice to the reversibility of the resemblances that Edward's funeral tableau sets up. The final scene of *Edward II* indicates the place of sovereign mortality through what it is not. Death is evoked on stage as the implicit third term between the living body of a prone actor (who is not dead) and the artificial copy of a severed head (which also is not dead, but in a significantly different way). This double failure suggests something more complicated than binaries between life and death, perpetuity and mortality, or king and traitor. The tableau acknowledges that sovereign death is always elsewhere. But it also suggests that it may be accessed through mimetic representations that partially evoke it.

Together, the two staging options of generic coffin and prone actor indicate that performances of sovereign dying are politically potent both because of how they fail and because of how they succeed. They fail to demonstrate the perpetuity associated with corporate sovereignty. But they do successfully recreate the dying king over and over again. There is no definitive royal death that emphatically ratifies demise. Instead, there are tentative echoes of the dead and dying king, which are always at risk of being overwritten by new performances. And out of these echoes, new potentials arise for alternative political formations that embrace ephemerality instead of resisting it.

Alternative Deaths and Performative Futures

I have argued that *Edward II* dramatizes a gradual transformation in understandings of sovereign mortality. The king's death is first evoked as a necessary component of a perpetual conception of the crown, but a component given less emphasis than discourses of succession, whether legitimate or deviant. The revelation that death is separable from demise triggers a political crisis. Finally, during and after the regicide, royal dying becomes an opportunity to experiment with alternative political settlements through performance. The various modes of dying assayed within the play demonstrate that the political ramifications of this evolution are uncertain. When he anticipates his death through sleep, Edward at first appears to fold violent political change into natural biological processes. But his sudden reawakening suggests that political consciousness might arise suddenly from the least expected locations. After his murder, imitative evocations of the dying king are employed for contrary ends. In some cases, otherwise marginalized figures, such as the child king Edward III or the imprisoned Isabella, mimic Edward in attempts to assume a degree of agency. These moments perhaps gesture toward some sort of incipient republicanism in which power is disbursed through the capacity of subjects to represent the sovereign momentarily. But the killings of Lightborn and Mortimer, along with the subsequent treatment of their bodies, demonstrate how mimetic potentials inherent in death can be used to disseminate death and so achieve repression or even terror by blurring distinctions between persons and objects. By the end of the play, the king's death matters. It is no longer merely a moment within the eternity of corporate sovereignty. Instead it reveals itself as a source of instability that supports quite different political projects because it offers an opportunity to revise the relationship between *zoe* and *bios* through performance.

Some of these alternatives are implicit in the text, in counterfactuals canvassed by the characters or in allusions to undramatized moments in the *Chronicle* that spur historically aware audience members to supplement what they actually see with different accounts of the action. But others seem to be products of historical distance and accident: Though the original company must have favored particular stagings of Edward's murder and funeral, there is no clear surviving evidence of what these were, and later productions and critical speculation can merely indicate a range of possibilities. This ambiguity might raise suspicions about my methodology. In imagining the political ramifications of different representations of Edward's hearse, I must be including alternatives that were not intended by the author or realized in the original enactments. Perhaps. But the conversation between Lightborn and Edward before the murder provides a precedent for treating the unknown and unspeakable aspect of death not as an impasse but rather as an opportunity for forming alternative communities that evade dominant discourses to forge new alliances and imagine new futures.

Whereas *Doctor Faustus* seems to respond to and partially endorse the movement Protestant theologians made from stage to print, *Edward II* proceeds in the opposite direction. The play opens with a letter that ratifies Edward's exclusive right to sovereignty following the decease of his father; it ends with a spectacularly staged funeral that threatens to distribute political power and mortality more widely. In the process, both sovereignty and mortality emerge as actions that must be performed rather than as matters of codified law. Because these performances are ephemeral and contingent, the play can anticipate nascent political developments along with possibilities that may never come to fruition. The continued theatrical power of *Edward II* and its capacity to be appropriated and adapted for new political purposes and moments by critics and directors suggest that this potential remains alive—though the repressive implications of some of the representations of sovereign death that I have outlined should serve as a caution to those inclined to read the play as utopian. *Edward II* demonstrates that individual deathbed performances may be ambiguous but suggests that the practice of dying offers an opportunity for political action. The next chapter discusses how Shakespeare responds to this suggestion by testing what forms of resistance a deliberately undertaken art of sovereign dying would enable and by investigating the political consequences of dying mimetically.

CHAPTER 3

Dying Representatively

Richard II and the Politics of Mimetic Mortality

Another history play, another imprisoned king suspended between demise and death.[1] Alone in his cell in Pomfret Castle, Shakespeare's Richard II struggles to comprehend his altered state. Where Marlowe's Edward had evaded recognizable narratives of sovereignty by retreating into bodily cares, Richard seeks a wider frame of reference. He has, he reveals,

> been studying how I may compare
> This prison where I live unto the world.
> And for because the world is populous
> And here is not a creature but myself
> I cannot do it; yet I'll hammer it out. (5.5.1–2)

For this king, to compare is to hammer. To draw connections and analogies between the isolated self and the populated world is to engage in effortful practices that forcefully beat self and world into conformity with each other. Initially he imagines himself as the father of a "generation of still breeding thoughts" that council him to resist, capitulate, and despair (5.5.8). But once dispossession has exposed a fissure between the king and the realm, Richard can only practice patriarchal rule in mockery, scarcely

controlling an incestuous and fractious family of ideas. Dissatisfied with
each of the alternatives they offer, he complains "Thus play I in one person
many people/And none contented" and fantasizes about exchanging the
personae of king and beggar (5.5.31–32). He concludes that

> whate'er I be
> Nor I nor any man that but man is
> With nothing shall be pleased till he be eased
> With being nothing. (5.5.38–41)

Sovereignty gives way to imitation and finally to the desire for death.

Seen in isolation, this soliloquy appears as a symptom of Richard's disease. Yet the king's speculative attempts to reconcile self and world through
mimicry and mortality are mirrored by more substantive efforts across the
play as a whole. Richard yokes imitation and death together when he invites
his followers to "sit upon the ground/And tell sad stories of the death of
kings" (3.2.151–52) and when he casts himself in the image of a martyr
during his assassination. Most of all, Richard repeatedly impersonates
Christ. Inhabiting the precedent of the Passion enables him to assert a
connection between monarchy and divinity, to condemn the followers who
have betrayed him—and perhaps to anticipate political resurrection.
While skeptical readers have found Richard's Christlike postures easy to
dismiss as acts of absolutist self-aggrandizement or refusals of political
reality, his behavior illuminates a range of early modern political institutions that struggle to incorporate individuals into larger communities.[2]
The Passion is at once a pattern for godly individuals to emulate in their
private behavior and the origin of Christian community. By dying like
Christ, Christians aspire to transform mortality from the most isolating of
human experiences into a universal fellowship that unites the living and
the dead. Since Kantorowicz's *The King's Two Bodies*, the Christological
models underpinning Richard's conception of kingship have been widely
acknowledged—though they are usually seen to lose potency following
Richard's deposition.[3] The question of how to reconcile solitary, creaturely
existence with the wider world, however, troubles Bolingbroke and the
other rebels almost as much as it troubles Richard, and devotional practices of mimesis continue to supply them with powerful frameworks for
government. The imitation of Christ and other holy exemplars underpins
institutions of governance and modes of power brought to oppose the
king, from the Parliament overseeing his abdication, to the prison in which
he is confined, and finally to the political vacuum that confronts his Lancas-

trian and Yorkist successors. Ultimately, *Richard II* suggests that twinned conceptions of death and mimetic representation remain central to modern political institutions.

My analysis of *Richard II* therefore travels in the opposite direction to my account of *Edward II*. Where Marlowe's play depicts a retreat inward from established narratives of dynasty into the more ambivalent political energies located in the dying body of the king, *Richard II* moves outward, from the mortal sovereign *corpus* to corporate political institutions and the nation as a whole. The play reveals how medieval and early modern conceptions of *imitatio Christi* and collective participation in the Passion influenced the development of political institutions and modes of governance into the sixteenth century and perhaps beyond. It shows the histories of religious imitation, dramatic mimesis, and political representation to be intertwined. To "play . . . in one person many people" can be conceived as a devotional, artistic, or political practice. Christ's Passion underpins Richard's naturalized conception of divine right. But it also animates institutions of representative governance, like Parliament, and sites of artistic expression and consumption, like the theater, that aspire to speak to and for a wide socioeconomic cross-section of the population. When Shakespeare casts the performance of the Passion as a political intervention, he situates death and representation together at the threshold of political participation. Politics and art must inevitably contend with and be limited by mortality. But the strategic re-creation of exemplary deaths can also spur political and artistic change. Performing the death of a figure from the past becomes a way to forge, or break, communities in the present. In the right circumstances, mimetic performances of dying become political representations.

Haunting the Hollow Crown

Richard is most concerned to appear Christlike when he is no longer indisputably sovereign. In consequence, his performances of the Passion seem out of joint. It is tempting to read this untimeliness as evidence of sacral kingship's bankruptcy or of Richard's personal failings. Yet the lamenting outbursts that immediately follow his return from Ireland in Act III, scene 2 present mimetic approaches to death as pragmatic responses to temporal dislocation.

Already, the king is too late. Richard had landed in England intending to repel Bolingbroke's invasion. But once on shore, he discovers that all is lost. His armies have disbanded. His friends have defected or else been captured. He can only wait for his inevitable encounter with the usurper. To understand his predicament, Richard turns to history and discovers there a succession of dying kings:

> For God's sake let us sit upon the ground
> And tell sad stories of the death of kings,
> How some have been deposed, some slain in war,
> Some haunted by the ghosts they have deposed,
> Some poisoned by their wives, some sleeping killed,
> All murdered. (3.2.155–60)

It is certainly a melancholy list. Succession effected through inheritance and justified by legitimate sexuality (the dominant discourse within *Edward II*) is never raised as a possibility; all that is visible is untimely death.[4] The kings that Richard imagines are passive victims, "All murdered." As the catalogue continues, moreover, their agency even in life appears to diminish. Kings involved in active political struggles (deposed or slain in war) give way to those who fail to control their families (poisoned by their wives) and finally those who already resemble death in their insensibility (sleeping killed). The list moves inward from the kingdom to the self, with each new instance revealing that the fortifications that are supposed to secure sovereignty, autonomous agency, and bodily integrity will not hold. In the previous chapter, I argued that Marlowe's dramatizations of Edward II's imprisonment and subsequent "sleeping" death suggest that political and biological existence might enter into what Agamben calls a "zone of indistiction."[5] Richard's list demonstrates that Edward's experience is in no way unique but might be incorporated into a larger taxonomy in which the reach of mortality can be felt at all levels of social organization.

The trajectory of Richard's list from war, to domesticity, to sleep replaces the sphere of political action with that of biological maintenance and prefigures some of the ideas of Hannah Arendt. In *The Human Condition*, Arendt contrasts the ancient Greek *polis*—a site promoting what she considers authentic political action—with modern conceptions of the social that obliterate meaningful distinctions between public and private. Within the *polis*, citizens were temporarily freed from bodily need and the day-to-day business of household management, both of which were seen as the concerns of the *oikos*.[6] Interacting with one another as equals and individuals, they exhibited "the human condition of plurality . . . the fact that men, not Man, live on the earth and inhabit the world."[7] Later Western cultures, according to Arendt, have debased this public realm into the social sphere by politicizing the household economy and the biological processes of the human animal. Instead of showcasing the unique words and deeds of individual political actors, modern societies police behavior to produce a "conformism . . . ultimately rooted in the one-ness of man-kind."[8] Action, as practiced by the Greek citizens, is dethroned in favor of forms of labor aligned with the management of biological life. Arendt's classical touch-stones map imperfectly at best onto the political power structures of the medieval royal court, so we should be wary of aligning her conceptions of *polis, oikos,* and the social precisely with Richard's litany.[9] Most impor-tantly, Richard understands his own capacity to act not in relation to other autonomous human agents but as a product of his exclusive connection to God. Nevertheless, his catalogue transforms kings from meaningful his-torical actors to members of a class. The promise of "sad stories" is unful-filled. Instead of the promised narrative, Richard offers only demography.

Yet this list also suggests a possible third option between fantasies of sovereign political autonomy on the one hand and homogenized popula-tions defined by biological exposure to death on the other. The kings "haunted by the ghosts they have deposed" stand out from the rest of the catalogue and partially resist incorporation into a trajectory of increasing passivity. On one level, they admittedly represent another narrowing of the scope of kingly autonomy; even victorious rulers find themselves exposed to fatal hauntings. Yet ghosts also display the untimely power of the deposed. Reading *Hamlet* alongside Marx, Derrida stresses the tempo-ral instability of specters, which "no longer [belong] to time" and so have the power to disrupt teleological narratives.[10] For Derrida, ghosts function primarily as emblems of skepticism about triumphalist histories. But they equally might counter narratives like Richard's and Arendt's that speak of decline. Resurgent revenants introduce stutters into the endless procession of regicides and anticipate Richard's later attacks on his successor. In reflection of the double life of a king, punctuated by both death and demise, the specter of the deposed king will haunt Bolingbroke in two different capacities and at two different moments. Imprisoned but alive, Richard persists as a constant source of political instability. Dead, his memory serves to justify rebellion through the rest of the second tetralogy. When kingly ghosts disrupt linear narrative, they reveal sovereign power's untimely basis and so intensify that power even in the act of challenging it. By evok-ing ghosts, then, Richard once again identifies the vulnerability that mor-tality exposes in kings but also suggests there may be agency alongside this weakness, in the fact that a ghost can be parasitic on the new monarch. Where other monarchs are subsumed into a progressive sequence of deaths, the ghost-kings force a switchback, which allows them to deploy the universal experience of mortality to specific political ends and to claim these deployments as paradigmatic manifestations of the self-constituting and untimely nature of sovereign power.

The power of Richard's ghosts stems not only from their general propensity to reemerge unexpectedly but also from a characteristically early modern belief that postures of dying are iterable. Ghosts threaten their victims because they have the capacity to transfer their own experiences of death onto other similarly situated individuals. The term Richard employs to describe the their actions, "haunt," emphasizes the importance of repetition in this process. The *Oxford English Dictionary* cites this passage as the earliest instance of what is now the most common sense of the word: "subject to the visits and molestation of disembodied spirits."[11] Older understandings of "haunt," which must still resonate in Richard's speech, include "to resort to frequently or habitually; to frequent or be much about (a place)" and "to practice habitually, frequently or regularly."[12] A ghost's repeated actions tend to blur boundaries between usurper and the usurped, as the specter treats the sitting king as a place to be occupied or as a practice to be put on. The resulting "murder" of the haunted king represents the seizure of the living body by the dead predecessor. Sovereignty and mortality merge through repetition of habitual postures.

What confirms both the untimely appearance of ghosts and the haunting forms of power they enable is Richard's realization that he is already haunted (both inhabited and practiced) by a sovereign whose rights he has attempted to usurp: King Death,[13]

> For within the hollow crown
> That rounds the mortal temples of a king
> Keeps Death his court: and there the antic sits,
> Scoffing his state and grinning at his pomp,
> Allowing him a breath, a little scene,
> To monarchize, be feared, and kill with looks,
> Infusing him with self and vain conceit,
> As if this flesh which walls about our life
> Were brass impregnable; and humoured thus,
> Comes at the last, and with a little pin
> Bores through his castle wall; and farewell, king. (3.2.156–66)

Mortality is not just the origin point for sovereignty, the necessary corollary to demise (as it was in *Edward II*). In Richard's understanding, it constitutes its entirety. King Richard and King Death are superimposed upon each other. As Zenón Luis-Martínez notes, Richard's reference to the "hollow crown" evokes both the royal regalia and the bony sphere of the king's skull.[14] Death and Richard occupy the same headspace, and as a result, their identities merge. Which of the two is the referent behind the pronouns designating "his court," "his state," and "his pomp" is never entirely clear. Their domains are contiguous.

The image insists that we can use a model of performance to understand the king's relationship to mortality. But it obfuscates how this performance is structured and what it achieves, offering two alternative possibilities. On one level, Death resembles an audience member and Richard an imperfect actor, performing his "little scene" at Death's royal pleasure. The inevitability of death must bring the monarchizing king to acknowledge the performative and constructed nature of social roles. Human action and kingly pretension are revealed as mere epiphenomena, while universal mortality is the only reality. As an auditor, Death is remarkable for enjoying of the power of patronage over the verisimilitude of the performance. Like Theseus watching the Rude Mechanicals in *A Midsummer Night's Dream*, he appears to derive a large part of his pleasure from the inadequacies of the king's royal impersonation, and the glimpses of the merely mortal actor under the role. When Shakespeare returns to the *theatrum mundi* conceit in *Macbeth*, this suggestion that mortal performance is most notable for its badness will be more explicit. Macbeth's "poor player / That struts and frets his hour upon the stage / And then is heard no more" is characterized not by the mimetic role he is attempting to evoke but by the effortful kinetic movements that index the bodily labor he has devoted to performance.[15] Additionally, Death relishes the bounded nature of Richard's scene. His grinning observation of the king seems sweetened by his awareness that he can use the "little pin" to terminate the action. Viewed in this light, the conceit emphasizes the differences of status and power that performance sustains within a system of patronage.

But we can also eye the image awry. Richard's allusion to Death's "antic" persona recalls the *danse macabre* tradition, in which skeletons arrest and lead away unwilling representatives of different estates and professions, always starting with the monarch (see Figure 2).[16] These grinning, antic skeletons are entertainers, and their exaggerated, parodic imitations of the postures of their dance partners function partly as forms of social critique but also as symbols of the uncanny proximity of life and death. In the dance of death, the living king at first supplies the original, authentic model, and the skeletal death the approximate and mocking imitation. However, the king is eventually brought to enter the dance and ape his

RP-P-OB-4509 D(R)+(v) H.99 7+8

Figure 2: Hans Holbein the younger, *The Emperor*, from *The Dance of Death*, 1538. By permission of the Rijksmuseum, Amsterdam.

initial skeletal imitator. The process of dying is represented through the accrual of increasingly mediated and increasingly incompetent imitations. Transi tombs and *memento mori* emblems similarly juxtapose the quick and the dead to imply that this process continues after the final moment of expiration. In doing so, they lend agency and perverse vitality to the grinning death's heads and decomposing corpses who reveal the pretensions of the living through satirical imitation. Once Death is revealed as a potential performer, the boundary between actor and auditor becomes more permeable and the balance of power and sources of pleasure more uncertain.

Taken as a whole, Richard's conceit insists that sovereign death is a performance but radically obscures what such performance achieves. Who is the player and who the played? Who wears the crown authentically and who in mocking imitation? Luis-Martínez reads the image as a baroque anamorphosis. Impossible topographies and perspectival shifts reflect Richard's inability to construct a coherent narrative of history.[17] Yet Richard's words imply he experiences his newfound awareness of the skull beneath the skin less as a strobing between two incompatible states and more as a convergence with death. His subsequent behavior then suggests that such a merging may enable political action rather than evacuate it, especially if the performance of death is approached as an imitation of the Passion. Though he remains trapped in the timeline of dying kings, Richard's haunting, mimetic performances of mortality will give him a limited opportunity to assert narratives of death that resist a purely demographic conception of royal mortality and so to remain a political actor through his deposition and beyond.

The Christian Practice of Mimetic Death

Once Richard has discovered a source of power in the idea of performing death, he turns to the Passion as his most important precedent. The usurped king embraces the practice of *imitatio Christi* to transform his self-sapping experience of being haunted by the spirit of Death into an affirmative performance of mortality that might advantage him spiritually or politically. In the process, he indicates how earthly communities as well as heavenly ones can be founded in the image of the Crucifixion.

Richard's practice has a long and complex historical lineage. Christianity starts with a death. Christ sacrifices Himself to expiate the sins of mortals, replacing the old law with the new, the letter with the spirit. The church is constituted around His corpse and the redemption it promises. The theological vision outlined in Paul's Epistles asserts that the events of the Crucifixion and Resurrection fundamentally alter the relationship between divinity and humanity. But to delineate this bare structure is to leave unanswered more difficult questions about how Christ's dead and risen body knits together a scriptural past, a living church, and an anticipated eschatology. How can a disparate collection of still-living, still-breathing sinners hope to participate in either the long-past agony of Christ or the future promise of salvation supposed to result from it? How can they participate in both at once?

Historians and literary critics trying to understand how people in the early modern era answered these questions have tended to focus on the bitter doctrinal contentions that arose over the meaning of the Eucharist. Polemics for and against transubstantiation help us see how believers in different sects could feel the Passion differently—whether through taste, touch, signification, or memory—and consequently how they might use Christ's body to forge different relationships to divinity and to one another.[18] Critical work on the Eucharist has yielded valuable insights into the affective dimensions of faith and the composition of early modern religious communities. But it would be a mistake to assume that the sacrament was the only avenue through which early modern people tried to encounter Christ's body. Other strategies may be less visible today precisely because they had a more oblique relationship to confessional identity and inspired less sectarian controversy.

Imitation of Christ, I suggest, is one of these.[19] The command to imitate Christ on the Cross is found in Mark's Gospel, where Jesus tells his listeners, "Whosoever will follow me, let him forsake himself, and take up his cross, and follow me. For whosoever will save his life, shall lose it, but whosoever shall lose his life for my sake and the Gospel's, he shall save it."[20] Similarly, Paul in the Letter to the Romans assures Christians, "if we be planted with him to the similitude of his death, even so shall we be to the similitude of his resurrection."[21] In both instances, the identities of Christ and the imitator converge at the moment of death, which through Christ becomes resurrection. Salvific Christian imitation of the Passion is predicated on the promise that, contra Heidegger, death can be relational. Christ can die for the good Christian so that in a good Christian's approach to death, he or she is with Christ.

The appeal of this idea is obvious. Nobody has to die alone. Yet devotional writers have struggled to articulate precisely what an imitation of Christ's Passion should entail. One option is to internalize mimesis. The *devotio moderna* movement of the late fourteenth and fifteenth centuries characterized imitation of the Savior as a private act of spiritual devotion. The most influential text within this tradition, Thomas á Kempis's *Imitatio Christi*, advised constant emulation of Christ's example through the humble and patient acceptance of suffering.[22] Significantly, the efficacy of these imitations was not necessarily predicated on outwardly visible resemblances to Christ's person or Passion; internalized or mystical forms of asceticism might be compatible with living in the world. Even the *Golden Legend* (elsewhere concerned to present martyrdom as a theatrically violent practice) insists that

> we may be martirs without yron yf we kepe veryly pacyence in oure courage Compassion of them that ben in affliction and tormentis wherof it is sayd who that hath compassyon of ony that is in necessyte he bereth the Crosse in his thought And he that suffreth vylonny and loueth his enemy is a martir secretely in his mynde.[23]

A similar perspective informs the very first medieval *ars moriendi* text. The *Tractatus Artis Bene Moriendi* emerged around the same time as á Kempis's *Imitatio Christi* and also assumed that Christ's presence could be evoked in the everyday occasion of the ordinary deathbed. Its advises that "suche thinges as Cryst dyde dyenge in the cros the saam shold euery man doo at 'his' laste ende, after hys konnynge & power."[24] An internal attitude of conformity to Christ's example at the moment of death can make a dying person one with the Crucifixion, despite stark differences in circumstances. It can be tempting to dismiss this approach as simply hypocritical, especially when taken up by the wealthy Londoners who composed the initial audience for the English-language *Tractatus*. Yet, as Amy Appleford shows, a disjunction between the imitator's material comfort and Christ's abjection could be understood as spiritually advantageous if it spurred mental detachment from external, worldly circumstances.[25] Devotional practices inspired by the *devotio moderna* promise to radically refigure relationships between internal and external postures, by making interior asceticism compatible with ordinary worldly engagement.

This interiorized ascetic tradition survived the Reformation in slightly modified form. Although the absolute inscrutability and omnipotence of the Calvinist God sometimes threatened to overshadow the mediating function of His Son, contemplation of Christ's example remained a necessary devotional practice, for Protestants as for Catholics. A large number of Protestant writers and thinkers sought inspiration from the *devotio moderna*, and some attempted to adapt á Kempis's *Imitatio Christi* for new confessional contexts.[26] The most commercially successful of these adaptations, Thomas Rogers's 1580 translation *Of the Imitation of Christ*, offers valuable insight into how Protestant writers understood their own relationship to their Catholic predecessors.[27] In his prefatory letters to the translation, Rogers initially sidesteps the problem of á Kempis's Catholicism by naturalizing imitative practices. He observes that "Who entereth into a due consideration of mans nature shal easilie perceaue that most

stranglie it is addicted vnto Imitation."[28] We are all, Rogers suggests, congenitally bound to imitate and have choice only over what examples we
attend to. While the holy actions of historical and biblical figures can offer
useful patterns for behavior, Christ stands as the ultimate exemplar. He
alone should "be folowed, and that alwaies, and necessarilie: alwaies, for
that he was most perfectlie good; and necessarilie, because both himselfe,
and his Apostles, haue commanded vs to do so."[29] Human nature and scriptural imperative justify the practice of *imitatio Christi* in terms amenable to
both confessions.

This is not the end of the matter, though, since Rogers insists there are
licit and illicit ways to imitate Christ. Here, as we might expect, sectarian
disputes reemerge, though their location is a little surprising. Rogers cautions that

> albeit I saie our Sauior Christ is always [to be imitated]; yet do I not
> saie in al things: and though necessarilie to be folowed; yet not as he
> was God. For he fasted fourtie daies and fourtie nights . . . he restored
> sight to the blind; health to the sicke; to the dead life; and manie other
> miracles by the almightie power of his Godhead he wrought, which
> are vnimitable (as I maie saie) of mortal man. In somuch that they
> offend greatlie, whether they do it of superstition, as Papists; or of
> meere zeale, as did the God of Norweigh, who dare enterprise to imi
> tate our Sauior in anie thing which he did miraclouslie as a God.[30]

Rogers locates the original split between what is permissible and impermissible not within fractured religious communities but within Christ's dual
aspects as man and God. When Catholics and zealots like Henry of Hasselt
(the "God of Norweigh") fall into error,[31] they do so because they have
either misrecognized the distinction between Christ's Godlike and manlike
behavior or have responded to that distinction inappropriately.[32] Heretics'
very efforts to render their imitations perfect lead them into perversion. In
their actions, as in Faustus's blasphemous parodies, the sacred and the
profane touch. Rogers wants to insist that such mistakes can be avoided,
since the distinction between God and Man is stark. However the word he
uses to define the boundary, "unimitable," is slippery. With it, Rogers tries
at once to claim that Godlike behavior is impossible to imitate (in which
case he is stating the obvious) and that it should not be imitated (in which
case he risks circularity). The danger of the inimitable is double. The imitator might fail to evoke Christ, falling into mere superstition as she
approaches His Godlike aspect. Or, even worse, she might horrifically
succeed in doing something that should be exclusively proper to the divine.

Although Rogers does not discuss the problem, the Passion is the most difficult instance for asserting such distinctions between God and man. In one sense, Christ's death fully realizes His assumption of human mortality. But by undergoing the most abject human experience, Christ paradoxically confirms His divinity and then refigures the law governing relationships between the human and the divine. Moreover, in crucial aspects His death is not like the death of a human. In John's Gospel, Jesus asserts that "No man taketh [my life] from me, but I lay it down of myself. I have power to lay it down, and have power to take it again."[33] Theologians from Augustine onward have read this verse as evidence that Christ died voluntarily.[34] Although human suicide constitutes an unforgiveable rejection of God's plan, Christ's willing death stands as that plan's fulfillment. And none of this can be imitated—except that the scriptures insist that it must be, because being planted with the similitude of the Passion is what allows believing Christians to triumph over death through union with Christ. The exceptional nature of the Passion threatens to scramble distinctions between what is appropriate and inappropriate. As a result, the conceptual challenges posed by *imitatio Christi* are likely to be starkest during encounters with mortality.

Alongside the private devotional practice of *imitatio Christi* stands another tradition that conceives of imitation as a public performance. In 1 Corinthians, Paul encourages his readers to "Be ye followers [*mimitai*] of me, even as I am of Christ."[35] Paul's own successful imitation of Christ brings him closer to God, while drawing in a wider network of other followers, at first as spectators and then as fellow performers. Taken one way, Paul's words even suggest that practices of imitation underpin the institutional formation of the church. The compliers of the Geneva Bible translate the Greek word *mimitai* as "follower" and so align practices of imitation with demonstrations of obedience to a higher authority.[36] Chains of public imitative performance can harden into formal ecclesiastical institutions. And as I will argue, similar networks of imitation can also sustain secular political communities.

Even as the institutional church aspires to support the Christian practice of all its members through generating networks of followers, it may complicate individual acts of Christlike imitation. The dyadic relationship an individual forges with Christ through mimesis is placed under stress by that individual's immersion in a wider network of fellow imitators and spectators. Like private, internalized practices of meditative imitation, outwardly visible performances of holy death risk being dismissed as insincere posturing. One sect's martyr is another's hypocrite, idolater, or suicide.

Observers who presume to judge practices of *imitatio Christi* also place themselves in danger. They may be fooled by charlatans and misrecognize true, passionate performances. Or, no longer mere onlookers, they may find themselves drawn into the enactment of the Passion—perhaps as fellow martyrs for Christ; perhaps as avatars for Pilate, Peter, or even Judas; and perhaps as all these things at once. The very etymology of the word "martyr" (from the Greek for "witness") troubles distinctions between observers and participants and implies that those who see the Passion will be compelled to emulate it.

The disputed circumstances surrounding the execution of Thomas Bilney illustrate this dynamic nicely. Bilney, a preacher of Lutheran ideas, was burned for heresy in Norwich in 1531. Following his death, controversy emerged about whether he had remained steadfast in his reformed faith or had returned to the Catholic fold.[37] Thomas More, who had ordered Bilney's punishment, attempted to discover the truth by questioning several eyewitnesses present at the execution. In *The Confutation of Tyndale's Answer* (1532), he draws on their accounts to assert that Bilney had publicly recanted.[38] While More was able to satisfy himself of Bilney's reclamation, surviving records of his interrogations suggest that his sources were more uncertain and in some cases strikingly keen to emphasize their own unreliability. Edward Rede, the mayor of Norwich, insisted he was unable to hear the proceedings properly; the alderman John Curratt rather absurdly claimed that he missed Bilney's final words because he was occupied by tying his shoelace.[39]

At the least, the witnesses' demurrals register uncertainty about what would constitute an authentic performance of recantation or of steadfastness. Brian Cummings persuasively suggests that we might be looking at a clash between different culturally available understandings of the profession of faith as a private or public act.[40] But my interest lies more in how the Lord Chancellor's interrogations forced Rede and Curratt to reconceive their observational stances as somatic performances. Rede's straining ears and Curratt's fumbling fingers are not just accidental details that fill out the scene around Bilney. The observers' bodies are made to bear responsibility for determining how Bilney's body witnesses Christ's. Bilney's performance of martyrdom in the image of the Passion inevitably generates additional complementary performances. (Variants of Pilate? Of Judas? Of future saints?) And the stakes of these various forms of participation are high, as Rede and Curratt's reluctance to commit themselves implies. Thomas More, the one person confronting this tableau who insisted its meaning could be fixed, would himself end up crossing the divide between executor and executed. The others scramble for precarious places of safety and end up suspended in postures of witnessing, between observation and participation.

The difficulties that Rogers, Bilney, Curratt, Rede, and More encounter in distinguishing the imitable from the inimitable and observation from participation suggest that the resemblances to Christ achieved through orthodox devotional practices of *imitatio Christi* and modern martyrdoms exist within a much wider field of possible similitudes. Significantly, some forms of resemblance—even to Christ—could be both unsought and unwanted. The precedent of the Crucifixion loomed over early modern Christian communities. Individuals might inadvertently wander into its shadow and find themselves suddenly confronted with the stark fact of Christ's death and their own obligation to respond to it in and through mortality. These accidental and undesirable identifications with the Passion serve as reminders that the promise of salvation through Christ's death has a paranoid underside. What if the Crucifixion stands not for redemption but instead its inverse: a debt so great it can never be repaid? What if being planted with the similitude of Christ entails losing yourself entirely?

While such fears seem antithetical to the salvific promise of Christianity, Roberto Esposito suggests that they factor heavily in the historical development of the institutional church out of Roman notions of *communitas*. In Roman jurisprudential discussion of *communitas*, the root word "*munus*" signifies an obligation that is owed but never directly reciprocated, "the gift that one gives because one *must* give and because one *cannot not* give . . . only the gift that one gives, not what one receives."[41] Rather than constituting a tangible, shared creation or benefit (a *res publica*), communities emerge around and perpetuate experiences of self-loss that threaten total annihilation. The Middle Ages simplified political understandings of community into the fixed territories of the *civitas* or the *castrum*, but something of the existential threat inherent in the classical concept inflected Pauline theology and remained an important part of the subsequent development of Christian doctrine and ecclesiastical institutions. In Paul's epistles, the Passion functions as the originary *munus* that draws members of Christendom together into a fellowship of gratitude. As Christians strive to enter into this fellowship, they discover that Christ's sacrifice hovers ambiguously between gift and debt. The Crucifixion demands a response, yet any merely human effort to reciprocate must fall short. In attempting to repay this gift, Christians must recognize that what they participate in isn't the glory of the Resurrection but the suffering and the blood of the Cross (1 Cor. 10:16; Phil. 3:10). Any possibility of appropriation is diminished; "taking part in" means everything except "to take"; on the contrary, it means losing something, to be weakened, to share the fate of the servant, not of the master (Phil. 3:10–11). His death.[42]

Reciprocal sacrifices made in Christ's name and image blur individual identities and create fellowship through universal exposure to death. But resemblance to Christ can never result in complete participation in the *Corpus Christi*, since the substances of man and God are infinitely heterogeneous.[43] In consequence, failure is inevitable. To become full members of the Christian community, individuals must give their all to the imitation of Christ, knowing that their efforts will always be insufficient.

Esposito claims that modern political theorists and institutions rediscover the problem of *munus* from the church, though he is not especially interested in explaining precisely how or when *communitas* is transformed once more from a sacred into a secular construct.[44] We can start to fill in the gap in his genealogy by considering how religious notions of *imitatio Christi* inform political conceptions of representation. In one sense, the imitation of Christ became markedly political in the early modern era simply because the Tudor state's efforts to control the spiritual life of the nation tended to invest all devotional acts and ecclesiastical institutions with political significance. The interpenetration of church and state power, already evident in More's interrogations of eyewitnesses, intensified greatly following the Act of Supremacy, and religious and political dissent became increasingly entangled in response. Yet the fact that deliberate similitudes of the Passion are matched by unwitting ones—that some of the communities that emerge in the image of Christ form spontaneously or accidentally—suggests that *imitatio* produces more complicated and unpredictable political effects than those that can be analyzed under models of governmental surveillance and resistance. To think carefully about what these effects are, and in particular about how politicized imitations of the Passion generate and sustain connections between mortality, sovereignty, community, and representation, I now turn back to *Richard II* for the remainder of this chapter.

Christ's Entry into Parliament

The political stakes of dying in the image of Christ become fully apparent when Richard gives up his throne in Act IV, scene 1. Richard draws on the precedent of Christ to suggest that abdication, imprisonment, and even regicide could perversely support sacred kingship. Critical disagreements over whether the ritual of abdication Richard invents should be read as a quasi-sacramental act, a politically strategic parody of ceremony, or a demonic profanation of divine forms attest both to the potency and the ambivalence of his performance.[45] But in focusing entirely on Richard's sovereign appropriation of Christological models and ignoring the context in which he speaks, critics risk wrongly restricting the play's focus to divinized monarchy and missing how political alternatives to Richard's notion of rule also grapple with the precedent of the Passion. In the abdication scene, imitation of Christ emerges as a potential model for multiple political institutions, including those that reject any notion of personal, divinized sovereign power.

The abdication of Shakespeare's Richard in front of a parliamentary assembly has no precedent in Holinshed. Instead, and in exhaustive bureaucratic detail, *The Chronicles* describe two distinct political mechanisms that together are used to ratify the transmission of power. Almost immediately after Richard's capture and imprisonment in the Tower, Bolingbroke calls a Parliament in the king's (that is, Richard's) name, which draws up a list of articles of Richard's crimes and concludes he is "worthie to be deposed from all kinglie honor, and princelie gouernement."[46] Meanwhile, Richard's remaining friends persuade him that active cooperation with the new regime will offer his best hope of survival. He agrees to author a "Bill of Renouncement" resigning his right to the Crown. When a parliamentary delegation (including Bolingbroke) enters the Tower to witness his signature of this document, they hear Richard state "if it were in his power, or at his assignement, he would that the duke of Lancaster there present should be his successour, and king after him" and see him place his signet ring on Bolingbroke's finger.[47] The delegation then returns to Parliament and proclaims Richard's voluntary abdication. Lords and Commons admit the report of the king's resignation, review the articles of his crimes, and pronounce a "publication of King Richard's deposing." Finally, Bolingbroke addresses the Lords, issuing a "challenge or claime to the crowne," which is accepted by the Archbishop of Canterbury, who leads him up to the throne "to the great reioising of the people."[48]

The Chronicles, then, describe two separate strategies for effecting demise, one focused on the person of the king enclosed in the Tower, the other focused on the representatives of the people assembled for the Convocation Parliament. The two centers of political activity are clearly connected and in certain respects mirror each other. Each is supported by its own

complement of commissioned officials, bureaucratic assistants, legal documents, and ceremonies designed to enact the symbolic transfer of sovereignty. Nevertheless, they reflect significantly different understandings of
the nature of political agency and action. In the Tower, sovereignty and its
termination are tied to the king's body as a locus of both power and vulnerability. Demise is the personal business of the ruler and his successor. The
process can be witnessed, and even shaped, by outsiders like Richard's
friends and the delegates who report back to Parliament. Nevertheless,
monarchical sovereignty, even in its revocation, remains personal and can
be transferred in only two ways: through an exceptional sovereign decision
or through a violent act of usurpation. By contrast, Parliament deperson-
alizes power. Although nominally summoned in the king's name (and
this fiction is particularly strained when that named king is imprisoned),
parliamentary representatives assert their right to pursue legal action
against him in the interest of the English people. Their collective power is
expressed through law rather than sovereign decision.

The Chronicles are careful to present these strategies in complementary
terms. The king in the Tower and the representatives in Parliament work
toward the same goal of Richard's demise. They are knit together by the
mobile figure of Bolingbroke, who shuttles back and forth between the two
spaces, acting as royal supplicant in the one and parliamentary plaintiff in
the other. Shakespeare's aim, however, seems rather different. He height-
ens the tensions between the two mechanisms of demise when he superimposes *The Chronicles'* two loci of power and moves Richard into the
parliamentary assembly. While Holinshed's adaptable Bolingbroke seems
equally capable of political action in both Tower and Parliament, Richard
describes his movement from one space to the other as a temporal, physical, and psychological dislocation:

> Alack, why am I sent for to a king
> Before I have shook off the regal thoughts
> Wherewith I reigned? I hardly yet have learned
> To insinuate, flatter, bow, and bend my knee.
> Give sorrow leave awhile to tutor me
> To this submission. (4.1.156–61)

In this complaint, Richard aligns entry into Parliament with self-
alienation. As a monarch, his social performances had been naturalized;
merely to think a regal thought had amounted to an act of reigning. Now
he must acknowledge the challenges involved in conforming the self to
the world and learning to perform submission. Summoned to this hostile

Parliament in an untimely fashion and already undergoing a disorienting constitutional reorganization, he casts around for a constant that might help him understand his altered state. He discovers one point of recognition in the "favors of these men," remarking, "Were they not mine? / Did they not sometime cry 'All hail!' to me?" (4.1.161–63). Yet, far from grounding him, recollection of former courtiers further undoes both his present and past selves.

In noting the "favors" of his former flatterers, Richard puns on the word's double senses of "distinguishing characteristics" and "signs of preference." Happily receiving Richard's rewards for past and anticipated future service, his followers had responded with expressions of appreciation, manifested particularly through their countenances. The faces that Richard had assumed would authentically identify loyal followers turn out to be false fronts concealing desires and interests that diverge from his. In this pun, Richard recognizes the nexus of royal gifts and flattery that underpins the political union of monarch and sycophants. As the different senses of favor infect one another, they erode distinctions between subjects and the donated objects they use to mark their mutual obligations to one another. All the men become interchangeable, and all appear more like things.[49] Moreover, under sorrow's tutelage, Richard too must learn to become masklike, to "insinuate, flatter, bow," and present a face to the world that diverges from his inner thoughts. Far from supplying a means to ground his experiences, Richard's recognition of the men he sees through their favors triggers a vertigo recalling his earlier sense of being haunted by King Death. Christopher Pye argues that *Richard II* reveals this dynamic's centrality to the very concept of personal sovereignty, at least at the level of representation. Shakespeare's continual recourse to images of mirrors, blots, and anamorphic perspectives reflect the impossibility of producing a coherent vision of the sovereign from within the field of his power. Even Richard needs the perspective of treachery and the refraction of despairing tears to understand the regal position he is losing.[50]

But Richard's dislocation is not complete. As his confidence in his ability to read the particular favors of those around him declines, he becomes more aware of the archetypes they resemble. The flatterers' hypocrisy makes them less readable as individuals but more recognizable as types. And as types, they evoke an exemplary narrative that promises to offer Richard his own role and script to perform. "All hail," as he makes sure to remind his listeners, was the greeting Judas used to betray Christ. The precedent of the Passion holds obvious political and psychological attractions for Richard. It allows him to register his sense of betrayal, to assert his innocence, and even to comfort himself with the thought of future resurrection. Additionally, it helps him articulate the discrepancies between the two modes of demise that Bolingbroke hopes to yoke together. As Marjorie Garber notes, Richard's performance of abdication exploits the overlaps between three possible definitions of the word "deposition": a forcible removal from power, a legal statement, and the descent of Christ's body from the cross.[51] When he deposes himself in the image of Christ, Richard lays bare the threats of violence and the acts of sacrilege that the rebels had hoped to cover over with parliamentary procedure. While Richard's identification with Christ has struck many audiences as narcissistic, I am less interested in accounting for his personal psychology than in considering what his words reveal about the structure of political communities founded on Christian conceptions of resemblance. More than a mere hyperbole, Richard's language of the Passion locates a life-sapping dynamic of treachery and obligation within the center of government.

To appreciate the significance of Richard's actions in Parliament, it is helpful to look briefly at an earlier moment in the play when he employs an embryonic version of this strategy. After failing to see his favorites Bushy, Greene, and the Earl of Wiltshire upon his return from Ireland, Richard lashes out at the courtiers for their apparent betrayal and accuses them of being "Three Judases, each one thrice worse than Judas" (3.2.127). In Richard's conceit, a multiplication of traitors entails an intensification of treachery. Guilt is not diminished when it is shared. Instead, it compounds. Importantly, though, Richard does not initially believe it to be universal. The caterpillars' betrayal implies the existence of a betrayed party, whose innocence will emerge secondarily as a response to their treachery. Bushy, Greene, and Wiltshire's resemblance to Judas confirms Richard's resemblance to Christ. Or more precisely, their excessive resemblance to Judas compensates for Richard's inadequate resemblance to Christ. The caterpillars acquire responsibility not only for their own treacherous actions but also for any hubris or failure involved in Richard's claim to be like the Savior.

The conceit fails because Richard is unfair. As Scrope puts it, Bushy, Greene, and Wiltshire have made peace "With heads and not with hands" (3.2.133). They have not betrayed Richard but—quite the contrary—died in his place. Bolingbroke's execution order had condemned them for their part in "mis[leading] a prince" (3.1.8), making them responsible for Richard's crimes. Once Richard's image recoils on him, the positions of Christ and Judas threaten to reverse. The ungrateful king looks more like a traitor, the courtiers like wronged innocents and sacrificial substitutes. However, the caterpillars gain no personal advantage from this alteration. They avoid the immediate charge of treachery only by assuming yet more guilt from Bolingbroke and by giving their lives in the king's stead. There is no way for them to survive the process of becoming like Christ, and in consequence they do not model a sustainable practice of *imitatio Christi* that Richard might adopt going forward. Nor do their deaths drain guilt out of the system. The reversal of Christ and Judas draws more guilty actors into the tableau. Bolingbroke assumes the role of Pilate when he publishes the caterpillars' guilt in order to "wash [their] blood/From off [his] hands" (3.1.5–6). And Richard's suggestion that guilt will compound as more people enter its field raises doubts about whether the courtiers' sacrifice will be sufficient to fully expiate the crimes they have been supercharged with. Can three heads make peace for multiple, intensified (and ever-multiplying, ever-intensifying) Judases?

In this instance, then, Richard succeeds in invoking Christ but gains no ostensible advantage from doing so. Christ does not appear in his standard political guise as a positive model for kingship. His precedent does not sanctify Richard's rule, redeem the body mortal with a mystical supplement, or anticipate a flow of benefits from the king to his followers. Rather, as Esposito had suggested, Christ functions as an "originary *munus*," a source of endless obligations that threaten to consume king and courtiers alike. All that Richard has achieved is to bring this threat into the court.[52] The parallels between sacred and secular institutions do not sacralize the king's rule or separate him from mere mortals but rather confirm his exposure, alongside that of his followers, to life-sapping, unavoidable guilt. If regal power in the play is, as Pye suggests, best viewed from traitorous perspectives, this dynamic does not merely reflect the limits of representation but also the centrality of debt and betrayal to Christological conceptions of sovereignty.

What happens to such guilt as the play moves away from the personal court to consider different political institutions? When Richard puns on the false "favors" of the men who surround him in the abdication scene, he hails them as members of the same courtly community as Bushy and Greene. Yet it is questionable if he is right to do so. While he recognizes those he sees as courtiers, they are now assembled in a different guise, as members of Parliament, representatives of the nation. And the difference may be significant. For some early modern jurists and historians—probably including the compilers of Holinshed's *Chronicles*—Richard II's protracted disputes with the Appellant Lords, culminating in the Convocation Parliament of 1399, offered an exemplary instance of Parliament's capacity to oppose tyrannical kingship. Annabel Patterson persuasively suggests that the exhausting attention paid by the *Chronicles* to the bureaucracy surrounding Richard's deposition has an ideological function. It serves to celebrate parliamentary authority grounded in law while denigrating less routinized expressions of the royal will.[53] Bolingbroke's easy movement between Tower and assembly promises to reconcile the Crown and the Commonwealth through the irresistible figure of the King in Parliament. Although this hope would never be realized in the remainder of Henry IV's rather fractious reign—in large part because the magnates who helped the king to the throne maintained their own personal political ambitions independent of either sovereign institution—the Convention Parliament existed in a certain Elizabethan protoliberal imaginary as an object of nostalgia and a precedent for future self-assertion.

Shakespeare's dramatization of Richard's abdication calls into question what it means for Parliament to represent the nation. The political concept of parliamentary representation emerged gradually over the medieval era. Early Norman parliaments were irregular assemblies of important magnates or else occasions for the king's direct tenants (great and small) to swear fealty. By the middle of the thirteenth century, however, the institution had expanded to include elected knights from every shire, individuals who over time came to think of themselves as representatives of the community of the realm. It also gained constitutional importance, since the king was increasingly expected to secure its consent to taxation, especially in support of military campaigns.[54] Parliament's fiscal authority was more rhetorical than real; while the members could dispute the nature, quantity, and use of a tax, they were unable to deny it absolutely. However, G. L. Harriss provocatively suggests that these very limitations may have "forced them to develop corporate identity as a political body representing the realm."[55] By the fourteenth century, certainly, parliamentary power (especially over Crown finances) was increasingly justified on the basis of the Commons' capacity to speak for the nation. The most widely circulating legal account of Parliament from this period, the *Modus Tenendi Parliamentum*, asserts that "two knights who come to Parliament for the shire have a greater voice in granting and denying than the greatest earl of England" because they represent "the whole community of England [*totam communitatem Anglie*]," while each magnate is in Parliament "for his own individual person, and for no one else."[56] This political "community" was sometimes understood through religious analogy. Analyzing legal, political, and literary texts from the fourteenth century, Matthew Giancarlo demonstrates how the voice of Parliament was repeatedly associated with "the

Pentecostal arrival of the Holy Spirit upon the assembled apostles." Members of the Commons resemble the Apostles because they have been visited by a spirit that empowers them to speak for the nation as a whole. The analogy implies that "the assembly can, and indeed should, rightly speak with the 'voice of the community' or *vox populi* at the same time that it adopts the functional identity of the *vox Dei*, and that the two can become mixed in the particular setting of Parliament."[57] Where the king aspires to represent the person of Christ directly, parliamentarians characterize themselves as the elected deputies who remain behind after Christ's ascension to continue His work. Through Pentecostal analogies, they position themselves as the lower and later supplements to the higher authority of the monarch. But, more radically, they could also hint at a process of historical succession, through which the individual charismatic person of the king must eventually give way to the collective institution of the people.

It is important not to overstate the material consequences of these notions of representation or to align them too neatly with later theories of parliamentary democracy. The notoriously murky textual history of the *Modus* ensures that its value as an account of actual parliamentary procedure is dubious at best.[58] An important and separate strand of late medieval political writing located the power of Parliament somewhere entirely different: the barons' capacity to act as chivalric defenders of the realm.[59] And in any case, before the franchise expansions of the nineteenth and twentieth centuries, the "community of England" actually bodied forth in the Commons was never more than a small, elite subsection of the populace.[60] Nevertheless, the concept of parliamentary representation outlined in the *Modus* acquired significant rhetorical importance in later disputes between Crown and Parliament. The increasingly absolutist ambitions of Tudor and Stuart rulers inspired their critics to mount contrary defenses of parliamentary sovereignty. Sixteenth- and seventeenth-century jurists domesticated their flirtations with classical and Italian modes of republicanism by aligning them with native traditions of mixed government, parliamentary representation, and the myth of the ancient constitution.[61] Repeatedly, throughout the constitutional crises of early modern England, the sovereign as the representative of God on earth squared off against Parliament as the voice of the people.

This context informs Shakespeare's representation of the deposition. As he prepares to abdicate before the assembled Lords and Commons, Shakespeare's Richard calls upon his listeners to consider the precise relationship between king and Parliament and the modes of representation upon which both centers of power purport to rely. He reiterates and even intensifies his audacious claim to have exceeded Christ's suffering, complaining that where Christ "in twelve [apostles] / Found truth in all but one; I, in twelve thousand, none" (4.1.161–62). Superficially, his words appear to repeat the same multiplicatory operations that wrongly condemned Bushy, Greene, and Wiltshire. Yet Richard's language here is far harder to dismiss as simple self-aggrandizement or ingratitude. The numbers he gives are not mere hyperbole but have an actual referent. "Twelve thousand" recalls the "twelve thousand fighting men" from Wales that Salisbury assures Richard would be there for him, could he only "call back yesterday, bid time return," and arrive back in England a day sooner (3.2.64–65).[62] As he recalls these missing soldiers in the presence of Parliament, Richard aligns the military force that failed to materialize with the assembled members to imply that the guilt of these two groups is shared. Perhaps he also reflects the particular obligation of the Commons to use their political voice to supply the Crown with military resources. Parliament's claim to represent the nation contextualizes Richard's Christological identification. It might seem absurd for Richard to view an assembly composed of a few hundred Peers and Commons and then condemn twelve thousand subjects as avatars of Judas. But it is also absurd for this small number of parliamentarians to pretend to speak for the nation as a whole. The king reworks Pentecostal models of parliamentary voice in a new and uncomfortable direction. In decrying the treachery of twelve thousand as an absurd intensification of the treachery of a single apostle, Richard casts judgment not just on individual acts of betrayal by former courtiers but on the fundamental claim made by the parliamentarians assembled before him to represent many men at once.

This particular critique of parliamentary representation becomes intensified within the theater. The few hundred parliamentarians attending and assenting to Richard's deposition are necessarily represented on stage by a far smaller number of players. By staging an inadequate dramatic approximation of Parliament, the play undermines the institution's claim to be representative. Additionally, Richard's remarks on the dissimulating favors of the men he sees around him reinforce long-established cultural associations between acting and falsity. The onstage parliamentarians are doubly unreliable, as insincere political operatives and as players. Their ability to dissimulate is necessary for them to function as actors and as courtiers but may generate skepticism about their integrity as national representatives. When superimposed, theatrical, courtly, and parliamentary modes of representation threaten to expose each other's limitations.

Having appropriated Parliament's claim to represent the nation in order to justify his own self-presentation as Christ, Richard then moves to prevent members from disputing his construction. He follows on from his accusation of betrayal by exclaiming,

> God save the King! Will no man say "Amen"?
> Am I both priest and clerk? Well then, Amen.
> God save the King, although I be not he
> And yet Amen, if heaven do think him me. (4.1.172–74).

The call to communal prayer invokes the parliamentary *vox populi* raised to *vox dei*. But it does so in a way that will inevitably cause that voice to falter. As Richard must realize, "Amen" cannot be spoken safely while the referent behind "King" is still so unclear. Whether those around Richard are genuinely concerned with providence or whether they merely desire to appear like good citizens of the new order, they must be silent. In their silence, they lose the opportunity to deny Richard's characterization of them as dissimulators and cede him the freedom to stage-manage his own abdication. Richard wins the right to perform in the image of Christ not by denying the parliamentary claims to political importance founded upon notions of representation but by acceding to them and shaping them to his own ends.

Richard's characterization of the parliamentarians as Judases, then, rests on a surer footing than his condemnation of the caterpillars. And at least initially, it also promises to return to him a limited degree of political agency. Richard wins by losing. He performs his abdication as a mimetic art of dying that promises resurrection with and in Christ while projecting questions about what constitutes an appropriate imitation of Christ onto those around him. In the space this behavior creates, Richard takes control of the abdication ceremony, maintaining a grip on the theater of monarchy even as he resigns the leading role and successfully evading Northumberland's demand that he read out his crimes.

Yet there are serious limitations to this strategy. First, Richard's resemblance to Christ is sustained by the parliamentarians' hard-heartedness. By relying on parliamentary Judases to ground his own representation of Christ, Richard casts the constitution of the nation as inherently divided, inevitably characterized by ingratitude. Going beyond Pye's suggestion that sovereignty requires treachery to understand itself or Greenblatt's claim that power works through stimulating and then containing subversion, Richard's Judas imagery imagines constant and inevitable betrayal and seems to anticipate the civil wars that punctuate the rest of the history plays. Second, the resemblances Richard has created are situational rather than structural. When Richard predicates his similarity to Christ more on his courtiers' similarities to Judas than on any notion of the divine right of kings, he positions himself as one actor among many and treats Christ not as a unique pattern of Christian piety but as one single possible exemplar in a field of potential behavioral models.

It quickly becomes clear that he does not have complete control of this field. Having equated himself with Christ and won an embarrassed, silent acceptance from those around him, Richard seems unable to rest in that pose. He admits that his own complicity in the abdication threatens to render him "a traitor with the rest" (4.1.241). As we saw with his earlier condemnation of the caterpillars, the polarities of Christ and Judas can flip quickly. But the resemblances that Richard does not, and indeed cannot, admit are perhaps more damning. Harry Berger observes that Richard's wish to be "a mockery king of snow / Standing before the sun of Boling-broke, / To melt myself away in water drops" and his doubt that the face he sees in the mirror was "the face / That every day under his household roof / Did keep ten thousand men?" constitute textual allusions to Mar-lowe's *Doctor Faustus* (4.1.259–61, 80–82).[63] In part, these echoes function as what Phyllis Rackin calls "double-edged" anachronisms, at once produc-ing an "illusion of presence" by "breaking the frame of historical represen-tation" and, in the same moment, reminding watchers "of the vast gulf of time and awareness that separates them from the historical events repre-sented on stage."[64] Through association with Marlowe's reprobate magi-cian, Richard becomes desacralized and disempowered. The allusion undermines his claims to Christlike singularity, reducing him to another reprobate confronting his end. Where he had hoped to function as an untimely, haunting figure hampering Bolingbroke's accession to the throne, he becomes the guiltily haunted. The local doubts these textual echoes raise about Richard's psyche and state of grace can help us recognize a more general phenomenon: Actors and audiences have complementary roles in creating and sustaining resemblances. When Richard justifies his imitation of Christ through recourse to the sustaining performances of his Judas-like courtiers and the awkward assent of his assembled audiences, he abdicates the power to control what he might resemble. He has won the temporary right to perform Christ, but he remains haunted by other fig-ures, some acknowledged and desired, some not.

Richard's evocations of unchristlike exemplars, moreover, do not only serve to diminish his own political agency through mechanisms similar to those he has used to undermine Bolingbroke and the parliamentarians; they additionally force audience members to consider the political impli-cations of their own positions as witnesses to the onstage representations.

Readers and watchers of *Richard II* have discovered a wonderfully large set of resemblances between the king and other biblical, literary, and historical analogues. Explicit references to Judas, Pilate, and Cain and Abel, as well as implicit ones to Thomas Becket, Henry VI, and Elizabeth I, reach backward into Genesis and forward to the time of the play's composition.[65] The apparent exploitation of this last resemblance by enemies of the queen during Essex's Rebellion should make the high stakes of these allusions evident.[66] As the figures haunting Richard become more removed from the immediate occasion of his demise, and especially as they emerge from nearer the present, they threaten to implicate audience members who recognize the ghosts in the ever-growing network of guilty representations. The prologue to *Henry V* famously pleads that

> since a crooked figure may
> Attest in little place a million;
> And let us, ciphers to this great accompt,
> On your imaginary forces work. (*Henry V*, Prologue 15–18)

When the Chorus invites listeners to "Piece out our imperfections with your thoughts" (23), it asks them to collaborate in constituting a transhistorical idea of nationhood. But where *Henry V* proposes that the suspension of disbelief will generate a nationalist affinity between actors and audience, *Richard II* casts audience collaboration in less encouraging terms. If audiences allow Richard to delineate the networks of representation within the play, they risk being implicated in a national Parliament of Judases. If they challenge the king's prerogative by identifying alternative resemblances, they do not avoid complicity. For watchers at a play, as for onlookers at the executions of heretics, the position of "witness" continually threatens to become a dangerously active one.

In part, then, the abdication scene illustrates how an imitative approach to demise modeled on Christ's Passion supplies Richard with a degree of agency and a model for political action in the face of death. But it also suggests that mimetic identifications are always contingent and that political emulation of Christ's sacrifice can be aligned with a variety of different political formations. In certain respects, Richard's behavior resembles Hobbesian absolutism more than it does the theopolitical forms of government with which his rule is most commonly associated. Hobbes derives the sovereign's absolute power not from any patriarchal or sacral assertion of a right to the throne but rather from a relationship between authorizing subjects and the fictive person of the sovereign who stands for them.[67] In other respects, the Passion in the Parliament evokes the various experiments in constitutional and representative governance that Patrick Collison talks about under the label of monarchical republicanism.[68] Though in the moment, Richard's challenge to the Lords and Commons to speak works to silence them, his words identify parliamentary representation as a constitutional force and so afford members the opportunity to create their own sacred and secular resemblances for their own political ends. Once the play replaces a fixed chain of analogies leading from earth to heaven with a network of shifting, interlocking resemblances, it threatens to render all forms of government contingent and unstable. The overthrow of hierarchy in *Richard II* anticipates both the civil wars of Henry IV's later reign and sixteenth- and seventeenth-century disputes between Crown and Parliament. The play primes viewers to react skeptically toward descriptions of either monarch or assembly as the supreme site of sovereign power. It suggests that because absolutism and republicanism both exploit Christological constructions of representation and community, they depend upon each other. Parliamentarians who draw on Pentecostal models to justify their claims to represent the nation must explain what happened to Christ. Conversely, Richard can only cast himself as a Christ figure because the parliamentarians are acting like false disciples.

Rather than illustrating the supersession of divine right and its replacement by protoliberal constitutional government, republicanism, or Machiavellian realpolitik, the abdication scene suggests that all possible constructions of government available within the world of *Richard II* are grounded in modes of Christian community that blur the distinctions between representation and participation. As in Richard's image of the court, *imitatio Christi* is always inadequate and always reversible. Christ may enter into Parliament, but then he disappears into a wider and more ambiguous field of resemblances. The residues he leaves behind are a disenchanted, delegitimized polity and guilt for the inevitable failure that accompanies all attempts to invoke him imitatively.

The Inimitable

In the following chapter, I will consider if such guilt can be avoided. Ben Jonson's *Volpone* explores whether approaching death as a private labor enables individuals to resist incorporation into the communities of obligation that form around Christ's example. The end of *Richard II*, however, moves in a contrary direction. As he confronts assassination, Richard no longer strives to mitigate the guilt involved in the emulation of Christ through displacement. Instead, he intensifies it. Embracing the sort of hagiographic narrative that Marlowe's Edward II evades at the moment of death, Richard takes on some of the ambiguous qualities of a Catholic martyr seen anachronistically from beyond the historical divide of the Reformation. His final speech invests his death with sacred and profane qualities simultaneously. He tells his murderer

> That hand shall burn in never-quenching fire
> That staggers thus my person. Exton, thy fierce hand
> Hath with the king's blood stained the king's own land.
> Mount, mount my soul. Thy seat is up on high
> While my gross flesh sinks downward, here to die. (5.5.108–12)

This speech moves in two contrary directions. Looking upward, Richard produces an apostrophe to his mounting soul that asserts certainty about his spiritual fate. The precedent of martyrdom allows him to reframe circumstances that might otherwise appear ignominious, most notably his deposition and imprisonment, as triumphs of patience in the image of Christ. Alongside his soul's ascent, though, Richard also narrates his body's descent. And his allusions to blood and gross flesh channel the precedent of martyrdom rather differently. Catholic devotional cults centered on the relics of martyrs frequently invested the bodies of dead saints with sanctifying and healing attributes. For Protestant reformers, these material residues acquired unsavory connotations of idolatry, ambition, and superstition. When Richard describes his corpse as "gross flesh," he alludes to the Pauline association of flesh with human corruption in a way that brings to mind this reformist suspicion of bodily relics. However, anti-Catholic discourses do not undermine his ability to present his regicide as a spiritual catastrophe with longstanding political implications for the nation. Quite the contrary, they secure it. Richard's appropriation of the postures of sainthood, along with his confident assertion that his soul is destined for heaven, may appear hubristic or even blasphemous to skeptical watchers. But any such doubts are localized, sloughed off, and left behind as a stain on Bolingbroke's realm. The dying king's polluted and polluting blood penetrates the ground, perhaps retaining just enough of the mystique of sainthood reinterpreted in a negative valence to substantiate his earlier conjuration that "This earth shall have a feeling, and these stones / Prove armèd soldiers" before rebellion succeeds (3.2.24–25). It anticipates the civil disorder that will be dramatized in the rest of the tetralogy.

In dying, Richard takes on some the attributes that Thomas Rogers condemned as inimitable. His end is politically potent precisely because it probably fails to realize the precedent of Christ appropriately. As in Rogers's discussion, though, it is unclear precisely where Richard's failures should be located. Is the problem that he is attempting something that he cannot do or that he is succeeding in something that he should not do? This uncertainty makes the threat he poses to Bolingbroke's future rule harder to define and harder to expiate. Moreover, as Richard's words anachronistically anticipate post-Reformation critiques of saints' cults, they invest his final performance with an untimely quality. Richard starts to move out of the linear progression of history and so to become more like the ghosts he imagined haunting their usurpers. Embodying rather than evading the guilt attached to the project of *imitatio Christi*, Richard leaves his decomposing corpse to pollute the land and establishes a *munus* at the heart of the commonwealth.

The final events of *Richard II* intimate some of the possible consequences of these sorts of dying performances for those who survive them. Exton immediately assents to the plausibility of Richard's presentation of events, confessing that his decision to spill "royal blood" was prompted by a hellish impulse (5.5.113). More significantly, the new Henry IV's attempts to devolve responsibility for the regicide lead him to perpetuate ideas and patterns Richard had instituted. When Henry IV banishes Exton by charging him "With Cain [to] go wander through the shade of night" (5.6.40), he performs a representational inversion that mirrors Richard's unstable emulation of both Christ and Judas. A series of allusions to Genesis 4 stretches through the play, from Bolingbroke's complaint in the first scene that the Duke of Gloucester's blood "like sacrificing Abel's, cries/Even from the tongueless caverns of the earth/To me for justice and rough chastisement" (1.1.104–6) to Richard's insistence that his blood has stained the land.[69] In Act I, Abel is Gloucester; Cain is nominally Mowbray but probably really Richard. By Act V, Abel has become Richard, while Cain is apparently Exton but actually Bolingbrook. As different deaths are reunderstood through the same scriptural model, they suggest open-ended processes whereby the slain are embodied and revived through imitation only to die again. In a double movement, the history depicted by the play moves forward, while the deaths it evokes become more ancient. Abel is the first human to die in the Bible, the model for all subsequent deaths, yet Christian authors frequently read him typologically to prefigure the Passion and subsequent martyrdoms.[70] His original death becomes anachronistically citational as subsequent Christianizing accretions overwrite but do not quite erase the original Jewish model. The allusion suggests that death, even from the start, was always mimetic and that the modes of imitative dying Richard and Bolingbroke appropriate for specific political purposes, along with the differences between Catholic and Protestant understandings of holy imitation, are only brief episodes in a much longer story typified by recursions and reworkings that continue indefinitely. Richard has left a fraught relationship to the Passion of Christ behind as his inheritance, and the new monarch must now take his own turn at being inhabited and haunted by King Death and the various other godly and reprobate figures who have previously performed arts of dying.

Later in Shakespeare's career, *Antony and Cleopatra* offers an illuminating counterpoint to Richard's martyrdom and suggests additional political arenas that are conditioned by religious imitation. Cleopatra's suicide is an equally theatrical and anachronistic royal death in the image of a religious icon, but it is one that occurs in a markedly different historical and geographical context. Throughout the play, Cleopatra asserts sovereign power through spectacular performances, some of which explicitly connect royalty with deity. Caesar, for example, reports that she appeared publicly in "th' habiliments of the goddess Isis" (3.6.17) to receive full possession of Egypt from Antony. Her suicide is equally showy. Immediately before she applies the asp to her breast, she asks to be dressed in her robe and crown, the symbols of her queenly authority. Her comportment inspires Charmian to compare her to Venus ("O eastern star!" 5.2.304). From Cleopatra's perspective, the two pagan goddesses work to divinize the Egyptian monarchy, much as the comparison to Christ sacralizes European kings. But early modern viewers would have been likely to supplement Venus and Isis with Christian archetypes, which complicate the symbolism of the queen's suicide. In particular, when Cleopatra connects royalty with maternity and quiets Charmian by comparing the asp to "my baby at my breast, / That sucks the nurse asleep" (5.2.305–6), she evokes images of the Virgin and child.

What should audiences make of this? As Drew Daniel observes, Cleopatra's death is generically impure. Her suicide by snakebite constitutes a savvy evasion of Octavius Caesar and a triumphant display of royalty. But it is also a cowardly pursuit of "easy ways to die" (5.2.352) and an extended sex joke. The position of Cleopatra's suicide at the end of "a spiral of bad mimesis" threatens to imbue it with a slapstick tone. It is an imitation of "Antony . . . imitating Eros's imitation of Cleopatra's imitation of self-killing."[71] Anachronistic allusions to Catholic and pagan modes of religious mimesis only add to this chain of resemblances and heighten generic ambiguity by encouraging divergent interpretations of the queen. Marian echoes would trigger nostalgia from some viewers and condemnation from others and so serve unpredictably to imply Cleopatra's nobility, presumption, or absurdity to different audience members.[72] Perhaps because of her proximity to comedy, or perhaps because of her gender, Cleopatra gains less clear political advantage from Mary's uncertain reputation than Richard did from his connection to martyred saints. Instead, Caesar is the character who leverages the ambivalent tone of her ending for political gain. Confronting the queen's body, he voices "pity" for the dead while simultaneously celebrating "his glory which / Brought them to be lamented" and orders her burial with Antony in a ceremony that combines the rituals of funeral and triumph (5.2.358–59). Though he pays some homage to the queen, he uses her death to assert his new status as the sole ruler of the Roman world.

But allusions to Mary also serve as reminders that he will not be in that position forever. Cleopatra's performances of Venus, Mary, and Isis displace her not just in time but also space and show how performances of mimetic dying might respond to territorial expansion as well as domestic usurpation. Once the play superimposes the Virgin on unchristian deities like Venus and Isis, it reinforces early modern Protestant associations of Catholicism with pagan idolatry, associations that troubled traditional distinctions between the Christian and heathen worlds after the Reformation. The unexpected appearance of the Virgin in Egypt locates Caesar's conquest within a longer history of conflicts around the Mediterranean, a history that features both antagonisms structured around religious difference and alliances between powers representing different faiths.[73] The play could be a spur to consider the importance of religious mimesis to nascent forms of imperialism as well as the difference gender makes in how saintly precedents are inhabited.

My readings of *Edward II*, *Richard II*, and *Antony and Cleopatra* illustrate how devotional arts of dying and traditions of *imitatio Christi* can be appropriated in situations of political instability to understand and respond to disempowerment. Edward and Richard each seek to accommodate themselves to political change through their approaches to death. While their efforts may incidentally grant them self-knowledge, they constitute practical interventions in the political sphere. Richard's practice in particular has a public dimension that makes the play a productive site for theorizing political community in the early modern era and beyond. His efforts to imitate Christ reveal less about his individual outlook or state of grace than about how different political frameworks employ notions of mimetic representation to understand and manage the demands of *communitas*. The king's personal sense of insufficiency—grounded in the awareness of being haunted by the spectral presence of death and of being merely a single term in a series of monarchs oriented toward mortality—is both inspired by and serves to perpetuate more complex forms of political organization. The nation, especially as it is instantiated by the King in Parliament, is ultimately cast as a community united in a guilty fellowship of death.

Once this model of politics has been instituted, it is hard to see how its negative consequences can be avoided. The end of *Richard II* implies that Henry IV will be subjected to the same forms of haunting as his predecessor, while characters in the later plays of the second tetralogy continually evoke the ghost of Richard to justify insurrection. However, as the demands of the community become more explicit and more insistent, so we might expect efforts to resist them to intensify. In the next chapter, I will discuss a protagonist who seeks to deny the claims of his neighbors and to hold himself apart from his social context by treating death as private property.

CHAPTER 4

Dying Communally

Volpone and How to Get Rich Quick

Why does Volpone counterfeit dying? For most readers, the answer has seemed obvious: He wants to make a profit. From his entrance, Volpone is marked as avaricious. His first action is to worship gold, and his fraud evokes a long tradition of literary misers extracting gifts from legacy hunters.[1] So far, so conventional, and of a piece with Jonson's characteristic satire of hypocrisy and greed.[2] However, Volpone himself cautions against this interpretation. Both he and Mosca note the ready availability of easier and more socially accepted strategies to make money outside their peculiar practice. Volpone insists that he gains "No common way" (1.1.33), while Mosca distinguishes their scam from the actions of usurers, who "devour / Soft prodigals" or "Tear forth the fathers of poor families / Out of their beds, and coffin them alive / In some kind, clasping prison, where their bones / May be forthcoming when the flesh is rotten" (1.1.40–47). While emphatically rejecting established paths to wealth understood as commerce in the actual or simulated death of others, Volpone trades in the death of the self.[3]

This chapter argues that these distinctions between the common and the singular are precisely what are at stake at Volpone's deathbed and in

Jonson's engagement with *artes moriendi*. Through Volpone's counterfeit, Jonson explores how the interpersonal obligations imagined to unite individuals within a community will be tested and deformed when a social world centered on informal local networks gives way to one composed of autonomous individuals and public institutions. To account for the fraud, I contrast the value-creating spiritual and material economies that devotional texts imagine to operate at the good communal deathbed with Roberto Esposito's account of the *munus*, the unending, life-threatening obligation to give embedded in community.[4] In my earlier account of *Richard II*, I discussed some of the reasons why the bonds that constitute community might be associated with the loss of the self. Volpone responds to the threat of community in a very different manner than does Shakespeare's deposed king. By imitating a dying man surrounded by concerned neighbors, he refigures dissolution into the common as a willed act that affirms separation and autonomy. Volpone's actions are punished once discovered. Yet, significantly, aspects of the economy he creates around the deathbed survive his condemnation. The court that sentences him does not neutralize his earlier challenge to informal commonality. Instead, it co-opts and extends it by confiscating Volpone's substance to support the public Hospital of the Incurabili and imprisoning him indefinitely in a state of mortification. Ultimately, *Volpone*'s treatment of the nexus between property, individuality, and dying suggests that distinctive aspects of the modern public sphere emerge as alternatives to or even rejections of traditional devotional activities but nevertheless retain core assumptions and strategies belonging to the practices they purport to supersede.

Analyzing the fraud in *Volpone* can clarify our understanding of Jonson's dramatic practice more generally. The interactions between the singular and the common at Volpone's deathbed provide insight into Jonson's understanding of the commercial theater, another space that can be seen as a site either of value-generating communal endeavor or of individualistic artistic, authorial, or critical aspirations. Since Jonah Barish's influential description of Jonson as an "anti-theatrical" playwright suspicious of spectacle and impersonation, critics have been inclined to read a condemnation of theatricality into the depiction of Volpone's fraud.[5] However, as I show, *Volpone* is less concerned with rejecting morally dubious mimetic deception than with exploring the nature of a selfhood that understands itself through its ability to deceive mimetically. An ethical critique of Volpone's actorly duplicity and avarice exists alongside an exploratory investigation into the unstable relations created between the performer's embodied impersonation, the author's words, and the audience's judgment. Jonson suggests that postures of institutionally mandated mortification may be proper both to Volpone and the player representing him.

Although Jonson's understanding of theater is often idiosyncratic, his treatment of mortality in *Volpone* illuminates the relationship between staged arts of dying and dramatic genre. Until now, this book has focused exclusively on tragedies, a decision that may seem unsurprising given widespread early modern understandings of them as "solemne play[s], describing cruell murders and sorrowes."[6] But death's occasional presence in Elizabethan and Jacobean comedy—from Bottom's parodic suicide in *A Midsummer Night's Dream*, to Barnadine's refusal to be executed in *Measure for Measure*, to Rafe's last words in *The Knight of the Burning Pestle*—also merits investigation. As Jonson defends the harsh "catastrophe" of *Volpone*, he clarifies the ethical and artistic stakes of rendering mortality comic as well as the political and economic forces that might push arts of dying toward comedy in the art of the modern era.

Dying Together

Volpone's fraud exploits a well-established theological and devotional assumption that a shared experience of Christian death strengthens communal bonds and generates communal benefits. As I mentioned in the previous chapter, Paul founds the Christian community on the dying body of Christ. The Crucifixion overwrites the inevitable link between sin and death under the law with a promise of eternal life to those who have faith: "For the wages of sin is death, but the gift of God *is* eternal life, through Jesus Christ our Lord."[7] When Paul calls for Christians to be "planted with [Christ] to the similitude of his death" so they can also share "*the similitude* of his resurrection," he evokes a community joined together by witnessing and participating in a shared experience of dying well.[8] Similarly, Augustine connects membership of the City of God with participation in communal death,[9] characterizing his fellow Christians as those who are "*consortium mortalitatis meae* [partners in mortality with me]."[10] In the notion of *consortium*, the individual Christian's relation to Christ in and through death also renders her a component of a larger heavenly and earthly community.

Early-seventeenth-century devotional culture developed these concepts along a number of different lines. Some texts imagine immaterial bonds of shared mortality that can unite communities of the dying and in the process transcend or redeem more earthly connections. In the *Devotions upon Emergent Occasions*, for instance, John Donne hears a bell tolling for an unknown man and praises God for making "*him* for whom this *bell* tolls, now in this dimnesse of his sight, to become a *superintendent*, an *overseer*, a *Bishop*, to as many as heare his *voice*, in this *bell*."[11] The process of dying as a Christian becomes an inspiration and object of contemplation for other nearby Christians as a spiritual community is created spontaneously by the sonic field of the bell. Moreover, when Donne characterizes the dying man as a "Bishop," he implies that a continuum exists between the spontaneous gatherings that happen to assemble around the sickbed, the formal organization of the established church, and the mystical community of all Christians. Later, Donne ascribes a place in heaven to the dead man, even though he has no knowledge of his character or circumstances, on the basis of his

> owne *Charity*; I ask that; & that tels me, *He is gone to everlasting rest,* and *joy*, and *glory:* I owe him a good *opinion;* it is but *thankfull charity* in mee, because I received *benefit* and *instruction* from him when his *Bell* told: and I, being made the fitter to *pray*, by that disposition, wherein I was assisted by his occasion, did *pray* for him.[12]

The bell establishes reciprocal postures of care and responsibility. The dying man is enabled by God to serve as an informal spiritual leader, while Donne (as an ordained minister, an actual leader within the church) prays for him in return. The interaction between Donne and the unknown man is transactional in character, since each gives something to the other. But although Donne feels obliged to offer a return for the benefits he has received, he does not appear to deplete his own resources by praying for his neighbor. This is not a contractual exchange in which both sides gain something and lose something, nor does there seem to be any scarcity in the economy brought into being by the bell. Rather, the coming together of Donne and the dying man around the occasion of the bell tolling creates spiritual value that did not previously exist.

The theological association of dying with community also has a concrete reflection in the practice of visitation of the sick. Early modern *artes moriendi* generally assume, or try to simulate, a communal deathbed extending benefits to witnesses as well as to the dying person. Eamon Duffy describes the medieval deathbed as "a communal effort, in which living friends and relatives and dead patrons and intercessors join hands to assist."[13] Though, in a post-Reformation Protestant context, patrons and intercessors drop away, the sense that dying is something family and friends do together remains. Thomas Becon's *The Sycke Mans Salve* (1561), a popular puritan dialogue, depicts a group of neighbors visiting a sick friend named Epaphroditus as an act of charity, "one of those works, whiche being don in the faithe of Christe shall be rewarded at the last day in the face of the whole worlde with then heritance of the heauenly kingdom."[14] The attendants comfort Epaphroditus as he sickens and dies. Concurrently, they also treat the deathbed as an occasion for spiritual reflection. After his friend's death, one onlooker observes, "A Christen and godly end made he. God geue vs al grace to make the like."[15] The deathbed strengthens bonds within a community of believers by instantiating a model of godly behavior that observers can mimic on their own deathbeds. As in Donne's *Devotions*, charity is presented as an obligation, but one that does not deplete its practitioners' resources or constitute a transactional exchange in which both sides gain something and lose something. Rather, the coming together of neighbors and the dying man creates spiritual benefits that did not previously exist. The *Salve* imagines a spiritual economy similar to that assembled by Donne's bell, but it locates it not in a sonic field but rather in the longstanding, informal, interpersonal relations within a group of like-minded Christians.

The impression that the deathbed generates value for all concerned persists even when Becon turns to financial matters. In Chapter 1, I discussed the intersection of legal and religious discourses in early modern wills. Many devotional texts on dying from the period discover spiritual value in the creation of bequests. One of the many obligations typically laid upon the dying person is to disengage from earthly concerns by settling disputes and debts and by disposing of worldly possessions and offices. In the context of a last testament, the transfer of property can mark a more important transfer of trust and care, an exhortation to the beneficiary to mirror the dying person in godliness and a denial of the significance of the very thing being handed over.[16] These understandings are emphasized in Epaphroditus's provisions for his wife:

> forasmuch as God hath blessed me with worldly substance, and she is mine own flesh, and whosoeuer prouideth not for his, hath denied the faith, and is worse than an infidell, I bequeth & geue vnto her for tearme of her life, this house wherein I nowe dwell, with the appurtenances, and all the housholde stuffe contayned therein [1 Tim. 5]. . . . Let this suffice for my wiues portion, whom I doubt not, God will take into his protection, and so prouide for her in the tyme of her short pilgrimage, that she shall want no good thing.[17]

Epaphroditus disposes of a substantial property but is doubly insulated from the sin of having economic intentionality with regard to it. First, his religious obligation to care for his dependents is rendered equivalent to the entire practice of faith and so loses all specificity as an actual financial transaction. Second, his claim that God will provide denies that his wife's material support is actually in question. Instead, the bequest becomes aligned with the assumption of Epaphroditus's bereaved family into a universal Christian community through union with God.

A similar understanding of deathbeds and wills as sources of community affirmation and reinforcement appears in testamentary law.[18] One prominent area of legal contention during this period surrounded the creation of "perpetuities." These are conditional clauses in property conveyances used by landowners to control the ownership and use of their land, and also the behavior of their heirs, beyond their own deaths. In the early modern era, they were typically created for dynastic reasons. Landowners sought to ensure that the title of head of the family and the property attaching to the family remained together in the hands of someone worthy of inheriting their status.[19] As in Epaphroditus's will, material property was understood to function as a signifier for expressions of love and for the perpetuation of a family identity.

This, at any rate, is the hope. However, as Jonson will emphasize, when real money is involved, such understandings of the communal deathbed can appear inadequate. Even in Becon's text, Epaphroditus risks looking simply hypocritical when he outlines a settlement for his daughters, saying, "If thei be godly brought vp, I doubt not, but if they liue, God will aboundauntly prouide for them. Notwithstanding I geue vnto eche of them .ii. C. pounds, of good & lawfull mony to be paid in the day of their mariage."[20] The proximity of material and spiritual economies invites exploitation of the deathbed scenario for gain. The problem arises more explicitly in the legal tradition. Perpetuities emerge as an issue precisely because they were so frequently litigated by plaintiffs seeking to decouple family identity and the material property being used to signify its persistence. Moreover, the terms in which case reports discuss these disputes indicate that at least some contemporary commentators linked the issue of perpetuities to more fundamental social and economic questions about the place of property (especially real property) in society. In some legal circles, perpetuities were condemned as a threat to the national interest in promoting the easy sale of land.[21] Edward Coke, one of the most prominent opponents of perpetuities, advocated making real property more easily alienable and celebrated the judgment in *Mary Portington's Case*, in which a class of perpetuities was invalidated, by saying, "the commonwealth rejoiced, that fettered freeholds and inheritances were set at liberty, and many and manifold inconveniences to the head and all the members of the commonwealth thereby avoided."[22]

It is tempting to align this language with a protoliberal sensibility and to see Coke as an early advocate for legal structures that would allow land to be understood as a form of capital. Yet while limitations upon perpetuities did increase over time, this trend cannot be understood to follow any simple, linear movement from status to contract or from feudalism to a market economy.[23] Coke made his name in *Shelley's Case*, where a complex family settlement that would have created a perpetuity was invalidated on the grounds that a clause that deeded property to a person "and his heirs" was equivalent to deeding it in fee-simple—that is, without any restrictions.[24] Coke champions an ideal of unfettered freeholds and argues for the invalidation of complex family settlements, but he does so by exploiting an ambiguity in the concept of an heir. In Coke's interpretation, a person's heirs are simultaneously to be chosen entirely at his own discretion and equivalent to himself. To name an heir is both to institute a contractual relation and to effect a transfer of status founded on an intimacy that almost rises to identity. This is precisely the ambiguity that Volpone will exploit.

Death for Sale

Over the course of his dramatic career, Jonson refers to *The Sycke Mans Salve* twice, both times to suggest that he is uncomfortable with how the text imagines and sustains group identity. In *Epicene*, while the School of Ladies is looking for something to read to Morose that might alleviate his afflictions, Lady Haughty recalls that her maid Trusty's "father and mother were both mad, when they put her to me. . . . And one of them, I know not which, was cur'd with the *Sick Man's Salve*; and the other with Green's *Groat's-worth of Wit*."[25] As evidence of the text's efficacy, she calls on Trusty, who confirms that every night her parents "read themselves asleep on those books."[26] In *Eastward Ho*, the newly penitent Quicksilver is described by his jailor as able to "tell you almost all the stories of the *Book of Martyrs*, and speak you all *the Sick Man's Salve* without book."[27]

Several parallels between these two episodes are worth stressing because they offer insight into how Jonson understands *artes moriendi*. First, in each play, the *Salve* is paired with another popular text advocating moral reformation (and in the case of *Eastward Ho*, with another textual touchstone for reform-minded Protestants). Rather than paying attention to the specific content of Becon's dialogue or the advice it gives about how to die, Jonson focuses on the role that reading it has in signaling membership of a devout community defined through familiarity with a distinctive set of shared texts. Second, he intimates that the integration of individuals into such communities through texts can be constrictive and coercive. Trusty's parents are undergoing treatment for insanity; Quicksilver is confined and threatened with execution and therefore has externally imposed reasons to enact repentance. Third, in both instances, Jonson credits the *Salve* with heavily ironized, but real, redemptive powers—only in a social register, rather than the spiritual one assumed by Becon. Trusty's parents are actually cured of madness, if only by the soporific nature of the tracts they read and a quasi-magical understanding of books as totemic objects. Quicksilver's repentance, if suspiciously self-interested and easily arrived at, is sustained until the end of the play and does finally win him mercy and a stay of execution. The efficacy of the tract is in some sense real and tied to the way in which it enables those who read it to act like members of recognizable puritan groups. Finally, the utility of the *Salve* is linked to imperfect mimicry. By falling asleep, Trusty's parents enact the loss of consciousness of dying. Quicksilver, speaking the words of *The Sycke Man's Salve* "without book," turns Becon's dialogic work into an actual piece of theater. As a result, questions about the nature and value of religious communities created through particular texts shade into questions about the nature and value of artistic, and especially dramatic, production.

Dennis Kezar draws on these examples to argue that Jonson distrusts the *artes moriendi* for encouraging forms of insincere self-fashioning that are exemplary of "the pervasive histrionics of his culture" and claims that skeptical allusions to the *Salve* reflect Jonson's more general suspicion of theatricality and socially constructed identity.[28] While I think that Kezar is right to note that Jonson's references to the practices of dying show a concern with the hypocritical performance of death, he is misleading in the way in which he ties this to the fashioning of the *self*. The constrictive uses to which the *Salve* is put in *Epicene* and *Eastward Ho* imply that hypocrisy is visible at a more general level, as the readers of the tract are attenuated and forcibly subsumed into communities that control what death can signify. There may be intimations of a purely personal insincerity, especially in the case of Quicksilver, but the *Salve* is used primarily as a form of social control or as a way of signaling submission to a particular communal perspective. This impression is intensified by the fact that the instances of Trusty's parents and Quicksilver drawing on the *Salve* are reported rather than seen. There are no selves onstage; the characters' performances of dying exist only as publicly expressed approval of their conformity.

Allusions to Becon in the London comedies primarily support a satire of puritan pietistic affectation. Jonson is most interested showing in how particular, identifiable social groups exert control through conventional notions of the good death. These satirical targets and the precise cultural practices of dying appropriate to this London milieu have little relevance in the Venetian setting of *Volpone*.[29] Instead, Jonson in this play explores a more constitutive aspect of the Christian model of a good death—the notion that the deathbed generates social and spiritual value through the affirmation of communal bonds—and in doing so suggests that the link made in *Epicene* and *Eastward Ho* between the dissolution of the self into the social and into nonbeing is not purely contingent. There may be deeper reasons why the deathbed becomes such an effective site of coercion.

Volpone and Mosca ironically evoke the art of dying well when they explain the fraud as an effort to resist the common way of public life and a retreat into retired contemplation of and preparation for mortality. Yet the deathbed they construct is actually governed by an economy of scarcity under which characters' postures of care become covers for purely self-interested actions. The fraud is the work of two collaborators with different understandings of what is at stake.[30] My argument focuses primarily on Volpone, since he is the more concerned with theorizing community and with finding ways to separate himself from it, though Mosca, whose identity is grounded in dependence and parasitism, offers ample reasons to be skeptical of Volpone's assertions of autonomy.

Volpone's initial description of his position indicates that, for him, the communal deathbed emblematizes the near relation between forms of collective existence and mortality:

> I have no wife, no parent, child, ally,
> To give my substance to; but whom I make
> Must be my heir; and this makes men observe me.
> This draws new clients daily to my house,
> Women and men of every sex and age,
> That bring me presents, send me plate, coin, jewels,
> With hope that when I die (which they expect
> Each greedy minute) it shall then return
> Tenfold upon them; whilst some, covetous
> Above the rest, seek to engross me whole,
> And counterwork, the one unto the other,
> Contend in gifts, as they would seem in love;
> All which I suffer, playing with their hopes,
> And am content to coin 'em into profit,
> And look upon their kindness, and take more,
> And look on that, still bearing them in hand,

Letting the cherry knock against their lips,
And draw it by their mouths, and back again. (1.1.73–90)

Volpone describes a hypothetical set of natural inheritors defined through preexisting and intimate relations to the dying person and then contrasts them to the heir that he will "make." He emphasizes his right to choose the destination of his property without reference to any extant ties of family and friendship. But by focusing on the title "heir" rather than on the action of economic dispensation, he acknowledges that writing a will is commonly understood as a transfer of status. In this context, his description of his wealth as "my substance" is important because it suggests the consequences such a transfer has for the original owner. The phrase recalls the Roman legal concept of *substantia*, meaning "the entire property of a person . . . or . . . an inheritance as a whole," and primarily indicates Volpone's material possessions.[31] Yet it also suggests Volpone's physical body and so indicates that naming an heir paradigmatically ratifies a familial sharing of substance in the form of biological inheritance. Additionally, the word evokes the Eucharist and therefore a community based on participation in the Passion. Though Volpone stresses his autonomy in choosing an heir, it nevertheless appears that by bequeathing his substance, he will lock himself into a particular set of interpersonal relations that will entail that his self is not entirely his own but instead part of a lineage and a Christian community. Volpone's claim that the legacy hunters "seek to engross [him] whole" further elides the distinction between his money and his person and, with a suggestion of cannibalism that again could be taken as implicitly Eucharistic, indicates the degree to which naming an heir, acknowledging familial ties, and participating in a communal deathbed threaten him with a loss of self.[32]

What family members Volpone does admit—a dwarf, a eunuch, and a hermaphroditic fool—appeal to him precisely because they diverge from such notions of inheritance, shared substance, or communal identity. Nano, Castrone, and Androgyno are alike only in being definitionally unalike, all marked physically as abnormal and so united by their status as grotesques.[33] When Mosca tells Corvino that all three are Volpone's disinherited bastards, "begot on beggars / Gypsies, and Jews, and blackmoors, when he was drunk/. . .but he has giv'n 'em nothing" (1.5.44–49), he brings the trio into a wider class of the excluded existing within and against European Christian society, and in particular he links them to nearly contemporaneous Shakespearean representations of Venetian social others in *The Merchant of Venice* and *Othello*.[34] Two of the three are presumably sterile, and when Nano and Castrato sing that "Your fool he is

your great man's dearling, / And your lady's sport and pleasure; / Tongue
and bauble are his treasure," their relationship to Volpone becomes sexualized (1.2.71–73).[35] As a consequence, the three stand not only for social,
economic, and religious exclusion but also for nonreproductive modes of
existence and incestuous relations between generations that can be set
against the ideal of legacy as a means to secure dynastic lineage or family
identity.

Moreover, this asociality becomes associated in Volpone's imagination
with immortality. On their first appearance, Nano and Androgyno perform
for Volpone's entertainment an interlude, composed by Mosca and presumably designed to appeal to Volpone's tastes and interests, that recounts the
metempsychosis of Pythagoras's soul through a number of religious and
philosophical groups, including Pythagoreans, Carthusian monks, and
puritans, until it comes to rest in Androgyno's body. The soul's survival
and persistence across time is directly associated with its transcendence of
communal identities. The trio oppose biological change and death by at
once incestuously superimposing generational positions, denying passage
between generations through inheritance, and resisting incorporation into
religious communities.[36]

Volpone's lack of a natural heir and his denial that the grotesques can act
as inheritors raises the question of how communal and lineal associations
might be created. Instead of a wife, parent, child, or ally, Volpone is visited
by an indiscriminate collection of "Women and men of every sex and age"
(1.1.77), all of whom hope to receive bequests through "their kindness"
(1.1.87)—that is, through expressions of care modeled on relations between
kin and Christian conceptions of charity. Yet the legacy hunters' gifts show
they ultimately share Volpone's complex understanding of his substance
and wish to exploit the slippages between the word's various connotations.
By presenting offerings to Volpone, they hope to be brought into relationships of virtual kinship as his heirs. Their kindness, however, is no more
than a cover for an investment that they expect to "return / Tenfold." The
phrase recalls Matthew 19:29: "And whosoever shall forsake houses, or
brethren, or sisters, or father, or mother, or wife, or children, or lands, for
my Name's sake, he shall receive a hundredfold more, and shall inherit
everlasting life." By taking the scriptural precedent literally (several legacy
hunters do disavow family members for Volpone's sake), they do the opposite of Epaphroditus. Where Becon's sick man metaphorizes his bequests as
signs of his faith and of the extension of Christian community to his family
and friends, Volpone and the legacy hunters materialize biblical precedent
as economic exchange. They undermine the notion of the good death not

by overtly rejecting it but by applying the precepts appropriate to it in strictly earthly terms under conditions of scarcity.

The legacy hunters' actions can also help us understand the reason for this scarcity. The rationale behind their gifts has been extensively discussed by Katherine Eisaman Maus. Maus contrasts Seneca's insistence in *De beneficiis* that the material gift is a mere signifier for the more important gift-giving intention with Marcel Mauss's claim that in archaic gift-giving societies, gifts demand reciprocation. Volpone exploits "gift-giving's big loophole: the giving of gifts seems to necessitate a response, but there is apparently no way to compel that response to occur."[37] The legacy hunters delude themselves that Volpone is obligated to make a return. But to attempt to raise that obligation to the formality of contract would stop the gift from functioning as symbol of love.

But Maus does not consider how asymmetric gift exchanges between two people function in a larger economic and social context.[38] In an exchange between two people, the receiver, at least, can gain something. But this effect dissipates as more people are added to the network. Jonson imagines constant donation that benefits nobody. By bringing presents, the legacy hunters do not only woo Volpone; they also "counterwork, the one unto another," and their aggregate effect is important. The insistent expressions of love that visitors offer to Volpone evoke the communal good deathbed as a shared experience where all work together and all gain together. However, the material benefits that are also being transferred at Volpone's bedside—and that are everyone's true focus—flow differently, in a way that reflects (and, again, interprets in material terms) the despairing underside of a practice of *imitatio Christi*: Christ's sacrifice creates an unpayable debt that demands servicing through imitative reciprocation but that can never be discharged.[39]

We learn from Mosca that Volpone knows "the use of riches" (1.1.62) and spends his gains freely, so that the gifts the legacy hunters make to him never accrue into an investment for the eventual heir but are instead wasted. Rather than being bound together as at a traditional deathbed by the opportunity for limitless heavenly benefits, the legacy hunters are united in a community of gift givers by limitless demands. Their recognition of one another as competitors is precisely what keeps their obligations open-ended; they need to keep giving so as not to be outdone. Volpone emphasizes the tantalizing nature of his practice when he describes "still bearing them in hand, / Letting the cherry knock against their lips / And draw it by their mouths, and back again" (1.1.88–90). Yet, however much he tries to elide the fact by emphasizing his control of the fraud, he too is

caught in the same pattern as his victims. The legacy hunters are attracted
to him for a reason. His mortality is inescapable, and ultimately his substance will have to be passed on to somebody. Maus's reading of the
dynamic of the gifts in *Volpone*, as intimating obligation without becoming
contract, holds true for each individual gift but needs to be qualified by
recognition of a wider gift economy in which obligations entirely eclipse
benefits.

In view of this dynamic, more suggestive models for the legacy hunters'
gifts and Volpone's deathbed can be found in Jean-Luc Nancy's and Roberto
Esposito's work on community. In *The Inoperative Community*, Nancy disputes the notion that community emerges around a shared common property, instead insisting that it is foremost a recognition that property cannot
be shared, a recognition that arises from an experience of the death of the
other.[40] Attempts to found operative communities working together on a
common ground can only universalize this death, since individuals are only
brought into stable immanent relation as dead matter.[41] Instead, true "inoperative" community will communicate ecstatically in and through an experience of incompletion in the presence of the other. Nancy, concerned with
the apparent failure of the left in the second half of the twentieth century,
imagines this ecstatic and always nonpresent community foremost as a possible alternative to totalitarianism or technocratic liberal capitalism. Consequently his account might not seem obviously relevant to the political and
economic situation of Jonson's theater. Esposito historicizes Nancy's core
association between community and loss. As we saw in Chapter 3, the root
munus in the word *communitas* refers under Roman law to a particular sort
of obligation, "the gift that one gives because one *must* give . . . only the gift
that one gives, not what one receives."[42] Rather than a *res publica*—that is, a
public thing individuals hold collectively—Esposito presents community as
an unfillable void to which members contribute not only defined goods or
services but even their very being as individuals.[43] The open-ended nature
of this obligation means that ultimately "the *communitas* carries within it a
gift of death."[44] Though Esposito finds a classical origin for his understanding of *communitas*, he associates fear of community and the desire to "immunize" against its obligations particularly strongly with modernity and the
emergence of a biopolitical sensibility under which power is exercised and
resisted through the management of bodies.[45] Significantly, he sees community and immunity as coimplicated, since immunization is only possible
through the incorporation of infected material, and this challenges Nancy's
stark distinction between the ecstatic, inoperative community and its operative, death-dealing perversions.

Volpone's account of the communal deathbed, where assumption into the community and assumption into nonbeing become equivalent, represents a very similar understanding to Esposito's. But it also raises questions about what is at stake in the passage from Nancy's ecstatic account to Esposito's biopolitical one. How exactly do the existential, material, and physiological obligations generated by community relate to one another? Can they be separated? And which has priority? I see Volpone's counterfeit as an attempt to neutralize the communal threat the deathbed represents— as an immunitarian response through which Volpone seeks dispensation from his debts to others. In Volpone's speech, as in Epaphroditus's will in *The Sycke Man's Salve*, the flow of material goods tracks the flow of more figurative and existential conceptions of the *munus*. When Volpone describes the legacy hunters, he evokes the Christian deathbed and familial inheritance ironically, suggesting they are covers for economic self-interest. The transfer of property is what matters, and everything else is just obfuscation. However, in trying to separate himself from the community, Volpone in effect follows Epaphroditus in treating money as a signifier for other obligations. Volpone's reaction to the interest the legacy hunters show in him is to try to privatize his death, to take the very thing that threatens to destroy his self and refigure it as a willed action undertaken for his own exclusive gain. Volpone undermines the deathbed community by profiting from it in order to satisfy his own avarice. But at the same time, he cultivates avarice as a way of separating himself from the community.

After observing the legacy hunters' interest in him and the nature of their attentions, Volpone remarks, "All which I suffer, playing with their hopes, / And am content to coin 'em into profit" (1.1.85–86). To suffer is to be in a passive state, subject to the predations of external forces. However, Volpone immediately recasts this suffering as "playing," under his control and reflective of his skillfulness. By understanding apparent passivity as a form of activity, he justifies "coin"ing the legacy hunters into profit for himself. The word "playing" additionally signals that Volpone's behavior relates to acting. Several critics draw on Barish's diagnosis of Jonson's "anti-theatricality" to argue that Volpone's histrionic character grounds an ethical critique of mimesis, where the protean figure of the actor is suspicious because it lacks an underlying moral self.[46] Yet Volpone's most longstanding imitation of the dying man sits oddly with this analysis and implies a more complex attitude to dramatic impersonation. Through Volpone's fraud, Jonson draws an analogy between arts of dying and arts of acting, but his main interest is not in unmasking histrionic counterfeit. In fact, the parallel points more emphatically to two quite different things. First, thinking about what people are doing when they are dying helps us think about what actors are doing onstage. And, second, the thing that actors *are* doing can be understood as an immunitarian activity that substantiates a core, inviolable self. Such immunitarian activity, moreover, may be portable to other contexts. To understand dying as an actorly practice is not so much to deny the existence of biological limitations to human agency as it is to search for ways to understand and exercise human agency through biological limitations. As a result, Volpone's fraud anticipates later understandings of possessive individualism—that is, belief that personal security and individual rights are grounded in possession of the body and of material property accrued through its actions.[47]

Barish identifies two core complaints behind Jonson's antitheatrical pronouncements: First, dramatic action promotes spectacle over words, and second, mimesis is hard to distinguish from lying.[48] But the impersonation of someone moribund, precisely because it is so minimal, can stand for acting in the purest sense—a sort of zero-degree acting—in a way that complicates these objections. To start with spectacle: Through Volpone's imitation of a dying man, Jonson creates a performance that in one sense is purely spectacular, since it is nonverbal, but in another sense, because of its minimalism, explores the limits of how far a performance can efface itself while still functioning as a performance. We see this when Corvino, who has been discussing Volpone's imminent demise with Mosca, worries that Volpone may have overheard them. Mosca demonstrates his patron's insensibility and nearness to death by shouting insults in Volpone's ear:

> Would you would once close
> Those filthy eyes of yours that flow with slime
> Like two frog-pits, and those same hanging cheeks,
> Covered with hide instead of skin—[*To Corvino.*] Nay, help, sir—
> That look like frozen dishclouts, set on end. (1.5.56–60)

Though the overt aim of Mosca's words is to reassure Corvino, they also obliquely compliment Volpone on the success of his spectacular impersonation (his achievement of suitably filthy eyes and hanging cheeks) while allowing Mosca a way to express genuine aggression toward his patron. Simultaneously, though, the speech underscores the degree to which Volpone's ability to maintain his body in a posture of inactivity is crucial to the fraud. Mosca's words are effective only if Volpone sustains them by not reacting. From one point of view, it does not matter what Mosca actually says, because the purpose of his words is to demonstrate that Volpone is insensible. In consequence, they draw attention to the self-control Volpone is exerting by resisting provocation and to the fact that his posture of inactivity is a piece of acting. When discussing his counterfeit, Volpone frequently emphasizes the effort it takes him to impersonate inactivity. As soon as another legacy hunter, Corbaccio, leaves his bedside, Volpone exclaims "Oh, I shall burst! / Let out my sides," so indicating the difficulty with which he has maintained his posture (1.4.133–34). Pretending to die, for Volpone, involves putting on a spectacle of the unspectacular.

Equally, Volpone's performance of dying is initially purely duplicitous. But it always has the potential to become real, not only because Volpone might choose to abandon mimesis but also because he might unwillingly be made to conform to what he has been representing without his onstage and offstage audiences recognizing that a change has taken place. In the first court scene, Volpone's prone, seemingly insensible body is brought before the judges as evidence that he could not have assaulted Celia. For the theater audience, this performance of incapacity looks almost identical to Volpone's earlier performance for Corvino. Yet on his return home, Volpone observes that "'Fore God, my left leg 'gan to have the cramp, / And I appre'nded, straight, some power had struck me / With a dead palsy" (5.1.5–7). We belatedly learn that some aspects of Volpone's performance had a nonmimetic significance for him. We have not only been watching an imitation of a sick man but also someone who might be becoming sick.

Volpone's impersonated art of dying, then, represents the full positive and negative potential of embodied, actorly, theatrical performance distinct from poetic text or authorial voice, and it is the nature of this performance that allows it to function as *immunitas*. The actorly effort involved in maintaining his bodily substance in a posture that is inactive yet mimetic is Volpone's self-justification for coining the legacy hunters. In a sense, he conceives of it as a form of work that entitles him to profit. Moreover, the cultivation of inactivity also serves to immunize him from the community because it affirms that he has control over this substance and can prevent the community's encroachment upon it. A practice of dying modeled on acting (or vice versa) becomes less concerned with feigning a new identity than with affirming an agential self able to feign identities. To say this is not to claim that Volpone's understanding of his agency and autonomy is uncontested. In particular, Volpone's dependence on Mosca's flattery— which in the instance I just cited, is deployed successfully upon himself and Corvino in the same moment—reveals significant limitations to his self-understanding of autonomous separation from the gulls and anticipates claims that Mosca will make on his substance by the end of the play. Nor is it to deny Jonson's ethical critique of Volpone's avarice and duplicity. But alongside that critique exists a more speculative investigation of the practices that enable avarice and duplicity to succeed.

Following Esposito's lead, we might take Volpone's rejection of tradition in the form of Christian and familial deathbed communities to indicate his alignment with modernity. I have already noted that Volpone's fraud depends on an understanding of the continuum between his person and his economic substance, an understanding that anticipates emergent understandings of possessive individualism or ownership as a safeguard of personal integrity.[49] However, my reading of Volpone's counterfeit has also demonstrated the extent to which his attack on the notion of the good death at the communal deathbed continues to draw upon it as a model not just through cynical, parodic imitation but also through the appropriation of representational and behavioral strategies appropriate to it. Volpone begins by subordinating religious and dynastic understandings of deathbed behavior to the flow of money, so implying that his project is one of demystification and that the only material reality in play is an economic one. Yet in carrying out the counterfeit, he appropriates the conception of dying as an effortful action, along with the sense that different forms of spiritual, familial, and economic inheritance can be made to track and signify one another, to justify his profit from the legacy hunters. This behavior reveals a far deeper homology with practices of dying well and renders the question of which register of discourse he is attempting to control more open. In consequence, *Volpone* should encourage us to be more cautious about linking given postures to modernity as such. The play shows traditional religious attitudes persisting in dialogue with secular ones rather than giving ground to secular modernity or being reappropriated for secular purposes.

Mortifying States

The ending of the play affirms the open-ended nature of this dialogue between sacred and secular understandings of mortality by showing devotional practices, economic activities, and secular institutions continuing to respond to and reshape one another. The Avocatori discover the fraud and punish Volpone and the other miscreants for their perversion of deathbed conventions. Yet their settlement reconfigures Volpone's counterfeit, just as his counterfeit reconfigured the traditional communal deathbed. In this process, the art of dying well persists in a modified form.

Volpone appears initially to have succeeded in manipulating the court just as comprehensively as he manipulated the legacy hunters, and by using very similar tactics. In the first court scene, the Avocatori are brought to credit Volpone's account of events by the pointed display of Volpone's inactive body and by the actions of the legacy hunters, who are again placed in a position of having to donate competitively to a shared purpose when they offer their testimony. However, as I note above, Volpone's private comments about his appearance in court indicate that the experience has rattled him. His cramp has caused him to doubt his ability to maintain mimetic self-difference between his posture and his reality. He explains the unpleasant effect the court has had on him, saying, "I ne'er was in dislike with my disguise / Till this fled moment. Here 'twas good, in private, / But in your public—*cavè*, whilst I breathe" (5.1.3–4).

The key source of Volpone's discomfort appears to lie in the public setting.[50] The courtroom exposes him to a greater level of scrutiny and a larger community than the bedroom. But more than that, it stresses fixed institutional and social roles over the private and informal cultivation of personal relationships. In the public court, power derives from professional and official identity. The Avocatori are unnamed, and even the legacy hunter Voltore appears in a new guise, as a highly competent advocate speaking a professionalized language. Instead of performing for an informal gathering of acquaintances, Volpone is exposed to the scrutiny of persons in an official capacity, and the relationship he bears to his associates alters under this pressure. He starts to collaborate with the legacy hunters, from whom he had earlier tried to separate himself, as all come together to offer an account of events that will incriminate Celia and Bonario. The two levels of hypocrisy Volpone had maintained at his deathbed collapse into a single plot to deceive in which the distinction between knaves and gulls is elided. Volpone's earlier manipulation of the community of the deathbed had relied on his skillful handling of shifting relationships between economic, religious, social, and legal understandings of his interactions with others. In his account of the public court, these different discourses converge in a single narrative outside his control. In Volpone's fear that his cramp is the work of "some power," the public authority of the court becomes aligned with divine sanction and the inevitability of biological decay. Whichever way he looks, his agency is diminished.

Volpone's fears lead directly to his disastrous decision to declare himself dead, and this decision leads equally directly to his subsequent uncasing. Mosca's betrayal reveals Volpone's belief that he has attained singularity and separation from community as illusory, since his actorly postures of dying were always dependent on Mosca's ratifying performances. Mosca, though in general far more ready than Volpone to acknowledge that his identity is defined through interpersonal relations, ultimately makes the same mistake as his master when he tries to discard his collaborator absolutely. Each misrecognizes the symbiotic relationship between host and parasite as one in which both parties maintain independent existence, when in fact it is another example of community formed around identity-sapping, open-ended obligation.

The judgment of the court justifies Volpone's apprehension that appearance in public marks a different and less controllable form of existence. The Avocatori punish the wrongdoers and set the innocent free. Affirming the association Volpone made earlier between public scrutiny and divine justice, they imply their judgment is sanctioned by heaven. The first Avocatore exclaims, "The knot is now undone, by miracle!" while Bonario notes that "Heaven could not long let such gross crimes be hid" (5.12.95, 98). The consonance between Volpone's imagined "power" and the reality of institutional punishment starts to look, at the very least, like cosmic irony, if not like a ratification of some link between heavenly and earthly justice. Volpone's punishment forces him to assume a position very like the dead palsy he worried about immediately after the first court appearance.[51] He is told he will be forced to "lie in prison, cramped with irons, / Till thou be'st sick and lame indeed" (5.12.123–24). Biological vulnerability manifested through cramping, the public sphere, and divine justice all work together to constrict and confine him.

Superficially, the Avocatori appear to reinstitute the conventional good death, alluding to the religious art of dying when they confine Corbaccio "To the Monastery of San' Spirito, / Where, since thou knew'st not how to live well here, / Thou shalt be learned to die well" (5.12.131–33). Yet this evocation of traditional forms and values barely masks important differences between the understandings of community implicit in the good communal deathbed and in their judgment. As Volpone recognizes, what we see here is a movement from the private sphere to the public. Because Volpone can successfully counterfeit a dying person and in doing so reveal weaknesses in the informal deathbed community, the court looks for a different mechanism to impose practices of dying upon him and Corbaccio. The Avocatori make no attempt to revive a community that could assemble spontaneously on the basis of shared personal knowledge and desire for mutual care. Instead, they turn to institutions. They deliver their judgments as official figures and link their judicial authority to a wider matrix of state and church power when they hand control of the various miscreants over to the Hospital of the Incurabili, an unnamed prison, and the Monastery of San Spirito. Personalized, mutually beneficial communities of the deathbed are replaced by anonymous civic institutions that have the power to cramp, to confine, and ultimately to mortify Volpone and Corbaccio.[52]

Though the play holds open the possibility that the authority of the Avocatori is divinely sanctioned, they are not valorized as characters. In their deference to Mosca when he is still the presumptive heir, they display exactly the same venality as the legacy hunters. However, their personal limitations do not compromise the effectiveness and validity of the justice they deliver. Indeed, that sound public judgment is compatible with private greed may be exactly what ratifies their authority and also what links their judgment to a broader political philosophy encapsulated in the myth of the Venetian republic. The capacity of prescribed political procedure to overcome personal interest is a recurring theme in Gasparo Contarini's account of the government of Venice, Jonson's primary source for information on the city-state.[53] This ability to contain self-interest distinguishes the public, institutional control exerted through the court from the moral frameworks created within the smaller, spontaneous communities that Volpone corrupts so effectively.

The Avocatori characterize as criminal Volpone's treatment of his own death as a commodity rather than as a spiritual event or the legal transfer of a lineage, but they implicitly concur that mortality has an alienable material value when they expropriate his "substance" (5.12.119). Importantly, the Avocatori use the same word as Volpone did in his earlier account of his fraud, and they exploit the same confusion between body and wealth. However, where Volpone had hoped to assert individuality, the Avocatori refigure his behavior in deindividuated, institutionalized terms. The money that Volpone has accrued from his imposture is to be transferred to "the hospital of the Incurabili," a state-endorsed institution dedicated to the management of the chronically ill (5.12.120). Contarini lists the Incurabili as one of the "Hospitals within the Citie," without describing it in more detail.[54] In fact, the hospital was founded in 1522, primarily to care for women suffering from syphilis. Though it was not initially sponsored by the state, regulations dating from 1521 compelled begging *incurabili* either to enter the hospital or suffer banishment from Venice.[55] Whether Jonson knew more about the hospital than its name is uncertain.[56] He might, however, have been inspired by parallel institutions at home. William Ingram notes that by the 1570s, London's hospitals had come under the control of the City, which supported them in part through fines levied on unauthorized dramatic performances.[57] At the least, Jonson encourages the audience to recognize resemblances between Volpone's earlier impersonation of a dying man and the positions of the hospital's patients. The Avocatori punish Volpone by taking the fruits of his counterfeit and using them to generate and support more declining bodies (his, Corbaccio's, the *incurabili*) out of the context of spontaneous deathbed communities and under the auspices of the Venetian civic authority.

The name given to these institutionalized bodies, *incurabili*, reflects an understanding of them strikingly different from conventional representations of the *moriens* on the traditional deathbed but perhaps more in line with how Volpone conceives of his own practice in opposition to communal models of care. Rather than defining persons heading toward death (*morientes*), as was common in Latin *ars moriendi* texts, the word *incurabili* places emphasis on the failure of those it designates to progress; they are characterized by the fact that they will not become healthy, that they will maintain an indefinite state of unwellness. At the same time, if we focus on the pastoral connotations of *cura*, we could also describe *incurabili* as those who cannot be cared for. *Incurabili* can be placed in opposition to the dying person at the good Christian deathbed who functions as a site generating earthly and heavenly care. Like Volpone, they linger indefinitely in a state of sickness and because of that lingering become confined to institutions, separated from traditional forms of community.

This resemblance between the *incurabili* and Volpone suggests that Volpone's sentence is not just an ironically apt punishment or a convenient way to fill state coffers but is in fact an intervention in a deeper dispute about whether the body is, or should be, a site of individual autonomy or institutional power. It is very tempting to see the judgment of the Avocatori as exemplifying the rise of biopolitics and of new forms of governmentality concerned with identifying and enforcing norms centered on the health of the body. In particular, the court's sentence would seem to support Esposito's insistence that the notion of the body politic is not just a metaphor but speaks to a real coimplication of politics and health.[58] Volpone, the *magnifico* who engages in fraud and attempts to undermine social institutions such as marriage, the family, and inheritance, represents a threat the Venetian republic must immunize itself against. The Avocatori carry out this immunization by aligning Volpone with a group (the *incurabili*) that has already been marked as physically unhealthy and that has been separated from the city in the institution of the hospital. Yet the means by which the Avocatori do so—simultaneously turning Volpone into someone "sick and lame indeed" and relying on his substance as a source of funding for the separation of the *incurabili*—indicates the aporia Esposito notes at the heart of all immunitarian strategies. Inoculation requires exposure to infectious material; ultimately *communitas* and *immunitas* will always presuppose each other.

Volpone's own response to the sentence, however, gestures toward something more like Nancy's inoperative community. He attempts to assert continuing agency and resist immunization by using figurative language. On being told that his goods will be seized and he will be confined until his illness is real, Volpone observes that "This is called mortifying of a Fox" (5.12.125). The multivalent pun on the word "mortifying" evokes spiritual discipline in preparation for death, a judicially imposed death sentence, the process through which rotting flesh decays either before or after death, and the tenderizing of meat for consumption.[59] Volpone simultaneously alludes to understandings of dying as an event and as a process that may culminate in death, begin after death, or continue through death in a way that denies special significance to the moment of death.[60] Additionally, he presents himself both as an individual with a social and spiritual identity and as mere matter. Volpone, through this pun, emphasizes the multiplicity of ways in which his position can be described. As in his earlier parody of deathbed behavior, we see an overlayering of different sacred, secular, and biological accounts of dying. Unlike in the earlier scenes, though, Volpone does not use any particular mode of discourse as a cover for another. He looks for a position from which he can resist absorption into the monitory narrative of the Avocatori and finds it in a linguistic ambiguity that affirms his near relation to death while absolutely refusing to specify what that relation is. To a point, his stance recalls Nancy's suggestion that both the common and the singular arise from a reciprocal experience of finitude that cannot become the basis of a substantive identity.[61] Volpone can acknowledge that mortification underpins his relation to community but deny that this mortification functions as a work—the production of institutionalized bodies for the benefit of the City of Venice—as the Avocatori hope. Instead, he hopes to use his proximity to death to render himself apparent as a singularity that, because it cannot be fully articulated, can retain some separation from the project of the state.[62] His behavior suggests that Esposito's insistence that the body politic and immunity are not just metaphors risks ignoring how metaphor can become an important field of interaction between individuals and communities. Esposito emphasizes the totalizing effect of the structural equivalence between different immunitarian strategies. Volpone, by contrast, retains personal agency in the face of annihilation precisely through inhabiting a linguistic and conceptual slippage between different understandings of approaches to death.

Community Theater

My discussion to this point has focused on what Volpone is doing when he is dying. However, a metatheatrical turn at the end of the play indicates that Jonson's focus is dual. Dying stands in for acting as much as acting stands in for dying. The epilogue raises questions about how the playing seen at Volpone's deathbed affects literary communities and dramatic genres. What challenge is made to communities of authors, readers, and auditors by a practice like Volpone's and its assumption that material economies are not subordinate to immaterial ones? Can critical and readerly charity survive in a commercial theater dependent on such actorly practices? Does the institutional settlement that would acknowledge and perhaps try to immunize against the realities of scarcity and of dissolution have a literary equivalent?

In his prefatory epistle to *Volpone*, Jonson attempts to allay such concerns by stressing the play's didacticism. He recalls classical comedies in which "oft-times the bawds, the servants, the rivals, yea, and the masters are mulcted; and fitly, it being the office of a comic poet to imitate justice and instruct to life, as well as purity of language or stir up gentle affections" (Epistle 90–92). These precedents justify a "catastrophe" that might otherwise "in the strict rigour of comic law, meet with censure" (Epistle 82–83) for its harshness. Jonson connects genre and ethics here, and to understand the implications of his claims, it is worth briefly comparing *Volpone*'s resolution to the sorts of poetic justice meted out at the ends of contemporary tragedies. In Chapter 1, I discussed how the homiletic tragedies of the 1570s and 1580s conclude with morally weighted deaths that clarify the ethical contours of their plots. Even if the workings of providence are obscured for some of the action, the event of a bad death reveals the reprobate and punishes him for his sins. Although later dramatists often follow Marlowe in raising doubts about the moral frameworks that bring dramatic villains to bad ends, their plots still frequently exhibit this familiar arc. Jonson's *Sejanus, His Fall*, for instance, takes the form of a *de Casibus* tragedy where Roman justice stands in ironically for providence. By the fifth act, Sejanus's ambition and self-regard have led him to believe himself above fortune, making it easy for Macro to separate him from his guards and turn the Senate against him. Jonson presents Sejanus's execution as a deserved punishment for his many crimes, but he also unmasks the corrupt political institutions that procure it. The "rude multitude" that desecrates Sejanus's corpse exposes the connection of senatorial justice to imperial tyranny and mob violence.[63] As the people collect and "deal small pieces of

the flesh for favours," they disseminate fragments of the corruption Sejanus represents in the form of relics, rendering him a perverse martyr to the
cause of ambition and anticipating later outrages from his devotees.[64]

For *Volpone*, Jonson adapts the climactic ending of *Sejanus* to the "scale"
of comedy by replacing beheading with extended imprisonment. As we
have seen, though, this substitution is not so much an evasion of death as a
reconception of its nature. When execution victims become *incurabili*,
mortality and punishment are transformed from events into processes.
And if these processes have more affinity with comedy than tragedy, then
so perhaps do modern strategies of immunity more generally. In *Eclipse of
Action*, Richard Halpern diagnoses a crisis in modern tragedy, which he
connects to the rise of the field of political economy. Aristotle famously
defined tragedy as "a representation of a serious, complete action";[65] when
Adam Smith and his followers devalue action in favor of production,
therefore, they incidentally strike at the basis of the genre.[66] Although
Halpern is primarily interested in the legacy of classical theories of tragedy, the different endings of *Sejanus* and *Volpone* suggest that the institutions of modernity exert similar pressures on inheritors of the *de Casibus*
and morality traditions. The forms of discipline that produce and manage
incurabili trigger repeated and proliferating poses of mortification, not
catharsis. These recall the chains of incompetent imitation seen in the
danse macabre or the spirals of bad mimesis that render Cleopatra's death
semihumorous. In his efforts to render *Volpone* morally improving, then,
Jonson reveals a deeper affinity between comedy and immunization. Even
as he defends himself from critics "that cry out 'We never punish vice in
our interludes'" (Epistle 87), he exposes his literary form as implicated in
the economic and social structures that enable modern viciousness.

But perhaps I am reading ungenerously. Jonson, after all, calls for "the
learned and charitable critic to have so much faith in me to think [the
catastrophe] was done of industry; for with what ease I could have varied it
nearer his scale, but that I fear to boast my own faculty, I could here insert"
(Epistle 84–86). In this appeal, Jonson evokes a community that functions
very like the good communal deathbed. Right-thinking critics will value
the catastrophe because of their excellence in learning and their charity—
that is, because of their faith in Jonson and willingness, based on a charitable understanding of human relations, to assume that his motives are
good. The play is thus an occasion for good critics and an industrious
playwright to identify, praise, and support one another through display of
their respective virtues. Literary criticism, literary production, and charity
are aligned.

Jonson's allusion to charitable critics here conforms to a pattern repeated throughout his lyric poetry. Stanley Fish suggests that many of Jonson's poems in praise of individuals strive to create a "community of the same" by asserting that the praiseworthy subject, readers, and author all share values that are further magnified through the occasion of the poem. Significantly, there is no scarcity within these communities, even when the poems are in fact celebrating a relationship based on patronage. Fish shows that for Jonson, the poetic recognition of identity in itself produces benefits; the virtues of both the addressee and the poet continuously magnify one another in a manner that makes the poet's receipt of patronage appear as great a benefit to the patron as to the recipient.[67] Such poetic communities closely resemble the idealized communal deathbeds of the *artes moriendi*, which generate value by affirming longstanding moral codes and strengthening existing bonds between individuals. Jonson's epistle implies that a similar community could emerge around *Volpone*.

That, at any rate, is the hope. However, a linguistic shift over the course of the passage from the Epistle that I have quoted shows Jonson struggling to define such a charitable community within the commercial theater as opposed to against it. The objectors Jonson would "snaffle" characterize the works they dislike as "interludes." Jonson in his response emphasizes the textual nature of his practice. Ancient "lines of example"—that is, precedents that exist in a written form—justify his treatment of vice, and in following these examples he is acting as a "comic poet" rather than as a creator of plays and certainly rather than as someone responsible for plays in performance. Though he hopes a positive literary community will form around *Volpone*, Jonson does not explain how it could do so within the space of performance as opposed to through the text.[68] Consequently, it remains unclear how these hypothetical critical communities relate to the assembly of author, paid actors, and paying auditors at the playhouse.

The epilogue spoken by Volpone addresses these problems in a different way. The speech questions what sort of community or public the theater is and how it judges the character of Volpone and his pretense of dying. If acting and dying are akin, what sort of theatrical institution could enable an audience to condemn Volpone's dying for profit while celebrating the acting for profit necessary to represent him? The epilogue asks if the audience assents to the judgment of the Avocatori:

> The seasoning of a play is the applause.
> Now, though the Fox be punished by the laws,
> He yet doth hope there is no suff'ring due

For any fact which he hath done 'gainst you;
If there be, censure him: here he doubtful stands.
If not, fare jovially, and clap your hands. (Epilogue 1–6)

By using the third person, the speech emphasizes differences between the actor speaking and the character he is embodying. We move out of the world of representation into what Robert Weimann would label presentation, as Volpone the character transforms into an actor addressing the audience directly on behalf of *Volpone* the drama.[69] Volpone's speech opens a gap between ethical and aesthetic judgments of the action. He alludes to the legal judgment against him and labels himself "the Fox," as he did in his discussion of his mortification. These echoes refer the audience back to the court's sentencing and ask it to consider how its own position relates to that of the Avocatori. The epilogue encourages watchers to question whether criminal or moral laws demanding Volpone's mortifying punishment can be aligned with aesthetic judgments. In drawing together the judgment of the Avocatori, Volpone's characterization of that judgment as the "mortifying of a fox," and the call for audience judgment in the epilogue, Jonson asks us to consider how the earlier analogy between acting and dying manifests within a wider, institutional context and gives way to a resemblance between theater and mortification.

Moreover, theater does not only resemble Volpone's mortification in having an institutional character. The epilogue generates postures of paralysis that, like Volpone's pun, are undetermined and maybe undeterminable. Jonson, like Volpone, uses this indeterminacy to locate a degree of authorial freedom from possible punishment. Volpone's final speech is cast in a subjunctive mode.[70] It does not assert that Volpone escapes the laws or the audience's condemnation; it asks the audience to decide whether Volpone escapes the laws and to consider the ethical implications of joining in censure of his crimes while enjoying and paying for the performance he has enabled. And like the court case, this results in a mortified, and mortifying, state of suspension encompassing author, actor, and spectators. The speech emphasizes the bodily constraint the end of the play puts on the lead actor who "doubtful stands" in front of the audience, and then it links it through rhyme to the bodily constraint of the auditors during the play, who will shortly be released to move freely and, if they choose, to "clap [their] hands." An account of how the organization of the theater relates to the judgment of the Avocatori is deferred and also made contingent upon the specific exigencies of a particular audience and a particular performance. In this way, Jonson deals with troubling questions about whether he, as an author economically reliant on actors and paying theatergoers, is somehow implicated in the antisocial aspects of Volpone's fraud—not by evading them but by asking for answers that will always appear provisional. Meanwhile, he leaves his protagonist hanging, waiting to see what sort of critical community will emerge around him.

Afterlife

Volpone, I have just argued, imagines the transformation of death from a communal experience into a private one. Over the course of the play, the project of collective participation in the image of Christ's Passion falters in the face of possessive individualism. Traditional forms of communal care lose their potency and find themselves exploited as opportunities for personal gain. Once the art of dying falls into abeyance, impersonal institutions like the law court and the hospital take over the responsibility for managing death from the community. Such management is no longer conceptualized as shared participation in a collective journey but instead as the confinement of those who can no longer be cared for.

Viewed from this perspective, the trajectory of the play appears to anticipate a more general story often told about death in modernity—namely, that the art of it has been lost. As far back as 1977, Philippe Ariès won widespread assent for claiming that the modern subject no longer knows how to die.[1] Impoverished late-capitalist understandings of agency rooted in consumer choice make it nearly impossible to conceive of death as an action. Meanwhile, the biomedical-industrial complex exerts ever-more efficient and pervasive forms of discipline over declining bodies.

Secularized, rendered hygienic, and monetized, death becomes an occasion of disempowerment rather than an opportunity for self-assertion. Even recent attempts to politicize postures of dying reflect this new paradigm. The activist group Black Lives Matter, to take a striking contemporary instance, powerfully insists on the innocence of the victims of police brutality, who have done nothing to bring about their deaths. Chants of "I can't breathe" and staged die-ins align innocence with suffering and inaction.[2] The potential for agency in death is pointedly and strategically denied.

But does modern death need to be so passive? The problem of medicalization is an old one. As far back as 1596, William Perkins complained "that in all places almost, the phisition is first sent for, and comes at the beginning of the sickenesse, and the Minister comes when a man is halfe dead."[3] In recent years, a growing number of organizations and individuals in Western Europe and North America have advocated alternatives to biomedical models of dying.[4] Paul Kalanithi's memoir *When Breath Becomes Air* (published posthumously in 2016) records the author's experience of terminal lung cancer[5] and weaves scientific inquiry together with life writing, sociology, and phenomenology to produce a holistic account of what it means to die. *The Art of Dying Well*, a website launched in 2016 by the Catholic Bishop's Conference of England and Wales, attempts to reimagine the original *Tractatus Artis Bene Moriendi* for a contemporary audience composed of believers and agnostics.[6] In a more secular vein, the Death Positive Movement, popularized by the mortician Caitlin Doughty, showcases scholarly, artistic, medical, and mortuary practices that demystify mortality.[7] These last two projects exploit the affordances of digital media to enable flexible and personalized approaches to dying. Hyperlinks highlight connections between different aspects of mortality, encouraging readers to develop customized approaches to death and suggesting that modernization and technological change have the potential to promote agency at the end of life as well as hamper it. The claim that we no longer know how to die often functions less as a diagnosis and more as a rhetorical gambit, serving as a prelude to the discussion of precisely the topic it asserts to be impossible.

Rather than assume an art of dying needs to be recovered from the past, then, I here analyze some later artistic responses to the *artes moriendi*, which might enable new forms of individual or collective action. In the first two parts of the epilogue, I focus on literary and artistic works from the seventeenth and eighteenth centuries that treat dying as a gendered phenomenon. The doctrine of coverture prevented most women from writing wills, while the nexus of sex, pregnancy, and death often increased female vulnerability to patriarchal predation. Denied legal and bodily autonomy, some female subjects discovered alternative forms of agency in mixed and impure selves, which mingle genders and generations, the womb and the grave, innocence and experience. In the final section, I discuss contemporary artworks that juxtapose signifiers of life and death to challenge assumptions that personal death is a linear process of decline and the longer cultural narratives that insist that arts of dying are extinct. Viewed together, the subjects of this epilogue demonstrate that modern art and literature continue to engage with mortality—as a thematic concern, a structural principle, and even a form of political action. The art of dying remains vital.

Winding Sheets and Women's Wills

Large numbers of people in the seventeenth century would have been unable to imagine themselves possessing the level of agency that Volpone exerts through his will. Among the lower classes, few had much to give, and the legal doctrine of coverture denied most women the ability to name heirs or dispose of property.[8] Patriarchal norms concentrated economic and social power in the hands of a small number of men and subsumed female identity within the family structure. Yet precisely because possessive individualism of the sort Volpone displays appeared untenable for women, their deaths could become fertile sites for exploring alternative understandings of the self. When women's deaths are connected to other gendered bodily experiences that disrupt bounded identities—including sexual intercourse, marriage, pregnancy, birth, and maternity—they become occasions for imagining new forms of community and agency.

In seventeenth-century literature, female will making was sometimes framed as a transgression against male authority. The heroine of John Webster's *The Duchess of Malfi*, for instance, uses the occasion of drafting a will to rebel against her brothers and propose marriage to her steward. The play casts Ferdinand and the Cardinal's demand that their sister remain unmarried as self-interested, if not incestuous.[9] But it also implicitly criticizes the Duchess and her lover for "jesting with religion" (3.2.319). The Duchess seeks to seduce Antonio by displaying her power, wealth, and autonomy as a woman not subject to coverture when she envisages disposing of her royal estates, "as 'tis fit princes should,/In perfect memory" (1.1.367–68). Like Volpone, she hopes to use a discourse of last things as a cover for the pursuit of worldly ends. When Antonio responds to the

Duchess's invitation, though, he modifies her language of princely obligations to draw attention to her fleshy and female body. His proposal that she
make a bequest of herself, not in one "winding sheet" but in "a couple"
(1.1.380), conflates shared bodily pleasures, pious will making, and burial
ritual. While Antonio presumably intends to encourage his mistress to
turn away from death toward life, he inaugurates a macabre pattern of
vanitas imagery linking the Duchess's sexual and fertile body to decay. Like
the bodies in the sheets, discourses of spiritual renunciation and worldly
corruption display a tendency to wind together throughout *The Duchess of
Malfi*. Boscola's apricots ripened in horse dung, which trigger the pregnant
Duchess's premature labor on an inauspicious day, connect birth, death,
eating, and excretion. His later attempt to bring the Duchess "By degrees
to mortification" (4.2.168) through a reminder that "Thou art a box of
worm seed, at best, but a salvatory of green mummy" (4.2.119–20) imagines her generating worms rather than children in a morbid inversion of
maternity.[10] Ultimately, the Duchess is unable to assert agency through the
practice of dying in the same way as Volpone because her body is not only
tied to mortality but also imbued with the intrinsically mixed qualities of
femininity, sexuality, and maternity, which render possessive individualism
and separation from community obligations unimaginable at the level of
her flesh.

When *The Duchess of Malfi* presents the Duchess's body as a site where
death, sex, and maternity become horrifically mingled, it participates in a
longer literary and artistic tradition of female grotesques. Early modern
writers frequently describe women's beauty practices, sexual desires, and
aging processes as doomed and disgusting attempts to deny mortality,
which, in that very act of denial, draw attention to its inevitability. Maternity and pregnancy were often characterized in especially monstrous
terms.[11] John Donne, for instance, offers a nightmarish vision of the uterus
as a site of deadly confusion in "Deaths Duell":

> in our mother's womb we are dead, so as that we do not know we live,
> not so much as we do in our sleep, neither is there any grave so close
> or so putrid a prison, as the womb would be unto us if we stayed in it
> beyond our time, or died there before our time. In the grave the
> worms do not kill us; we breed, and feed, and then kill those worms
> which we ourselves produced. In the womb the dead child kills the
> mother that conceived it, and is a murderer, nay, a parricide, even after
> it is dead. And if we be not dead so in the womb, so as that being dead
> we kill her that gave us our first life, our life of vegetation, yet we are

dead so as David's idols are dead. In the womb we have eyes and see not, ears and hear not. There in the womb we are fitted for works of darkness, all the while deprived of light; and there in the womb we are taught cruelty, by being fed with blood, and may be damned, though we be never born.[12]

Donne sees pregnancy as a phenomenon that troubles stable binaries between human and inhuman, self and other. The womb is a site of dynamic exchange in which mother and child simultaneously protect and attack each other. Possessing only a vegetable life that can plausibly be read as a form of death, the fetus is more like an idol than a person. Structural homologies between the womb and the grave offer readers reminders not just of the complex interplay between maternal and fetal life but, more fundamentally, of the spiritual state of fallenness that has transformed the uterus into a place of violence, darkness, cruelty, and damnation.

Later in the text, Donne inverts this description of the mortifying womb to produce a uterine (and disturbingly vital) image of the grave. Under the earth, buried bodies quicken and give birth to worms that partake of "my mother, and my sister and myself."[13] The antagonism between confining mother and parricidal child in the womb anticipates the complete breakdown of familial order in the incestuous, vermicular grave. Antonio and the Duchess's erotic vision of smiling bequests and coupled winding sheets seems recast by Donne as a horrific breakdown of distinctions between individuals and generations and a collapse of death and life into each other. Donne's echoing images deny linear temporality and stable familial hierarchies. The womb—like the grave it mirrors—is associated with a confusion of genders and generations. It reveals the human to be riven by the alien and opens a perspective from which life is indistinguishable from death.

It might seem perverse to attempt to cast Donne's understandings of womb and grave in more affirmative terms. Yet in some respects, his language finds echoes in recent theorists who discover utopian possibilities in somatic confusion. In "The Biopolitics of Postmodern Bodies: Constitutions of Self in Immune System Discourse," Donna Haraway insists that bodies must be recognized as historical constructs if we are to understand how they are turned to political ends. To substantiate her argument, she contrasts nineteenth-century descriptions of the body as "a system of work, organized by the hierarchical division of labour, ordered by a privileged dialectic between highly localized nervous and reproductive functions," with postmodern accounts of it as "a coded text, organized as an engineering communications system, ordered by a fluid and dispersed command-control-intelligence network."[14] Prostheses and medical implants, theories of genetics that locate natural selection at the level of the gene rather than the person, and shifting understandings of the immune system all undermine beliefs in individual autonomy and organic self-sufficiency as radically as Donne's reminders that all of life is a form of death. But where Donne diagnoses sin, Haraway treats shifting biomedical paradigms as opportunities to pursue liberatory projects that unsettle traditional gender identities and gender roles. Whereas nineteenth-century medical-advice texts construct the female subject around "the maternal function and the physical site of the uterus" (282), contemporary evolutionary biology insists that replication occurs at the level of genes as well as individuals and sees the body as no more than a phenotypic expression of an underlying genetic code. Stressing the latter model over the former offers Haraway a means to challenge heteronormativity and the patriarchal power structures it enables.

While Haraway considers the uterus solely in relation to nineteenth-century constructions of the feminine, Esposito builds on her work to show how contemporary biomedical models of pregnancy also challenge essentialized and bounded identities in ways that can be turned to utopian ends. Modern immunology suggests the fetus is protected from the maternal immune system by an unusual set of maternal antibodies that mask its alien nature:

> Far from being inactive [in pregnancy], the immunity mechanism is working on a double front, because if on the one hand it is directed toward controlling the fetus, on the other, it is also controlling itself. In short, by immunizing the other, it is also immunizing itself. . . . The mother is pitted against the child and the child against the mother, and yet what results from this conflict is the spark of life.[15]

The fetus exists as a foreign occupant within the uterus, confronting the mother internally with that which is external to her and so contesting the notion of the bounded self in sole possession of the body. The unfamiliarity of the fetus triggers the maternal immune system to become self-divided and go to war with itself. So far this sounds rather like Donne's account of incestuous wombs and graves—except that the antagonistic actions of the immune system ultimately produce a protective, and communal, equilibrium that allows the pregnancy to progress. Esposito suggests that this process opens up "a perspective . . . within immunitary logic" from which "nothing remains of the incompatibility between self and other" (171).

Pregnancy, in this account, reveals community and immunity to be inextricable at the level of the cell.

Seventeenth-century understandings of the biology of pregnancy differ radically from modern ones, of course. But like Esposito, some early modern writers find hopeful ways to think about the confusion of mother and child and of life and death. In 1622, Elizabeth Jocelin learned that she was pregnant for the first time—and responded by buying herself a winding sheet and secretly composing a conduct book to be given to her child in the event she did not survive to raise it.[16] Jocelin was not particularly unusual in recognizing the harsh medical reality that made birth a dangerous endeavor for mother and child.[17] Many women treated pregnancy as an occasion to contemplate last things. Diaries, spiritual autobiographies, and conduct books record them composing prayers for safe delivery, making provision for their offspring who might be left orphaned, writing wills, and anticipating their own burials.[18] In Jocelin's case, such fears were horribly prophetic. She died of puerperal fever nine days after giving birth to a daughter. Her text was found by her husband and published in 1624 as *The Mother's Legacie, to her Unborn Childe*.

Jocelin's conceit of her tract as a legacy raises familiar questions about the agency and propriety of female testatrices. Thomas Goad, whose "Approbation" serves as a preface to *The Mother's Legacie*, notes that as a married woman under coverture, Jocelin had no right to own or dispose of property (A3r). Nevertheless, he allows her literary testament to stand on the grounds that

> corruptible riches, even to those who have capacity of alienating them,
> bring onely a ciuill propriety, but no morall & vertous influence for
> the wel dispensing, or bestowing them: whereas vertue and grace haue
> power beyond all empeachment of sex or other debility, to enable and
> instruct the possessor to employ the same vnquestionably for the
> inward inriching of others. (A4v)

The pattern by now should be familiar. Virtuous individuals are able to employ worldly forms like wills to analogize spiritual forms of care, and as Wendy Wall notes, such analogies can offer marginalized individuals like Jocelin entry into public forums from which they are otherwise excluded.[19] While Webster and Jonson show how easily the material vehicle may overwhelm the spiritual tenor, Jocelin's text ultimately resists the trajectory that I have traced through the plays toward privatization of the deathbed.

Teresa Feroli reads *The Mother's Legacie* as a despairing record of "the self-loss that is consistent with maternity," in which Jocelin imagines dying as a means of mourning the erasure of identity occasioned by mother-hood.[20] But such self-loss need not only be approached mournfully—nor, I think, is it purely a source of grief within Jocelin's writing. Precisely because pregnancy renders notions of identity rooted in exclusive posses-sion of the body untenable, it can generate new types of community. In *The Mother's Legacie*, Jocelin exploits homologies between the bodily connec-tion of pregnant mother and fetus and the mystical fellowship of living and dead Christians in order to acquire spiritual authority despite her gender and to retain a line of communication to her child even after her death. Although she presents her project as a purely domestic intervention—and indeed disavows more public roles for women when she rejects scholarly education for girls as a dangerous temptation to pride (B4r–B5r)—the dynamics she exploits can suggest more broadly applicable forms of agency rooted in self-difference.

In purchasing herself a winding sheet on learning of her pregnancy and in writing her text in double contemplation of birth and death, Jocelin performs the analogy of womb and grave that Donne describes. Her *Lega-cie* additionally echoes "Deaths Duell" by refusing to respect boundaries between genders and generations. At times, Jocelin mirrors Donne in confusing parents and children to signal depravity. She exhorts her child to obey its parents by arguing that neglect of the sixth commandment amounts to committing both murder and adultery, and her language places disobedient children in incestuous and parricidal positions to emphasize their sins:

> thou canst not bee a disobedient childe, but thou art a murderer, a
> double one: first of nature in thy selfe, which if thy wicked purposes
> doe not smother, will of her selfe breake forth into that duty. For an
> example, the story of *Aeneas* shewes how much it was obserued by
> them that receiued not the Commandement from Gods owne mouth,
> as did the Iewes, yet he exposed himselfe to all dangers rather than
> hee would forsake his father. Secondly, thou art a murtherer of thy
> father, who hauing stored vp all his ioy in thee, hath by thy disobedi-
> ence his gray head brought with sorrow to the graue; which God for-
> bid. And what difference, shall I say, is there betweene a disobedient
> childe, and an adulterer? The one forsakes her, by whom he giueth
> being vnto others; the other despiseth those from whom hee had his
> owne being. (94–95)

But at other points in the *Legacie*, the conjunction of pregnancy and death allows Jocelin and her text to occupy multiple subject positions that are rhetorically and spiritually advantageous. In the prefatory letter to her husband, for instance, Jocelin describes her writings as "a deputed Mother for instruction, and for solace a twinne-like sister, issuing from the same Parent, and seeing the light about the same time" (B8v–B9r). The text, like the worms in Donne's grave, constitutes mother, sister—and also infant who occasions its composition and whom it hopes to mold. It is able to do so precisely because death and pregnancy are proximate. Here, though, generational and temporal collapse serves not to mark human depravity but rather to afford Jocelin the opportunity to communicate with her child from beyond the grave and induct it into a community of believers that aspires to transcend time.

Clarissa's Passing

Criticism has long treated texts like Jocelin's as important antecedents for the eighteenth-century novel. For Ian Watt, Protestant habits of private devotion anticipate and inculcate notions of character essential to psychological realism.[21] Nancy Armstrong goes further, asserting that connections between conduct literature and domestic novels are not merely stylistic but also ideological. The two genres work in concert to inculcate a historically specific notion of femininity that grounds a new political understanding of the emergent middle class.[22] *Ars moriendi* traditions certainly influence some prominent eighteenth-century novelists and no doubt contribute to these developments. But in doing so, they also complicate critical assumptions about the sorts of characters and domestic ideals that conduct books aspire to produce. Samuel Richardson's *Clarissa* refers explicitly to Jeremy Taylor's *Rules and Exercises of Holy Dying* (1651), and the five hundred pages of the book that track the heroine's gradual progress toward exemplary death show her conforming in many respects to Taylor's ideals.[23] Yet while employing *ars moriendi* models, Richardson also acknowledges forces within his culture that would dismiss such devotional traditions as old-fashioned and insincere. The first character in the novel to allude to Taylor's tract is Clarissa's rapist, the libertine Lovelace, who employs it instrumentally. When Clarissa subsequently attempts to redeem the genre that Lovelace has traduced, she does so not by rejecting the cynical terms in which he understands Taylor's text but by adopting them. Her use of Taylor suggests that *ars moriendi* texts can support more unstable understandings of gender identity and female agency than Armstrong's account of conduct books admits, understandings that retain something of the uncomfortable mixtures of Webster, Donne, and Jocelin.

Holy Dying makes an inauspicious first appearance in *Clarissa*. Clarissa has escaped from Mrs. Sinclair's brothel, where Lovelace had confined her, and found temporary refuge at a rooming house. When Lovelace discovers her whereabouts, he visits her with two ladies, whom he presents as his female relations. (They are in fact disguised prostitutes, working in concert with Lovelace to dupe Clarissa into returning to Mrs Sinclair's.) Lovelace incorporates a copy of Taylor's tract into his performance of benign intentions. Clarissa describes seeing him "looking into a book which, had there not been a preconcert, would not have taken his attention for one moment. It was *Taylor's Holy Living and Dying.*"[24] Precisely because conduct manuals prescribe codes of behavior, they have always been susceptible to instrumental use. As we have already seen, Quicksilver from *Eastward Ho* recites passages from Becon's *Sycke Man's Salve* in order to demonstrate his repentance and win his freedom. The play shows little interest in the sincerity of Quicksilver's religious conversion; it is enough that Becon's text offers a culturally legible script for performing contrition.

But where Quicksilver's recitation of Becon works singly, Lovelace uses Taylor to create two contrary social performances. He insincerely pretends to religious feeling while simultaneously treating Taylor as a prop to demonstrate libertine wit. Although Lovelace's initial "preconcerted" perusal of *Holy Dying* forms part of his hypocritical effort to present himself as redeemable, his account of the text to Clarissa attempts to situate Taylor's project in the modern world:

> A smart book, this, my dear!—This old divine affects, I see, a mighty flowery style upon a solemn subject. But it puts me in mind of an ordinary country funeral, where the young women, in honor of a defunct companion, especially if she were a virgin, or *passed for such*, make a flower-bed of her coffin. (1002, emphasis Richardson's)

Lovelace ironically praises the disjunctures within Taylor's style. The incompatible and affected aesthetic modes implied by smartness, floridity, and solemnity bring to his mind the "ordinary" funeral of the woman who passes (in the double senses of "appears" and "dies") as a virgin. Taylor, in this reading, exemplifies an outdated form of piety, but one that, precisely through its anachronisms, becomes an apt emblem for modern hypocrisy. *Ars moriendi* would be irrelevant to the libertine milieu that Lovelace inhabits—except that in its very contradictions it comes to represent that world's modes of passing.

The funereal image anticipates Lovelace's later sexual assault and encourages readers to see Clarissa's rape in the context of a larger—and markedly gendered—project of immunization from death. For Lovelace, passing is perversely linked to authenticity. Discovering a libertine subtext within a devotional work allows him to stay true to his irreligious principles even as he obfuscates them behind a show of piety. Successful social performance demonstrates rakish self-possession. Female passing, however, functions differently. As Laura Baudot notes, Lovelace's image of the floral coffin evokes the *carpe diem* tradition. The ephemeral flower conventionally stands both for female virtue and human life, neither of which are able to resist the destructive and homogenizing forces of seduction and mortality.[25] Whereas the rake constructs his own character, the seeming virgin has significance imposed upon her.[26] By linking his own freedom as a libertine to the deflowering and death of a female victim, Lovelace (very much like Volpone) limits his own exposure to mortality by forcing it on a dupe. He affirms his ability to instrumentalize the devotional forms that purport to incorporate individuals into a Christian community and to recast them as personal works. Simultaneously, he displaces vulnerability onto a feminized other. This project appears in its full horror in the act of rape. Sandra Macpherson demonstrates the close link *Clarissa* assumes between the seduction or sexual assault of female characters and their deaths, arguing that the novel relies upon legal notions of strict liability to make Lovelace guilty of Clarissa's murder.[27] Rape also appears like murder from the perspective of the victim. As Stephanie Hershinow notes, the drugs that Lovelace uses to incapacitate Clarissa cause her to lose consciousness during the assault. Rape, then, becomes akin to death not just because the chastity it destroys is a fundamental part of Clarissa's identity but also because Clarissa, placed in a deathlike stupor, is denied the capacity to experience it.[28] Lovelace imposes sexuality and mortality upon her simultaneously.

Clarissa's progress toward death reclaims this imagined funeral—not by repudiating the mocking terms in which Lovelace describes it but rather by inhabiting them. She plans and then enacts a holy death and burial that redeems Lovelace's conception of passing by discovering personal agency and spiritual value within it. Clarissa commissions an ornately decorated coffin that perpetuates the association Lovelace created between death, loss of chastity, and floral ephemerality, but she contests the gendered terms through which he understood it. She applies the principle of transience to a male subject by including the device of "the head of a white lily snapped short off" above the inscription "The days of man are but as grass. For he flourisheth as a flower of the field," and she feminizes the agency that conceived the device by connecting it to her design of "needleworks" (1306).

Later, thwarting Lovelace's attempts to possess her in death by embalming her corpse and preserving her heart "in spirits" (1384), Clarissa legally prescribes the treatment of her body. In her will, she states that "the occasion of my death not admitting of doubt, I will not on any account that it be opened; and it is my desire that it shall not be touched but by those of my own sex" (1413). The female corpse dressers recall the "young women" in Lovelace's funeral image. In Clarissa's revision, however, they no longer collude in feminine deceit but instead protect female virtue from masculine violation.

Clarissa's insistence on preserving the integrity and wholeness of her body reflects her desire to reconstitute herself as an autonomous agent. However, her public assertion that autopsy is unnecessary because the occasion of her death does not admit doubt throws the novel's silence about the state of her body and the medical reasons for her decline into sharper focus. Among other things, we never learn if Lovelace has made her pregnant.[29] Clarissa's ignorance of the event of her rape is mirrored by readers' ignorance of the bodily consequences of the rape and therefore of the precise relationship between death and sex within the novel. As Jonathan Kramnick notes, the novel's sustained interest in causation makes its reticence here particularly hard for readers to accept.[30] Many of the possibilities that critics have projected onto the lacuna threaten to infect Clarissa's good end with more negative understandings of mortality. Terry Castle, for instance, observes that Belford's lurid account of Mrs. Sinclair's death intrudes jarringly on Clarissa's progress toward the grave in a manner that blurs distinctions between the two women.[31] Both characters are associated with images of rupture. The fracture in Mrs. Sinclair's leg echoes the cut lily on Clarissa's coffin as well as the fragmented narrative that emerges from her correspondence. Castle reads the affinities that emerge between Mrs. Sinclair and Clarissa in the context of the novel's more general silencing of female voices. Clarissa is unable to determine her narrative progress toward the grave exclusively through her words and actions and instead becomes fissured and infected by the negative example of the despairing madam. Taking a quite different tack but still affirming Castle's sense that Clarissa fails to sustain purity or self-sufficiency in death, Jolene Zigarovich attributes necrophiliac impulses to both Clarissa and Lovelace.[32] In this reading, the beautiful death is not a rejection of sex but its perverse apotheosis.

I think it is possible to acknowledge the force of these observations while refusing to interpret them as signs of failure or pathology. Ann Louise Kibbie argues persuasively that the novel's obsessive attention to Clarissa's body is less reflective of morbid psychology than of legal and philosophical questions about how the inalienable self is constituted in relation to alienable property.[33] As we have seen, similar problems show up in *Volpone* and the *artes moriendi*. Clarissa's approach to death sustains the compromises, impurities, and vulnerabilities to externally imposed meaning that are inherent in Lovelace's notion of female passing. Richardson, like Jocelin, acknowledges that the feminization of death—and its association with other embodied experiences that are coded as female—tends to militate against any performance of pure autonomy and self-sufficiency. But this impurity can be a source of strength. It allows Clarissa to acknowledge and embody self-difference and contradiction and so recast the assumptions Lovelace used to abuse her in redemptive terms. The novel does not deny Lovelace's charge that Taylor's tract is both archaic and self-divided. Rather, Richardson shows how Clarissa labors to reconcile its disparate elements with one another and with her inhospitable surroundings. As Kramnick observes, the novel's reticence about what is happening to Clarissa's body foregrounds questions about the relationship between mental intentions and physical effects.[34] Death becomes invested with the richness of Richardsonian psychology not despite but through the anachronistic qualities of *Holy Dying* that Lovelace finds so easy to ridicule and the confusions of persons that possible pregnancy implies. More abstractly, Richardson's appropriation of Jeremy Taylor offers a general framework for understanding the persistence of religious precedents within the novel and other largely secular genres. To follow the fate of the *artes moriendi* to the present need not only entail tracking artistic displays of religiosity—or even, necessarily, artistic depictions of death. It requires tracing a genealogy of devotional forms that have come to hold content entirely different from their originals. Such tracing, moreover, could offer a riposte to those like Ariès who insist that because death is no longer talked about directly, the art of it is no longer practiced. The practices of reconciling this world to the next are woven into the novel form and survive in modern habits of reading.

Look up Here, I'm in Heaven

The music video for David Bowie's single "Lazarus" opens with a shot of a closet, doors slightly ajar. A hand emerges from the dark interior, before the camera cuts to a prone figure lying on a bed and pans up slowly, from an anonymous bulk hidden under blankets, to a pair of wrinkled hands, and finally to Bowie's face (see Figure 3). The skin is papery. The eyes are

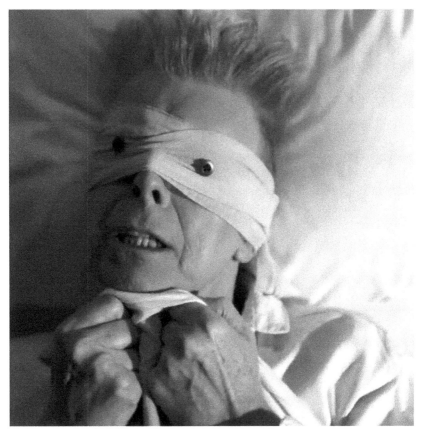

Figure 3: David Bowie, "Lazarus," dir. Johan Renck, filmed 2015, YouTube video, 4:09. https://www.youtube.com/watch?v=y-JqH1M4Ya8.

hidden under bandages, secured with buttons on top of the sockets. "Look up here, I'm in heaven," Bowie sings. "I've got scars that can't be seen."[35] "Lazarus" was released in December 2015 as the second single trailing the album *Blackstar*, which came out on January 8, 2016, Bowie's sixty-ninth birthday. Two days later, the singer would be dead from liver cancer. His illness had been concealed from the public.

The biographical fact of Bowie's death immediately altered critical interpretations of *Blackstar*. In Simon Critchley's words, the album "simply sounded different."[36] On January 7, Ryan Dombal's review of *Blackstar* in *Pitchfork* had commended Bowie for "embrac[ing] his status as a no-fucks icon, a 68-year-old with 'nothing left to lose,' as he sings on 'Lazarus.'"[37]

Dombal here reads the allusion to the biblical Lazarus as a parable of resurrection that nods to Bowie's multiple personae and continual stylistic reinvention. Signs that Bowie is aging are performative markers of a new "no-fucks" avatar. More generally, Dombal and other early reviewers understand the album as a comeback. On January 11, by contrast, Bowie's long-time producer Tony Visconti characterized the record as a "parting gift" and added, "His death was no different from his life—a work of art."[38] Chris Roberts at *The Quietus* built explicitly on Visconti's statement to commend *Blackstar* as "a bold and brilliant way to go."[39] Visconti later complicated his account at the biographical level by noting that Bowie only learned his cancer was terminal after the recording of *Blackstar* (and the filming of "Lazarus").[40] Yet, with a few exceptions,[41] this interpretation of the album as an immediate performance of personal mortality stuck. Critchley, while acknowledging that the change he perceived in *Blackstar* was "obviously absurd," insisted: "If a death can be a work of art, a statement completely consistent with an artist's aesthetic, then this is what happened on January 10th, 2016. . . . This was a noble death in the gift of privacy with all of his fans listening to his new album."[42] Allusions within the album to death, or heaven, or hospitals, or, well, anything became reunderstood as "clues" to the imminence of the singer's end—never mind the prevalence of these themes in Bowie's music from the sixties onward.

The trajectory of Bowie's career partly explains this collective impulse to connect the artist's biological death to his musical output. As a performer, Bowie frequently collapsed distinctions between art and life. The personae he crafted—Ziggy Stardust, Aladdin Sane, the Thin White Duke—might have been conceived as performative fronts for particular musical projects. But on many occasions Bowie blurred the line between their characters and his or implied that "David Bowie" was equally constructed. When pressed in interviews on his relationship to his alter egos or on the details of the authentic self supposedly underlying them, Bowie could often be flippant, deliberately dense, or contradictory.[43] Liner notes on the singer's 1995 album *1. Outside* echo Roland Barthes and announce to the reader: "All art is unstable. Its meaning is not necessarily that implied by the author. There is no authoritative voice, there are only multiple readings."[44] For the many cultural critics predisposed to see Bowie as an instantiation of Baudrillard's simulacrum, "Lazarus" might represent another instance of the power of postmodern representation to subsume reality.[45] Alternatively one could view the single and music video as final, redemptive gestures of authentication. While I find both these perspectives unsatisfactory—the first risks cynicism, the second mawkishness—I do not believe it is possible to discount the conjunction of Bowie's death and the release of *Blackstar* as mere coincidence. Building on my readings of Donne and Jocelin, I propose that baroque aesthetics and *artes moriendi* offer critics a more flexible vocabulary for explaining the complex and shifting relationships Bowie generates between art, life, and death as well as ways to understand what is at stake in his project.

Bowie is certainly not the first artist to document and perform his own mortality. In its temporally unmoored representation of a dying body, "Lazarus" echoes John Donne's preparations for death. Donne's biographer Izaak Walton describes how in the final weeks of his life, Donne commissioned a portraitist

> to draw his picture, which was taken as followeth.—Severall Charcole-fires being first made in his large study, he brought with him into that place his winding-sheet in his hand, and having put off all his clothes, had his sheet put on him, and so tied with knots at his head and feet, and his hands so placed as dead bodies are usually fitted for the grave. Upon this Urn he thus stood with his eyes shut, and so much of the sheet turned aside as might shew his lean, pale, and death-like face, which was purposely turned toward the East, from whence he expected the second coming of our Saviour. Thus he was drawn at his just height; and when the picture was fully finished, he caused it to be set by his bed-side, where it continued, and became his hourly object till his death.[46]

This portrait then served as the model for Donne's monument in St. Paul's as well as the engraving by Martin Droushout that became the frontispiece for the 1632 publication of "Deaths Duell" (see Figure 4).

In *John Donne: Body and Soul*, Ramie Targoff emphasizes the peculiarities of Donne's portrait, which, she insists, "is hardly a standard image for deathbed contemplation." Where the conventional *vanitas* image is the bony skull stripped clean of flesh, Donne both displays and regards his body. Rather than standing purely as a reminder of the inevitable destination of the grave, the image gives Donne access to "the strange thrill of being simultaneously dead and alive."[47]

I want to bring greater precision to Targoff's notion of simultaneity. Donne does not simply merge liveness with deadness; he orchestrates a complex and dynamic exchange between the two states. The creation of the picture disrupts the orderly temporal progression of mortality so as to allow Donne to move unpredictably from sickbed, to grave, to resurrection. As Helen Gardner cautions, we should be wary of treating Walton's

Figure 4: John Donne, *Deaths Duell* (London, 1632), frontispiece. By permission of the Photo Negative Collection, Beinecke Rare Book and Manuscript Library, Yale University.

anecdote as strictly factual.[48] Instead, *The Life of John Donne* supplies a narrative framework that allows Donne's picture to participate doubly in the genres of *ars moriendi* and *memento mori*.

First, posing for the portrait offers Donne an opportunity to pursue a practice of dying that closely resembles the dramatic *artes moriendi*. Walton's detailed descriptions of the work done to produce Donne's costume

and posture serve as reminders that *ars moriendi* is always active and effortful. Indeed, it is hard not to suspect that the demands placed on Donne's
debilitated body by this process—stripping down to a sheet in March!
balancing on an urn!—would have hastened his actual demise. "Practice"
in the sense of preparation for death becomes "practice" in the sense of
performance of death; as in *Clarissa*, two senses of passing infect each
other. Second, the picture functions as a *memento mori*, but one that further blurs distinctions between action and inaction and raises questions
about how we should understand the temporality of dying. Staring at the
picture of himself in a winding sheet, Donne appears to be looking at an
image of death. Except the picture is really of someone alive. And more
than that, the Donne contemplating the picture from his deathbed is closer
to the moment of his biological end than the Donne pictured. Compara-
tively, this is a picture of health. By contemplating a picture that shows him
both where he has come from and where he will go, Donne situates his
present self in relation to past and future. Contemplation thus draws
Donne's attention, and our attention, to the process of dying. Since Donne
is doing little else, it can even *become* the process of dying. While I have
separated out the moments of posing and contemplation sequentially in
order to explain them more clearly, they will necessarily overlap. As Donne
poses, he also contemplates. As he contemplates, he poses, if not for the
artist, then for Walton, his spiritual biographer. Finally, as Donne's practice of dying is remediated and disseminated through Walton's prose narrative and Droushout's engraving, it becomes a warning and exemplar for
readers, who must anticipate their own deaths.

Some twentieth-century artists achieve similar effects using photogra-
phy but seek to connect their own approaches to mortality to social and
political questions about whose deaths are displayed and whose are hidden.
David Wojnarowicz's self-portrait *Untitled (Face in Dirt)* is one of a series
of photographs and paintings through which the artist appears to anticipate his death from AIDS (see Figure 5). In it, Wojnarowicz's visage, partially obscured by dirt and stones, rises out of (or perhaps sinks into) what
looks like a shallow grave. Like Donne's image, the picture functions at
once as *ars moriendi* and *momento mori*. But Wojnarowicz evokes these two
traditions for explicitly political ends. The partial burial of the face speaks
to the cultural silencing of queer communities ravaged by AIDS. The continued visibility of Wojnarowicz's features implies his refusal to submit
passively to his own erasure. In this instance, then, the temporal eddies
enabled by a staged deathbed portrait do not simply reflect the paradoxes
that surround the personal contemplation and practice of mortality. Wojn-

Figure 5: David Wojnarowicz, *Untitled (Face in Dirt)*, 1990, silver print, 18 ×19 inches, Liz and Eric Lefkofsky. Courtesy of the Estate of David Wojnarowicz and P.P.O.W, New York.

arowicz uses temporal instability to contest the premature consignment of those with HIV to oblivion and to demand a political resurrection.

Hannah Wilke explores similar dynamics in *Intra-Venus*, a photo and video series documenting the progress of the lymphoma that would eventually kill her. Her images confront the viewer with unflinching, even exhibitionist, displays of her sick body. They at once record the predations of disease and subvert traditional representations of the female form. The diptych *July 28, 1992/February 19, 1992*, for instance, juxtaposes two color portraits of Wilke (see Figure 6). In the image on the left, the artist stares directly out from a blue background. Naked (apart from the IV port on her right hand), she confronts viewers with both her gaze and the physical markers of her sickness. In the image on the right, Wilke is wrapped in a

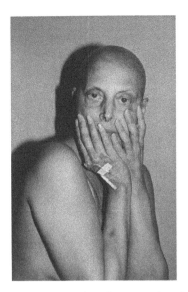 

Figure 6: Hannah Wilke, *Intra- Venus Series No. 4, July 26 and February 19, 1992*, 1992–1993. Performalist self- portrait with Donald Goddard. Two chromogenic supergloss prints, 71½ × 47½ inches each. Courtesy of Donald and Helen Goddard and Ronald Feldman Gallery, New York.

blue blanket, her eyes now closed in what could be sleep or death. Where the first picture ironizes the idealized feminine forms of classical nudes, the second calls to mind beatific images of the Virgin and other female saints. Wilke at once protests the reduction of women to idealized archetypes within the Western art tradition and inhabits those archetypes in order to explore the narratives that attach to illness. To support the project of destabilization, Wilke also plays with time. The title associates each of the images with a date, approximately four months apart, and presumably reflecting when the photographs were taken. But Wilke's position of the later picture on the left and the earlier one on the right disrupts the usual Western practice of reading texts and images from left to right, while the shared palates of the two images serve to bring the two moments of time into proximity. The deathlike pose on the right exists at once before, after, and coexistent with the alert one on the left. The juxtaposition challenges assumptions that the passage from life to death is linear. And like Wojnarowicz, Wilke seems to discover political agency in this disruption. As she alters the timeline of her lymphoma, she also subverts the historical traditions of Western art that have determined how women are seen.

In one way, the resemblance of "Lazarus" to the portraits of Donne, Wojnarowicz, and Wilke resolves the question of how Bowie's life and art converge. "Lazarus," like Donne's picture, functions doubly as *ars moriendi* and *memento mori*, muddling action with contemplation and signs of vitality with images of death.[49] We see the same effortful, performative construction of a living person as an emblem of mortality. Moreover, the genre conventions of the music video—in particular the eschewal of linear narrative in favor of successive cuts back and forth between thematically related images—disrupt the timeline of any steady progress to the grave. Shots of Bowie prone on the bed are interspersed with shots of him standing and dancing or of him writing at a desk under the gaze of a skull. Even if "Lazarus" was not conceived as a literal artistic rendition of Bowie's biological death or a parting gift to fans, the video anticipates temporal reorganization and represents the transformation of contemplation into action, so as to incorporate Bowie's death and the death of the watcher— whenever these events should occur.

But in noting these connections, I arguably only displace the question of what "Lazarus" represents into a different register, one of influence and tradition. Is Bowie deliberately evoking Donne's postures? Or is the similarity between them merely coincidence? While I have not been able to find any evidence of Bowie's familiarity with Donne's portrait, the title he gave to one of the songs on *Blackstar*, "'Tis Pity She Was a Whore," suggests some interest in baroque aesthetics. Nevertheless, Bowie's video implies a very different spiritual frame of reference to Donne's picture. Donne turns his face toward the east to anticipate the appearance of the second coming. Bowie's bandaged eyes imply ignorance of afterlife, and the buttons that secure them recall the pagan world of Charon's obol. If he echoes Donne, he does so while ignoring the promise of "the second coming of our Savior," which for Donne would have been the most important element of the deathbed performance. Once we shift focus to the late-twentieth-century artworks, the problem of articulating the position of "Lazarus" within a tradition of *ars moriendi* images acquires an insistently ethical dimension. Both Wilke and Wojnarowicz use postures of dying to contest the marginalization of women and queer people in histories of Western art. When Bowie adopts similar strategies in a mass-market product, it is unclear whether he amplifies their actions or travesties and appropriates them to commercial ends. The trajectory is at once a fulfillment and a betrayal.

More fundamentally, this double movement is already reflected in the artworks, all of which display awareness of the complex temporalities necessarily involved in the artistic anticipation of dying and recognition of the inevitable gaps between representation and reality. It is precisely in these disruptions of tradition and moments of bad faith that the forms of agency I have been discussing in *ars moriendi* and the early modern stage seem to persist into the present. The temporal disjunctions and perspectival shifts within Bowie's video and Wilke's and Wojnarowicz's photographs suggest that this process of reconfiguration will never be entirely complete and never entirely subsumed by any single ideological project. One *memento mori* begins another *ars moriendi*. We are all dying with—and through—Faustus, Edward, Richard, Volpone, Jocelin, Clarissa, Wojnarowicz, Wilke, and Bowie. Audiences, readers, performers, and creators all participate in a constant search for a satisfactory approach to the end.

ACKNOWLEDGMENTS

Everybody helped.

Hugh Epstein at Richmond College, and Luke Thurston and Judy Weiss at Robinson College, Cambridge, helped get me on this path. At Johns Hopkins University, Amanda Anderson, Sharon Cameron, Stephen Campbell, Simon During, Frances Ferguson, Christopher Nealon, Elizabeth Patton, Gabrielle Spiegel, and Mark Christian Thompson modeled forms of rigorous scholarship and critical engagement that I'm still struggling to emulate. In particular, this book would not exist without the guidance of Richard Halpern and Drew Daniel, both of whom continue to be unfailingly generous and supportive. Many thanks to my colleagues at Case Western Reserve University, including Kim Emmons, Denna Iammarino, T. Kenny Fountain, Sarah Gridley, Kurt Koenigsberger, John Higgins, Megan Jewell, William Marling, James Newlin, Erika Olbricht, John Orlock, Thrity Umrigar, Athena Vrettos, Anthony Wexler, John Wiehl, and Martha Woodmansee for their support and advice. I'm especially grateful to Michael Clune and Chris Flint for their mentoring and eagle-eye editing.

I'm also grateful to friends elsewhere for their intellectual, emotional, and logistical support throughout. David Hershinow, Stephanie Insley Hershinow, Wendy Beth Hyman, William Cook Miller, Benjamin Parris, and Andrew Sisson were unspeakably free with their time, knowledge, attention, and friendship. They all read large portions of the manuscript (in some cases, repeatedly), and the book is far stronger for their insightful responses and continuous encouragement. The project also benefited enormously from Patricia Cahill's and Will Stockton's generous reader's reports on the entire manuscript and from Gail Kern Paster's and Will West's responses to versions of individual chapters. Keith Angelino listened to me complain and kept me supplied with wine and Italian food. As members of the Renaissance Reading Group at Johns Hopkins, Rebecca Buckham, Marisa O'Connor, and Samuel Smith offered a vital sounding board. Conversations with Nick Bujak, Jacob Israel Chilton, Robert D. Day, Patrick Fessenbecker, Roger Maioli, Doug Tye, and Kara Wedekind were vital influences during the initial phases of the project. More recently, I have benefited from the insights of Alice Dailey, Lawrence Manley, Jim Marino, Debapriya Sarkar, Katherine Schaap Williams, and Arielle Zibrak. Chris Geekie helped enormously with the Latin. James Kuzner generously offered advice on an early version of my book proposal. Brooke Conti also read the proposal and (with Wendy) has been an invaluable writing partner and confidante in Cleveland. David Schley and Jessica Valdez held me accountable. Sarah Hanson and Charlie Messum offered guidance on art, while Ben Newman assisted with the music. Recently, Jermaine Xaba has been a source of dogs, love, and boundless enthusiasm.

I gratefully acknowledge the support of the librarians at Case Western Reserve University's Kelvin Smith Library. In particular, Bill Claspy, as research services librarian for English, has been a stellar resource. Mark Clemente and Jared Bendis in the Freedman Center for Digital Scholarship have helped enormously with the images. The publication of this book was supported by a grant from the W. P. Jones Presidential Faculty Development Fund of Case Western Reserve University.

Chapter 1 appeared as "*Doctor Faustus* and the Art of Dying Badly," *Renaissance Drama* 45, no. 1 (2017): 1–23. A version of Chapter 4 appeared as "'This is called mortifying of a fox': *Volpone* and How to Get Rich Quick by Dying Slowly," *Shakespeare Quarterly* 65, no. 2 (2014): 140–63. Thanks to the editors for their permission to reprint.

Many thanks to the brilliant people at Fordham University Press for nurturing this project. Thomas Lay has been everything I could ask for in an editor. Eric Newman has kept the project running smoothly. Rob Fellman did wonders as a copy editor. Thanks to Bryan Kvet for indexing.

My greatest debts are to my sisters, Becky and Hannah, and my parents, Donna and Richard, for their unflagging support. This book is dedicated to them.

NOTES

INTRODUCTION: THE ART OF DYING

1. Sigmund Freud, "Mourning and Melancholia," in *The Standard Edition of the Complete Psychological Works of Sigmund Freud*, ed. and trans. James Strachey (London: Hogarth, 1957), 14:246. Although Freud only alludes to *Hamlet* in passing, when he typifies the attitude of the melancholic individual through the quotation "Use every man after his desert, and who shall scape whipping," Kenneth Reinhardt and Julia Lupton persuasively argue that Shakespeare is fundamental to his conception of melancholia: "Freud speaks through Hamlet, but *sotto voce*, in an 'undervoice' that projects Hamlet, the philosopher of melancholy, as Freud's ghostly double. The introjection and projection illustrated by the quotation are exemplified by Freud's treatment of the quotation." Kenneth Reinhardt and Julia Lupton, *After Oedipus: Shakespeare in Psychoanalysis* (Ithaca, NY: Cornell University Press, 1993), 26.

2. For Benjaminian readings of early modern drama in general and *Hamlet* in particular, see Reinhardt and Lupton, *After Oedipus*, 34–59; Hugh Grady, "Hamlet as Mourning-Play: A Benjaminesque Interpretation," *Shakespeare Studies* 36 (2008): 135–65; Susan Zimmerman, *The Early Modern Corpse and Shakespeare's Theatre* (Edinburgh: Edinburgh University Press, 2005), 195–97.

3. Hamlet was the only *Trauerspiel* hero "who corresponded to this dichotomy between the neo-antique and the medieval light in which the baroque saw the melancholic." Walter Benjamin, *The Origin of German Tragic Drama*, trans. John Osborne (London: Verso, 1998), 158.

4. Herbert Blau, *Take Up the Bodies: Theater at the Vanishing Point* (Urbana: University of Illinois Press, 1983).

5. Alice Rayner, *Ghosts: Death's Double and the Phenomena of Theater* (Minneapolis: University of Minnesota Press, 2006), xvii.

6. Rayner, *Ghosts*, xx.

7. Peggy Phelan, *Mourning Sex: Performing Public Memories* (New York: Routledge, 1997), 3.

8. Peggy Phelan, *Unmarked: The Politics of Performance* (New York: Routledge, 1993); Phelan, *Mourning Sex*; Joseph Roach, *Cities of the Dead:*

Circum-Atlantic Performance (New York: Columbia University Press, 1996); Nicole Loraux, *The Mourning Voice: An Essay on Greek Tragedy* (Ithaca, NY: Cornell University Press, 2002); Rebecca Schneider, *Performing Remains: Art and War in Times of Theatrical Reenactment* (New York: Routledge, 2011).

9. Phelan, *Mourning Sex*, 163.

10. William Shakespeare, *Hamlet*, in *The Norton Shakespeare*, ed. Stephen Greenblatt, Walter Cohen, Suzanne Gossett, Jean E. Howard, Katherine Eisaman Maus, and Gordon McMullan, 3rd ed. (New York: Norton, 2016), 1.5.99. Further references to Shakespeare's plays will be from this edition unless otherwise specified and given parenthetically.

11. According to Livy, Lucretia committed suicide following her rape by the king Sextus Tarquinius. Her death inspired a rebellion, which overthrew the Roman monarchy. Livy, *The History of Rome*, trans. B. O. Foster (Cambridge, MA: Harvard University Press, 1919), 1.57–59.

12. "*Sed ita haec causa ex utroque latere coartatur ut, si extenuatur homicidium, adulterium confirmetur; si purgatur adulterium, homicidium cumuletur* [But then the case is reduced to a dilemma: if the murder is less heinous, then the adultery is confirmed; if the adultery is extenuated, the charge of murder is aggravated]." Augustine, *City of God*, trans. George E. McCracken (Cambridge, MA: Harvard University Press, 1957), 1.19.

13. Though less explicit, different performance traditions that represent Gertrude's death as an accident or as a deliberate act to defy Claudius and protect Hamlet raise similar questions.

14. Most commentators suggest that he alludes to the litigation following the suicide of Sir James Hales. See Luke Wilson, "Hamlet, Hales V. Petit, and the Hysteresis of Action," *ELH* 60, no. 1 (1993): 17–55.

15. Q2 lacks a stage direction here.

16. Mark 8:34–35. All biblical quotations are from the Geneva Version unless otherwise noted.

17. Margareta de Grazia surveys the shifting (and sometimes incompatible) "modernities" to which *Hamlet* has been aligned and argues for a historicized approach to the play, one that decenters the Prince, in *"Hamlet" without Hamlet* (Cambridge: Cambridge University Press, 2007).

18. Amy Appleford offers a comprehensive introduction to the genre in the excellent *Learning to Die in London, 1380–1540* (Philadelphia: University of Pennsylvania Press, 2015), although, unlike me, she does not consider post-Reformation Protestant texts. Also see Mary Catherine O'Connor, *The Art of Dying Well: The Development of the* Ars Moriendi (New York: Columbia University Press, 1942); Nancy Lee Beaty, *The Craft of Dying: A Study of the Literary Tradition of the* Ars Moriendi *in England* (New Haven, CT: Yale University Press, 1970); David William Atkinson, *The English* Ars Moriendi

(New York: Peter Lang, 1992); Austra Reinis, *Reforming the Art of Dying: The Ars Moriendi in the German Reformation (1519–1528)* (Burlington, VT: Ashgate, 2007).

19. O'Connor, *The Art of Dying Well*, 56. O'Connor's monograph remains the most comprehensive pan-European survey and bibliography of *artes moriendi* texts.

20. O'Connor, *The Art of Dying Well*, 191.

21. This is not to deny that the deathbed sometimes functioned as an important site for the assertion of sectarian identity. See M. A. Overell, "The Reformation of Death in Italy and England, circa 1550," *Renaissance and Reformation/Renaissance et Reforme* 23, no. 4 (1999): 5–21. On texts that consider death in relation to gender and social status, see Lucinda M. Becker, *Death and the Early Modern Englishwoman* (Burlington, VT: Ashgate, 2003), esp. 103–28.

22. William Perkins, *A Salve for a Sicke Man: or, a Treatise Containing the Nature, Differences, and Kindes of Death* (Cambridge, 1595).

23. Peter Lake, *Moderate Puritans and the Elizabethan Church* (Cambridge: Cambridge University Press, 1982), 10.

24. Perkins, *A Salve for a Sicke Man*, 90.

25. Elaine Scarry, *The Body in Pain: The Making and Unmaking of the World* (Oxford: Oxford University Press, 1985), 4. By taking torture as her paradigmatic example of a painful situation, Scarry associates pain particularly with political oppression.

26. On the spatialization of the *artes moriendi*, see Kristen Poole, *Supernatural Environments in Shakespeare's England: Spaces of Demonism, Divinity, and Drama* (Cambridge: Cambridge University Press, 2011), 58–94.

27. Although Perkins and other writers typically gender dying figures as male, *artes moriendi* stress mortality as a universal experience and insist that their contents can and should be adapted to different circumstances. To reflect this universality, I use male and female pronouns interchangeably.

28. Perkins, *A Salve for a Sicke Man*, 58–59.

29. Phil. 3.10; 1 Cor. 12:27.

30. Appleford's recent book shows that this situation is changing in medieval and early Tudor studies. Two other notable recent analyses of early modern literature in relation to *artes moriendi* are Poole, *Supernatural Environments*; and Dennis Kezar, *Guilty Creatures: Renaissance Poetry and the Ethics of Authorship* (Oxford: Oxford University Press, 2001), 139–72.

31. Michael Neill, *Issues of Death: Mortality and Identity in English Renaissance Tragedy* (Oxford: Clarendon, 1997), 48.

32. Neill, *Issues of Death*, 35. Robert N. Watson similarly claims that classical philosophy offered a "rationale for exploring taboo topics, and a conveniently distant screen on which to project current doubts about Christian

providence and statecraft." Robert N. Watson, *The Rest Is Silence: Death as Annihilation in the English Renaissance* (Berkeley: University of California Press, 1994), 33.

33. "*Mors me sequitur, fugit vita; adversus hac me doce aliquid. Effice, ut ego mortem non fugiam, vita me non effugiat.*" Seneca, "On the Shortness of Life," in *Epistulae Morales*, trans. Richard M. Gummere (Cambridge, MA: Harvard University Press, 1917), XLIX.

34. G. R. Morgan, "A Critical Edition of Caxton's *The Art and Craft to Know Well to Die* and *Ars Moriendi* Together with the Antecedent Manuscript Material," PhD diss., Oxford University, 1972, 2:6.

35. Appleford, *Learning to Die*, 82.

36. Some commentators argue that the endorsement of suicide exposes contradictions within Stoic ethics. As Terrance Irwin notes, the Stoic projects of detachment aspire to separate the personal pursuit of virtue from external circumstances entirely. While this separation does not necessarily mean that suicide is to be condemned, it raises questions about why a true sage would ever find it necessary. See *Classical Thought* (Oxford: Oxford University Press, 1988), 177.

37. John Donne, *Biathanatos*, ed. Ernest W. Sullivan II (Newark: University of Delaware Press, 1984). On early modern responses to Stoic suicide, see Eric Langley, *Narcissism and Suicide in Shakespeare and His Contemporaries* (Oxford: Oxford University Press, 2009); Brian Cummings, *Mortal Thoughts: Religion, Secularity, and Identity in Shakespeare and Early Modern Culture* (Cambridge: Cambridge University Press, 2013), 252–65.

38. Perkins, *A Salve for a Sicke Man*, 169.

39. For instance, see William E. Engel, *Mapping Mortality: The Persistence of Melancholy and Memory in Early Modern England* (Amherst: University of Massachusetts Press, 1996); Watson, *The Rest Is Silence*.

40. Martin Heidegger, *Being and Time*, trans. John Macquarrie and Edward Robinson (New York: Harper & Row, 1962), 83 (H 56).

41. Heidegger, *Being and Time*, 294 (H 250). It is debatable how closely Heidegger's conceptions of death and authenticity can be tied to biological and anthropological accounts of mortality. *Being and Time* is insistent that the ontological phenomenon of death must be distinguished from the ontic one of "demise"; to die, in his sense, is very different from the mere biological process of becoming a corpse or from any of the customs and rituals that surround that process. Heidegger defines "demise" as what happens when Dasein "end[s] without authentically dying"—in other words, what we would think of as the biological death of the human (291 [H 247]). A particularly helpful discussion of the differences between death and demise appears in Carman Taylor, *Heidegger's Analytic: Interpretation, Discourse, and Authen-*

ticity in Being and Time (Cambridge: Cambridge University Press, 2003), 276–84.

42. Heidegger, *Being and Time*, 303 (H 258–59).

43. Heidegger, *Being and Time*, 311 (H 266).

44. Emmanuel Levinas, *God, Death, and Time*, trans. Bettina Tergo (Stanford, CA: Stanford University Press, 2000), 10.

45. Levinas, *God, Death, and Time*, 16–17.

46. "*At, nescio quomodo, verso deinde aliorsum aspectu, visus es eciam illi sanctissimus martir Erasmus, quem forte speciali venerabatur devocione, ea forma qua a carnificibus tortus depingi solet in ecclesiis, ipsis iam quasi renovates passionum torturis, iuxta iacere.*" *Henrici VI Angliae Regis Miracula Postuma*, ed. Paulius Grosjean (Brussels: Societe des Bollandistes, 1935), 100. The translation is from Eamon Duffy, *The Stripping of the Altars: Traditional Religion in England c.1400–c.1580* (New Haven, CT: Yale University Press, 1992), 180. In fact, Walter was able to evade death in this instance thanks to miraculous intervention.

47. John Jewel, *A defence of the Apologie of the Churche of Englande conteininge an answeare to a certaine booke lately set foorthe by M. Hardinge, and entituled, A confutation of &c* . . . (London, 1567), 311–12.

48. For instance, see my discussion of Thomas Bilney's execution in Chapter 3.

49. Hannah Arendt, *The Human Condition* (Chicago: University of Chicago Press, 1998), esp. 313–25.

50. Michel Foucault first articulates this idea in *The History of Sexuality, Volume 1: An Introduction* (New York: Vintage, 1978) and elaborates it further in *Society Must Be Defended, Lectures at the Collège de France 1975–76* (New York: Picador, 2003) and *Security, Territory, Population: Lectures at the Collège de France, 1977–78* (New York: Palgrave Macmillan, 2007).

51. Foucault, *The History of Sexuality, Volume 1*, 137.

52. Using slightly different terminology and taking Western imperialism rather than the Holocaust as his central example, Achille Mbembe encourages us to recognize that in many colonial situations, life-promoting forms of biopolitics are less important than the "necropolitics" that justifies and promotes imperialist terror, indigenous displacement, racial and ethnic violence, and genocide. See his "Necropolitics," *Public Culture* 15, no. 1 (2003): 11–40. Because of the colonialist focus of his analysis, Mbembe has had less of an impact on early modern studies than the other theorists I discuss. Nevertheless, his historical analyses of entire political systems that were grounded upon death are invaluable models for thinking about the place of death within the political more generally. Without discounting the unique horrors of colonial experience, I would suggest that we might productively look for other necropolitics at work in other contexts.

53. Giorgio Agamben, *Homo Sacer: Sovereign Power and Bare Life* (Stanford, CA: University of California Press, 1998), 109, 181. Note that Agamben uses the term "bare life" somewhat inconsistently, sometimes appearing to treat it as a synonym for *zoe* while at other times, as here, distinguishing it.

54. Predictably, the precise origin point for modernity turns out to be rather fungible. Foucault locates an important epistemic shift from sovereignty to governmentality in the seventeenth century (*The History of Sexuality, Volume 1*, 139). Arendt claims that the same period saw a devaluation of action in favor of contemplation, which eventually opened the space for biologically inflected manifestations of political economy, though the *animal laborans* does not gain true ascendency until the nineteenth century with the rise of secularization (*The Human Condition*, 320–25). Agamben suggests that sovereignty and bare life function transhistorically as two mutually supporting moments within any political system; nevertheless, when he asserts that the concentration camp is the "'nomos' of the modern," he implies both that manifestations of bare life are historically contingent and that there is a peculiarly intense formation specific to the modern moment (*Homo Sacer*, 166).

55. Paul Kottman, *A Politics of the Scene* (Stanford, CA: Stanford University Press, 2007); Patricia Cahill, *Unto the Breach: Martial Formations, Historical Trauma, and the Early Modern Stage* (Oxford: Oxford University Press, 2008); Eric Santner, *The Royal Remains: The Peoples' Two Bodies and the Endgames of Sovereignty* (Chicago: University of Chicago Press, 2011).

56. Giorgio Agamben, *The Highest Poverty*, trans. Adam Kotsko (Stanford, CA: Stanford University Press, 2013), 107.

57. Agamben, *The Highest Poverty*, 115.

58. See Appleford, *Learning to Die in London*, 104.

59. Roberto Esposito, *Communitas: The Origin and Destiny of Community*, trans. Timothy Campbell (Stanford, CA: Stanford University Press, 2010), 8.

60. Esposito, *Communitas*, 12.

61. For accounts of how executions were used to contest religious and political ideology in the period, see J. A. Sharpe, "'Last Dying Speeches': Religion, Ideology, and Public Execution in Seventeenth-Century England," *Past and Present* 107, no. 1 (1985): 144–67; T. W. Laquerer, "Crowds, Carnival, and the State in English Executions, 1604–1868," in *The First Modern Society: Essays in Honor of Lawrence Stone*, ed. Lee Beier, David Cannadine, and James Rosenheim (Cambridge: Cambridge University Press, 1989); Peter Lake and Michael Questier, *The Antichrist's Lewd Hat: Protestants, Papists, and Players in Post-Reformation England* (New Haven, CT: Yale University Press, 2002).

62. Stephen Greenblatt, *Renaissance Self-Fashioning: From More to Shakespeare* (Chicago: University of Chicago Press, 1980), 74–114. Kezar similarly discusses death as an act of self-fashioning in *Guilty Creatures*, 139–71.

63. Julia Lupton does not ascribe especial importance to executions or martrydoms, perhaps because she had already examined the Catholic martyrological tradition represented by *The Golden Legend* in her *Afterlives of the Saints: Hagiography, Typology, and Renaissance Literature* (Stanford: Stanford University Press, 1996).

64. Julia Lupton, *Citizen-Saints: Shakespeare and Political Theology* (Chicago: University of Chicago Press, 2005), 4.

65. On the politics of the exception, see Carl Schmitt, *Political Theology: Four Chapters on the Concept of Sovereignty* (Chicago: University of Chicago Press, 2005); Agamben, *Homo Sacer*. On its relevance to early modern political culture, see Graham Hammill and Julia Lupton, eds., *Political Theology and Early Modernity* (Chicago: University of Chicago Press, 2012).

66. For a survey of different editorial decisions, see Christopher Shirley, "Sodomy and Stage Directions in Christopher Marlowe's *Edward(s) II*," *SEL* 54, no. 2 (2014): 279–96.

67. For instance, see Patrick Ryan, "Marlowe's *Edward II* and the Medieval Passion Play," *Comparative Drama* 32, no. 4 (1998–1999): 465–95.

68. James Kuzner, *Open Subjects: English Renaissance Subjects, Modern Selfhoods, and the Virtue of Vulnerability* (Edinburgh: Edinburgh University Press, 2011); *Shakespeare as a Way of Life: Skeptical Practice and the Politics of Weakness* (New York: Fordham University Press, 2016).

69. Joseph Campana, *The Pain of Reformation: Spenser, Vulnerability, and the Ethics of Masculinity* (New York: Fordham University Press, 2012); Joseph Campana, "The Child's Two Bodies: Shakespeare, Sovereignty, and the End of Succession," *ELH* 81, no. 3 (2014): 811–39.

70. Kuzner, *Shakespeare as a Way of Life*, 6–7.

71. Philippe Ariès, *The Hour of Our Death*, trans. Helen Weaver (New York: Knopf, 1981), 583–601.

1. DYING BADLY: *DOCTOR FAUSTUS* AND THE PARODIC DRAMA OF BLASPHEMY

1. Christopher Marlowe, *Doctor Faustus*, ed. Michael Keefer, 2nd ed. (Peterborough, Ont.: Broadview, 2006), 5.2.33–36. Further references will be given parenthetically and are from the A text unless otherwise specified. I focus on this more predestinarian version of the play because it questions the status of human action and agency more insistently. However, I note significant variations in the B text when relevant. For discussion of textual issues, see Keefer's introduction (63–69).

2. For Calvinist readings, see Alan Sinfield, *Literature in Protestant England, 1560–1660* (Beckenham: Croom Helm, 1983), 116–20; Jonathan Dollimore, *Radical Tragedy: Religion, Ideology, and Power in the Drama of Shakespeare*

and His Contemporaries (Chicago: University of Chicago Press, 1984), 109–19; John Stachniewski, *The Persecutory Imagination: English Puritanism and the Literature of Religious Despair* (Oxford: Clarendon, 1991), 292–331. For accounts of how diverse religious cultures inform the theater, see Robert Hunter, *Shakespeare and the Mystery of God's Judgments* (Athens: University of Georgia Press, 1976), 44; Huston Diehl, *Staging Reform and Reforming the Stage: Protestantism and Popular Theater* (Ithaca, NY: Cornell University Press, 1997); and Jeffrey Knapp, *Shakespeare's Tribe: Church, Nation, and Theater in Renaissance England* (Chicago: University of Chicago Press, 2002). For a rebuttal of Stachniewski and other predestinarian readers, see T. McAlindon, "*Doctor Faustus:* The Predestination Theory," *English Studies* 76, no. 3 (1995): 215–20. For interesting recent readings of *Doctor Faustus* and non-Calvinist theologies, see Angus Fletcher, "*Doctor Faustus* and the Lutheran Aesthetic," *English Literary Renaissance* 35, no. 2 (2005): 187–209; and John Parker, "Faustus, Confession, and the Sins of Omission," *ELH* 18, no. 1 (2013): 29–59. For readings of Faustus as a freethinker, see Harry Levin, *The Overreacher: A Study of Christopher Marlowe* (Cambridge, MA: Harvard University Press, 1952); William Empson, *Doctor Faustus and the Censor:* The English Faust Book *and Marlowe's* Doctor Faustus (Oxford: Blackwell, 1987); and John S. Mebane, *Renaissance Magic and the Return of the Golden Age: The Occult Tradition and Marlowe, Jonson, and Shakespeare* (Lincoln: University of Nebraska Press, 1989), 113–36. Robert Ornstein and Andrew Duxfield split the difference and see *Doctor Faustus* as the site of contention between religious and secularizing forces. Robert Ornstein, "Marlowe and God: The Tragic Theology of *Doctor Faustus*," *PMLA* 83, no. 5 (1968): 1378–85; Andrew Duxfield, "'Resolve me of all ambiguities': Doctor Faustus and the Failure to Unify," *Early Modern Literary Studies* 16 (2007): 7.1–21.

3. "Our good lives always with Thee, from which when we are avert we are perverted." Augustine, *Confessions*, trans. William Watts, ed. W. H. D. Rouse (Cambridge, MA: Harvard University Press, 1912), 4.16.

4. Martin Luther asserts "free choice in all men alike has the same limitations: it can will nothing good." Martin Luther, *The Bondage of the Will. Luther and Erasmus: Free Will and Salvation*, trans. Philip S. Watson (Philadelphia: Westminster, 1969), 228. Similarly, Jean Calvin writes: "We hold that all human desires are evil, and we charge them with sin not in as far as they are natural, but because they are inordinate, and inordinate because nothing pure and upright can proceed from a corrupt and polluted nature." John Calvin, *Institutes of the Christian Religion*, trans. Henry Beveridge (London, 1599), 3.3.12.

5. J. C. Scaliger, *Poetices Libri Septem* (Santandrean, 1594), I.42; Mikhail Bakhtin, *The Dialogic Imagination*, trans. Michael Holquist (Austin: University

of Texas Press, 1981); Mikhail Bakhtin, *Rabelais and His World*, trans. Hélène Iswolsky (Bloomington: Indiana University Press, 1984).

6. Giorgio Agamben, *Profanations*, trans. Jeff Fort (New York: Zone, 2007), 41.

7. To be clear, I am not arguing that *Doctor Faustus* is, strictly speaking, a Calvinist play. But I do think it grapples with questions of human agency that became newly urgent in the wake of Calvinist articulations of predestinarian theology.

8. See Hugh Gazzard, "An Act to Restrain Abuses of Players (1606)," *Review of English Studies* 61, no. 251 (2010): 495–528.

9. On Elizabethan antitheatricality, see Jonas Barish, *The Anti-Theatrical Prejudice* (London: University of California Press, 1981), 80–131; Peter Lake and Michael Questier, *The Antichrist's Lewd Hat: Protestants, Papists, and Players in Post-Reformation England* (New Haven, CT: Yale University Press, 2002), 425–82. Diehl rightly notes that puritanism and antitheatricality are not synonymous (*Staging Reform and Reforming the Stage*, 5–8).

10. Paul Whitfield White, *Theatre and Reformation: Protestantism, Patronage, and Playing in Tudor England* (Cambridge: Cambridge University Press, 1993), 166.

11. On ancient Greek conceptions of *parodos*, see Fred W. Householder Jr., "αρωδια," *Classical Philology* 39, no. 1 (1944): 1–9.

12. See Mark Burde, "The *Parodia Sacra* Problem and Medieval Comic Studies," in *Laughter in the Middle Ages and Early Modern Times: Epistemology of a Fundamental Human Behavior, Its Meaning, and Consequences*, ed. Albrecht Classen (New York: de Gruyter, 2010), 224.

13. Martha Bayless, *Parody in the Middle Ages: The Latin Tradition* (Ann Arbor: University of Michigan Press, 1996), 211–12. Also see E. K. Chambers, *The Mediaeval Stage* (Oxford: Oxford University Press, 1903), 1:330; Bakhtin, *Rabelais and His World*, 13–15; Barbara Newman, *Medieval Crossover: Reading the Secular against the Sacred* (Notre Dame: University of Notre Dame Press, 2013), 168–69.

14. Scalinger, *Poetices Libri Septem*, I.42.

15. Margaret A. Rose, *Parody: Ancient, Modern, and Postmodern* (Cambridge: Cambridge University Press, 1993), 9–10.

16. Ben Jonson, *Every Man in His Humour*, folio version, ed. David Bevington, in *The Cambridge Edition of the Works of Ben Jonson*, vol. 4 (Cambridge: Cambridge University Press, 2012), 5.5.24.

17. *Tudor Royal Proclamations*, ed. Paul L. Hughes and James Francis Larkin (New Haven, CT: Yale University Press, 1964–69), 1:302. For details of the campaign against festivals of misrule, see Max Harris, *Sacred Folly: A New History of the Feast of Fools* (Ithaca, NY: Cornell University Press, 2011), 180–238.

18. Philip Stubbes, *The Anatomie of Abuses* (London: 1583), 244.

19. Stubbes, *The Anatomie of Abuses*, 236.

20. Stubbes, *The Anatomie of Abuses*, 237.

21. Plato, *The Republic*, trans. Paul Shorey (Cambridge, MA: Harvard University Press, 1942), 597e.

22. See, for instance, Michael Bristol, *Carnival and Theater: Plebeian Culture and the Structure of Authority in Renaissance England* (New York: Methuen, 1985), 150–55; and Suzan Last, "Marlowe's Literary Double Agency: *Doctor Faustus* as a Subversive Comedy of Error," *Renaissance and Reformation / Renaissance et Réforme* 24, no. 1 (2000): 26–27.

23. Mikhail Bakhtin, *The Dialogic Imagination*, 59.

24. Mikhail Bakhtin, *The Dialogic Imagination*, 60–61.

25. Burde, "The *Parodia Sacra* Problem," 234–40.

26. Agamben, *Profanations*, 48.

27. Agamben, *Profanations*, 42.

28. Although Agamben does not explicitly make the connection, his understanding of parodic mystery evokes the mystical tradition of negative theology associated with Pseudo-Dionysius the Aeropagite that seeks to produce an account of God through describing what he is not.

29. This locational instability is apparent even within Bakhtin's and Agamben's understandings of parody. In Bakhtin's account of the emergence of heteroglossia, populist appropriations of high culture understood on a vertical axis are figured as dialogues between different idiolects occurring on a horizontal axis. Though Agamben defines parody in terms of juxtaposition, his description of the mystery it responds to persistently evokes catabasis.

30. On the effect of the Reformation on *ars moriendi*, see Philippe Ariès, *The Hour of Our Death*, trans. Helen Weaver (New York: Knopf, 1981); Eamon Duffy, *The Stripping of the Altars: Traditional Religion in England c. 1400–c. 1580* (New Haven, CT: Yale University Press, 1992); Ralph Houlbrooke, *Death, Religion, and the Family in England* (Oxford: Oxford University Press, 2000); Brad S. Gregory, *Salvation at Stake: Christian Martyrdom in Early Modern England* (Cambridge, MA: Harvard University Press, 1999); and Austra Reinis, *Reforming the Art of Dying: The* Ars Moriendi *in the German Reformation (1519–1528)* (Burlington, VT: Ashgate, 2007). Appleford warns against reading the medieval tradition as homogenous and identifies different laicized and ascetic strands. For examples of Protestant attacks on Catholic superstition, see Thomas Becon, *The Sycke Mans Salve* (London: 1561), 176–83; William Perkins, *A Salve for a Sicke Man: or, a Treatise Containing the Nature, Differences, and Kindes of Death* (Cambridge, 1595), 84–94.

31. For cross-confessional comparisons of martyrs, see Gregory, *Salvation at Stake*; and Lake and Questier, *Lewd Hat*, 223–80.

32. For instance, see the dispute between Thomas More and John Foxe over Thomas Bilney's behavior during his execution. Thomas More, *The Co[n] futacyon of Tyndales Answere* (London, 1532), 2C4v; John Foxe, *The Unabridged Acts and Monuments Online* (Sheffield: HRI Online Publications, 2011), bk. 8, 1033.

33. Angus Fletcher suggests "Calvinists were living in the future anterior tense, acting now (in their present) so that they *will have been saved* (in their future)." Angus Fletcher, *Time, Space, and Motion in the Age of Shakespeare* (Cambridge, MA: Harvard University Press, 2007), 57.

34. Mary Catherine O'Connor, *The Art of Dying Well: The Development of the* Ars Moriendi (New York: Columbia University Press, 1942), 191.

35. *Here begynneth a treatyse how ye hye fader of heuen sendeth dethe to somon euery creature to come* (London, 1528).

36. David Bevington, *From Mankind to Marlowe* (Cambridge, MA: Harvard University Press, 1962), 162.

37. Bevington, *From Mankind to Marlowe*, 247.

38. W. Wager, *Enough Is as Good as a Feast*, ed. Seymour de Ricci (New York: G. D. Smith, 1920), 1401. Further references will be given parenthetically.

39. Compare Luther: "If [the ungodly] did good works for the sake of obtaining the Kingdom, they would never obtain it, but would rather belong among the ungodly who with an evil and mercenary eye 'seek their own' in God" (*The Bondage of the Will*, 152–53). Also see, on the tradition of blood money, John Parker, *The Aesthetics of Antichrist: From Christian Drama to Christopher Marlowe* (Ithaca, NY: Cornell University Press, 2007), 87–95.

40. See Ariès, *The Hour of Our Death*, 189–90; Lloyd Bonfield, *Devising, Dying, and Dispute: Probate Litigation in Early Modern England* (Burlington, VT: Ashgate, 2012), 22–25.

41. Becon, *The Sycke Mans Salve*, 147.

42. Different predestinarian sects assumed individuals would have different levels of knowledge about their election, so this uncertainty could manifest in a variety of different ways. For an account of different culturally available varieties of predestinarianism, see Sean Hughes, "The Problem of 'Calvinism': English Theologies of Predestination, c. 1580–1630," in *Belief and Practice in Reformation England*, ed. Susan Wabuda and Caroline Litzenberger (Aldershot: Ashgate, 1998). Though Wager obliquely registers the problem, the play is insufficiently interested in doctrinal niceties to be aligned with a specific sectarian position.

43. On the reception of Spiera in England and on the continent, see M. A. Overell, "The Reformation of Death in Italy and England, circa 1550," *Renaissance and Reformation/Renaissance et Reforme* 23, no. 4 (1999): 5–21;

Kenneth Sheppard, "Atheism, Apostasy, and the Afterlives of Francis Spira in Early Modern England," *The Seventeenth Century* 27, no. 4 (2012).

44. Nathaniel Woodes, *The Conflict of Conscience* (1581), ed. Herbert Davis and F. P. Wilson (London: Malone Society Reprints, 1952), 1977.

45. Woodes, *The Conflict of Conscience*, 2220.

46. For speculation on the reasons for the rewrite, see R. G. Hunter, *Shakespeare and the Mystery of God's Judgments*, 36.

47. Ruth Lunney, *Marlowe and the Popular Tradition: Innovation in the English Drama before 1595* (Manchester: Manchester University Press, 2002), 124–57.

48. This variety might superficially sound like Bakhtinian heteroglossia, but Faustus's actions rarely align with Bakhtin's account of parody. *Doctor Faustus* admittedly contains carnivalesque episodes, like the interruption of the Pope's feast, but it does not valorize Faustus's iconoclasm in any sustained manner.

49. For accounts of Faustus's actions in terms of demonic parody, see Stephen Greenblatt, *Renaissance Self-Fashioning* (Chicago: University of Chicago Press, 1980), 214; Pompa Banerjee, "I, Mephastophilis: Self, Other, and Demonic Parody in Marlowe's *Doctor Faustus*," *Christianity and Literature* 42, no. 2 (1993): 221–41.

50. Edward A. Snow, "Marlowe's *Doctor Faustus* and the Ends of Desire," in *Two Renaissance Mythmakers: Christopher Marlowe and Ben Jonson*, ed. Alvin Kernan (Baltimore, MD: Johns Hopkins University Press, 1977), 78.

51. Stachniewski, *The Persecutory Imagination*, 296–97. Note this speech is significantly reworked in the B text to allow more Arminian interpretations. On the theological effects of the revisions, see Leah Marcus, *Unediting the Renaissance: Shakespeare, Marlowe, Milton* (London: Routledge, 1996), 38–68.

52. Parker, *The Aesthetics of Antichrist*, 1–42.

53. Although as Parker notes, its classicism can be overstated. The speech also has significant apocryphal intertexts. By evoking Simon Magus's relationship with a Helen in the *Acts of Peter* and the Wisdom of Solomon, it troubles distinctions between classical and scriptural heritage. See Parker, *The Aesthetics of Antichrist*, 235–37.

54. Richard Halpern, "Marlowe's School of Night: *Doctor Faustus* and Capital," *ELH* 71, no. 2 (2005): 455–95, 119–21.

55. Lucian, *The Dialogues of the Dead*, in *Lucian VII*, trans. M. D. Macleod (Cambridge, MA: Harvard University Press, 1961), 5.409.

56. Mephastophilis endorses this possibility by promising Faustus that he will inflict as much punishment as he can on the old man's body (5.1.79).

57. And here Marlowe might be following the spirit of Lucian's *Dialogues*. Although the vision of Helen's skull can be accommodated with early

modern conceptions of *vanitas*, Lucian generally advocates a distinctively playful approach to death. In Dialogue 20, as other dead souls are stripped of their beauty, wealth, and pretentions, Menippus is allowed to take his "independence, plain speaking, cheerfulness, noble bearing and laughter" into the underworld (20.373).

58. Giorgio Agamben, *The Highest Poverty*, trans. Adam Kotsko (Stanford, CA: Stanford University Press, 2013), 109–22.

59. Michael Neill, *Issues of Death: Mortality and Identity in English Renaissance Tragedy* (Oxford: Clarendon, 1997), 207–11.

60. This reading, admittedly, seems less plausible in the B text, where the scholars confront Faustus's mutilated body (5.3).

61. Compare Augustine: "For [the second death of the damned] consists not in the separation of soul and body, but in the union of both in eternal punishment. There, by contrast to their present state, men will not be before death or after death, but always in death, and, for that reason, never living, never dead, but endlessly dying." Augustine, *The City of God against the Pagans*, trans. and ed. R. W. Dyson (Cambridge: Cambridge University Press, 1998), 13.11.

62. Troni Grande argues that such dilation is a touchstone of Marlovian poetics. Troni Grande, *Marlovian Tragedy: The Play of Dilation* (Lewisburg, PA: Bucknell University Press, 1999).

63. Graham Hammill, *Sexuality and Form: Caravaggio, Marlowe, and Bacon* (Chicago: University of Chicago Press, 200), 127.

2. DYING POLITICALLY: *EDWARD II* AND THE ENDS
OF DYNASTIC MONARCHY

1. The scholarship on politics and sexuality in *Edward II* is too extensive to survey fully here. But see, in particular, Alan Bray, *Homosexuality in Renaissance England* (New York: Columbia University Press, 1982); Jonathan Goldberg, *Sodometries: Renaissance Texts, Modern Sexualities* (Stanford, CA: Stanford University Press, 1992), 105–45; Stephen Orgel, *Impersonations: The Performance of Gender in Shakespeare's England* (Cambridge: Cambridge University Press, 1996), 46–48; Mario DiGangi, *The Homoerotics of Early Modern Drama* (Cambridge: Cambridge University Press, 1997), 107–15; Meredith Skura, "Marlowe's *Edward II*: Penetrating Language in Shakespeare's *Richard II*," *Shakespeare Survey* 50 (1997): 41–55; Curtis Perry, "The Politics of Access and Representations of the Sodomite King in Early Modern England," *Renaissance Quarterly* 53 (2000): 1054–83; Jonathan Crewe, "Disorderly Love: Sodomy Revisited in Marlowe's *Edward II*," *Criticism* 51, no. 3 (2009): 385–99.

2. Critical awareness of how deployments of sexuality further political projects can ultimately be traced back to Foucault, who distinguishes between

the premodern exercise of power through a "symbolics of blood" in support of sovereignty and a modern deployment of an "analytics of sexuality" in support of biopolitical governance. Michel Foucault, *The History of Sexuality, Volume 1: An Introduction* (New York: Vintage, 1978), 148. However, even in *The History of Sexuality*, sexuality was in fact just one regime through which bio-power, defined more generally as "a power to *foster* life or *disallow* it to the point of death," might be exercised (138).

3. Jean Bodin, *The Six Bookes of a Common-Weale*, trans. Richard Knowles (London, 1606), 84.

4. The following is merely an indication of how such debates could be couched in terms of perpetual sovereignty rather than a comprehensive historiographical survey. On the succession crisis, see Marie Axton, *The Queen's Two Bodies: Drama and the Elizabethan Succession* (London: Royal Historical Society, 1977); Christopher Highley, *Catholics Writing the Nation in Early Modern Britain and Ireland* (Oxford: Oxford University Press, 2008), 98–108. On the Jacobean union, see Neil Cuddy, "Anglo-Scottish Union and the Court of James I, 1603–1625," *Transactions of the Royal Historical Society* 39 (1989): 107–24. On disputes between Charles and Parliament, see Ernst Kantorowicz, *The King's Two Bodies: A Study in Mediaeval Political Theology* (Princeton, NJ: Princeton University Press, 1957), 20–23; Kevin Sharpe, *The Personal Rule of Charles I* (New Haven, CT: Yale University Press, 1992), 714–30.

5. The perceived ephemerality and instability of republics was a common argument against them. "The one thing most clearly known about republics was that they came to an end in time, whereas a theocentric universe perpetually affirmed monarchy, irrespective of the fate of particular monarchies." J. G. A. Pocock, *The Machiavellian Moment: Florentine Political Thought and the Atlantic Republican Tradition* (Princeton, NJ: Princeton University Press, 2003), 53–54. On literary manifestations of republican impulses, see Andrew Hadfield, *Shakespeare and Republicanism* (Cambridge: Cambridge University Press, 2005); Patrick Cheney, *Marlowe's Republican Authorship: Lucan, Liberty, and the Sublime* (Basingstoke: Palgrave Macmillan, 2009). Though I accept the argument that republicanism had a greater influence on Elizabethan political thought than has sometimes been recognized and that *Edward II* may contain republican elements, I consider the play to be interested primarily in monarchy as a perpetual institution.

6. Kantorowicz, *The King's Two Bodies*, 7–23.

7. See David Norbrook, "The Emperor's New Body? *Richard II*, Ernst Kantorowicz, and the Politics of Shakespeare Criticism," *Textual Practice* 10 (Summer 1996): 342.

8. See Lorna Hutson, "Imagining Justice: Kantorowicz and Shakespeare," *Representations* 106, no. 1 (2009): 118–42; Victoria Kahn, *The Future*

of Illusion: Political Theology and Early Modern Texts (Chicago: University of Chicago Press, 2014), 55–83. Axton also reads the theory as a restriction on royal power in the specific context of the succession question in *The Queen's Two Bodies*.

9. Giorgio Agamben, *Homo Sacer: Sovereign Power and Bare Life* (Stanford, CA: University of California Press, 1998), 96.

10. This is acknowledged by Axton, *The Queen's Two Bodies*, 20; Norbrook, "The Emperor's New Body," 343.

11. Julia Lupton links Kantorowicz's conception of the crown's minority to modern environmentalist characterizations of the earth as a rights-bearing entity requiring stewardship in *Thinking with Shakespeare: Essays on Politics and Life* (Chicago: University of Chicago Press, 2011), 212–13. Campana does not discuss Kantorowicz's treatment of minority but arrives at a rather similar account of how children can become symbols of sovereignty in Joseph Campana, "The Child's Two Bodies: Shakespeare, Sovereignty, and the End of Succession," *ELH* 81, no. 3 (2014): 811–39.

12. Kantorowicz, *The King's Two Bodies*, 378.

13. Kantorowicz, *The King's Two Bodies*, 372–73.

14. Kantorowicz, *The King's Two Bodies*, 379.

15. John Cowell, *The Interpreter: Or Book Containing the Signification of Words* (Cambridge: 1607), Qq1r. *The Interpreter*, which denigrates the common law and Parliament in favor of the ecclesiastical courts and the prerogative, was condemned by the Commons for its quasi-absolutist account of royal power and then censured by royal proclamation in 1610. For a discussion of the arguments around its suppression, see Cyndia Susan Clegg, *Press Censorship in Jacobean England* (Cambridge: Cambridge University Press, 2001), 137–43. Clegg plausibly argues that the furor around Cowell's book was motivated more by political exigencies than by any truly radical definitions and suggests that it may have remained in circulation.

16. For example, the Master of the Ward of Courts and Liberties is required "not to take or receiue of any person any gift or reward in any case or mater depending before him, or wherein the king shall be party, whereby any preiudice, losse, hinderance, or disherison shall be or grow to the king." Cowell, *The Interpreter*, Vv2r.

17. For instance, Edmond Borlase records a 1644 petition from Irish Protestants, who complain that Charles is acting to the disherison of his crown by failing to suppress the Irish rebellion, in *The History of the Execrable Irish Rebellion* (London, 1680), 63. John Digby, Earl of Bristol, justifies his Civil War royalism on the grounds that "The Militia belongeth to the King, as unseparable from the Crown, without which he cannot protect nor punish, withstand Enemies or suppress Rebels; The Lords and Commons cannot

assent in Parliament to any thing that tends to the disherison of the Crown."
John Digby, *An Apology of John, Earl of Bristol* (s.l., 1657), Appendix, 20.

18. Lee Edelman, *No Future: Queer Theory and the Death Drive* (Durham, NC: Duke University Press, 2004), esp. 1–31.

19. See Andrew Hadfield, *Shakespeare and Renaissance Politics* (London: Thompson Learning, 2004), 40. The exception that proves the rule is Plowden's *Treatise of Succession*, which argues that the king is uniquely barred from altering the line of his succession away from his "natural" inheritors (Cotton MS Caligula B. IV). However, precisely because the text argued for an understanding of dynasty that would have placed the descent of the crown outside the control of any monarch, it could only circulate covertly, in manuscript form. See Marie Axton, "The Influence of Plowden's Succession Treatise," *Huntingdon Quarterly Library* 37, no. 3 (1974): 209–26.

20. Robert Filmer, *Patriarcha, or the Natural Power of Kings* (London, 1680). On Filmer's relation to his intellectual contexts, see James Daly, *Sir Robert Filmer and English Political Thought* (Toronto: University of Toronto Press, 1979), 15–27.

21. Margreta de Grazia, *"Hamlet" without Hamlet* (Cambridge: Cambridge University Press, 2007); Katherine Eisaman Maus, *Being and Having in Shakespeare* (Oxford: Oxford University Press, 2013).

22. Christopher Marlowe, *Edward II*, ed. Mathew R. Martin (Peterborough, Ont.: Broadview, 2010), 1.1–2. Further references to the play will be given parenthetically.

23. Goldberg, *Sodometries*, 123; Digangi, *The Homoerotics of Early Modern Drama*, 108.

24. For instance, Bray argues that "Marlowe describes in this play what could be a sodomitical relationship, but he places it wholly within the incompatible conventions of Elizabethan friendship, in a tension which he never allows to be resolved." Alan Bray, "Homosexuality and the Signs of Male Friendship in Elizabethan England," *History Workshop Journal* 29 (1990): 10. Goldberg (*Sodometries*, 123) disagrees, arguing the play "institutes a sodomitical regime" that renders all interpersonal relations sodomical. Perry ("The Politics of Access") demonstrates how *Edward II* negotiates the changing political role of the favorite through established discourses of friendship and sodomy that work in tandem. Crewe ("Disorderly Love," 392) calls for recognition that the playtext also evidences "phobic accompaniments and traumatic consequences to male-male sexual relations."

25. Though my turn from sex to death here might superficially appear to recapitulate Edelman's distinction between heteronormative reproductive futurity and the queered death drive, important differences exist between what count as legitimate sexual and social relations in the sixteenth century

and the present. Though heterosexual marriage was necessary for the production of children, there is extensive evidence of a widespread cultural distrust of female sexuality and a corresponding privileging of male-male homosocial relations and fantasies of patrilineal parthenogenesis. See Janet Adelman, *Suffocating Mothers: Fantasies of Maternal Origin in Shakespeare's Plays*, Hamlet *to* The Tempest (New York: Routledge, 1992).

26. Perry ("The Politics of Access," 1065) suggests that from an Elizabethan perspective, this appeal to tradition is specious: "Though Mortimer Junior authorizes his rebellion with reference to long-established hierarchies of blood, it is Edward himself whose political ideas seem most traditional."

27. This commitment is more explicit in the historical record, where the barons complain that Edward "acted 'in disherison of the Crown.'" Kantorowicz, *The King's Two Bodies*, 373.

28. Marie Rutkoski similarly argues Mortimer's threat to the prince is sexualized in "Breeching the Boy in Marlowe's *Edward II*," *SEL: Studies in English Literature, 1500–1900* 46, no. 2 (2006): 293.

29. See Christopher Marlowe, *Edward II*, ed. W. Moelwyn Merchant (New York: Hill and Wang, 1968), 3.2.162–3n.

30. Ps. 80:14–15.

31. Grande notices the similarities and reads both extended death scenes as experiments with the form of tragedy. Troni Grande, *Marlovian Tragedy: The Play of Dilation* (Lewisburg, PA: Bucknell University Press, 1999), 110–11.

32. Plowden, *Commentaries*, Hill v. Grange, 177a. This passage is discussed by Kantorowicz, *The King's Two Bodies*, 407.

33. Plowden, *Treatise of Succession*, 3r.

34. "The scatological site of punishment for the sodomite is further fabricated to parody and ridicule anal eroticism with the filth and waste of the castle's cloaca." David Stymeist, "Status, Sodomy, and the Theater in Marlowe's *Edward II*," *SEL: Studies in English Literature, 1500–1900* 44, no. 2 (2004): 245.

35. Discussing the House of Alma in Spenser's *Faerie Queene*, Schoenfeldt takes modern critics to task for reading the early modern body primarily in terms of genital sexuality, when in many instances ingestion, digestion, and excretion may be just as symbolically significant. Michael Schoenfeldt, *Bodies and Selves in Early Modern England: Physiology and Inwardness in Spenser, Shakespeare, Herbert, and Milton* (Cambridge: Cambridge University Press, 2000), 62–63.

36. See Skura, "Marlowe's *Edward II*," 44–45; Mark Thornton Burnett, *Edward II* and Elizabethan Politics," in *Marlowe, History, and Sexuality*, ed. Paul Whitfield White (New York: AMS, 1998), 96.

37. Agamben, *Homo Sacer*, 1.

38. Agamben, *Homo Sacer*, 109.

39. "If he that attempteth to depose his Soveraign, be killed, or punished by him for such attempt, he is author of his own punishment, as being by the Institution, Author of all his Soverign shall do." Thomas Hobbes, *Leviathan*, ed. Richard Tuck (Cambridge: Cambridge University Press, 1991), 122. My reading of Hobbes is heavily influenced by Roberto Esposito, *Communitas: The Origin and Destiny of Community*, trans. Timothy Campbell (Stanford, CA: Stanford University Press, 2010), 20–34.

40. Marjorie Garber, "'Here's Nothing Writ': Scribe, Script, and Circumscription in Marlowe's Plays," *Theater Journal* 36, no. 3 (1984): 319–20.

41. For a survey of different editorial decisions, see Christopher Shirley, "Sodomy and Stage Directions in Christopher Marlowe's *Edward(s) II*," *SEL* 54, no. 2 (2014): 279–96.

42. Raphael Holinshed, *The First and Second Volumes of Chronicles* (London, 1587), 6:341.

43. Orgel, *Impersonations*, 47; Andrew Hadfield, "Marlowe's Representation of the Death of Edward II," *Notes and Queries* 56, no. 254 (2009): 40–41.

44. For readings of Edward's death as *contrapasso*, see Patrick Ryan, "Marlowe's *Edward II* and the Medieval Passion Play," *Comparative Drama* 32, no. 4 (1998–1999): 478; Stymeist, "Status, Sodomy, and the Theater," 245–46; Crewe, "Disorderly Love," 392–96. For arguments that sodomy passes to Mortimer, see DiGangi, *The Homoerotics of Early Modern Drama*, 114; Rutkoski, "Breeching the Boy," 295.

45. Hadfield, "Marlowe's Representation," 41.

46. Rutkoski, who argues that Marlowe's presentation of Prince Edward blurs distinctions between the homoerotic narcissism characteristic of Edward II's relation to his minions and heterosexual reproductive narcissism and so undermines the distinction between dynasty and eroticized challenges to dynasty, is a notable exception ("Breeching the Boy," 288–89).

47. For readings of Edward's death as a sincere or parodied evocation of martyrdom, see Ryan, "Marlowe's *Edward II* and the Medieval Passion Play"; Tom Pettitt, "'Skreaming like a pigge halfe stickt': Vernacular Topoi in the Carnivalesque Martyrdom of Edward II," *Orbis Litterarum* 60 (2005): 79–108.

48. Benjamin Parris, "'The Body Is with the King, But the King Is Not with the Body': Sovereign Sleep in *Hamlet* and *Macbeth*," *Shakespeare Studies* 40 (2012): 101–42.

49. I thank Patricia Cahill for this suggestion.

50. Lee Edelman suggests a somewhat similar dynamic within *Hamlet* in "Against Survival: Queerness in a Time That's Out of Joint," *Shakespeare Quarterly* 62, no. 2 (2011): 148–69. The Ghost saddles the prince with the impossible task of "liv[ing] from the outset an after-life as ambassador of the

dead without, in the process, becoming a mere ambassador of death" (167) and so demonstrates the untenable position in which the ideology of reproductive futurity places the child. However, where such demands precipitate a crisis for Hamlet, they appear to empower Edward III, perhaps suggesting ways that a figure might be able to take on the negativity Edelman discovers within queerness while embodying dynastic hope. This might suggest that Edelman's conception of the queer is less constitutively radical than he wants to argue or at least that its nearest analogues within Elizabethan texts are more amenable to normative constructions of futurity.

51. Lise Hull, *Britain's Medieval Castles* (Westport, CT: Praeger, 2006), 55.

52. On the disciplinary effect of executions, see Michel Foucault, *Discipline and Punish: The Birth of the Prison*, trans. Alan Sheridan (New York: Pantheon, 1977); J. A. Sharpe, "'Last Dying Speeches': Religion, Ideology, and Public Execution in Seventeenth-Century England," *Past and Present* 107, no. 1 (1985): 144–67.

53. Cheney, *Marlowe's Republican Authorship*, 148–64; Thomas A. Anderson, "Surpassing the King's Two Bodies: The Politics of Staging the Royal Effigy in Marlowe's *Edward II*," *Shakespeare Bulletin* 32, no. 4 (2014): 585–611.

54. Cheney, *Marlowe's Republican Authorship*, 160. Anderson ("Surpassing the King's Two Bodies," 600–1) expands on Cheney and notes that Marlowe departs from the *Chronicle* sources by presenting Isabella's arrest and Mortimer's execution as simultaneous. In doing so, he simultaneously gestures toward absolutism and republicanism.

55. Anderson, "Surpassing the King's Two Bodies," 597.

56. While making a case for an original staging that he thinks plausible, Anderson acknowledges that his claims about the appearance of an actor as effigy are necessarily speculative.

57. Alan C. Dessen and Leslie Thomson, *A Dictionary of Stage Directions in English Drama, 1580–1642* (Cambridge: Cambridge University Press, 1999), s.v. "hearse."

58. Jonathan Goldberg, *Sodometries*, 125–26.

59. Anderson, "Surpassing the King's Two Bodies," 602.

60. Susan Zimmerman, *The Early Modern Corpse and Shakespeare's Theatre* (Edinburgh: Edinburgh University Press, 2005), 93.

61. Elsewhere, Zimmerman (*The Early Modern Corpse*, 148–49) discusses how Webster exploits the analogous performance techniques used to represent corpses and effigies to unsettle the audience's perception of theatrical reality in *The Duchess of Malfi*.

62. This seems especially true if Richard Rowland is right that the sledge used by Marlowe's company to represent Edward's hearse is the same

they used to represent criminals being conveyed to execution. See Christopher Marlowe, *Edward II*, in *The Works and Life of Christopher Marlowe*, ed. Richard Rowland (New York: Gordian, 1930), 6:206n52.

63. Dessen and Thomson, *A Dictionary of Stage Directions in English Drama*, note that Henslowe's inventory included a number of prop heads (s.v. "head").

64. Stephen Greenblatt, "Invisible Bullets," in *Shakespearean Negotiations: The Circulation of Social Energy in Renaissance England* (Berkeley: University of California Press, 1989).

3. DYING REPRESENTATIVELY: *RICHARD II* AND THE POLITICS OF MIMETIC MORTALITY

1. On the parallels between *Edward II* and *Richard II*, see James Shapiro, *Rival Playwrights: Marlowe, Jonson, Shakespeare* (New York: Columbia University Press, 1991), 85; Madhavi Menon, "*Richard II* and the Taint of Metonymy," *ELH* 70, no. 3 (2003): 653–75.

2. For a representative (but in no way comprehensive) sampling of sympathetic and unsympathetic critical responses to Richard's predicament, see E. M. Tillyard, *Shakespeare's History Plays* (New York: Macmillan, 1946), 244–64; Ernst Kantorowicz, *The King's Two Bodies: A Study in Mediaeval Political Theology* (Princeton, NJ: Princeton University Press, 1957); Harry Berger, *Imaginary Audition: Shakespeare on Stage and Page* (Berkeley: University of California Press, 1989); Zenón Luis-Martínez, "Shakespeare's Historical Drama as *Trauerspiel*: *Richard II* and After," *ELH*, 75, no. 3 (2008); Lorna Hutson, "Imagining Justice: Kantorowicz and Shakespeare," *Representations* 106 (2009); David Womersley, *Divinity and State* (Oxford: Oxford University Press, 2010), 285–99; Eric Santner, *The Royal Remains: The Peoples' Two Bodies and the Endgames of Sovereignty* (Chicago: University of Chicago Press, 2011), 43–50.

3. Kantorowicz, *The King's Two Bodies*, 24–41 (on *Richard II*), 42–86 (on Christ-centered models of kingship).

4. Andrew Hadfield draws attention to the lack of legitimate rulers within Shakespeare's history plays in *Shakespeare and Renaissance Politics* (London: Arden Shakespeare, 2004), 40–41.

5. Giorgio Agamben, *Homo Sacer: Sovereign Power and Bare Life* (Stanford, CA: University of California Press, 1998), 109.

6. Hannah Arendt, *The Human Condition* (Chicago: University of Chicago Press, 1998), 32. Arendt acknowledges that this sphere of action is necessarily elitist and dependent on the work of those excluded from it (especially women and slaves).

7. Arendt, *The Human Condition*, 7.

8. Arendt, *The Human Condition*, 46.

9. For Arendt's discussion of the Middle Ages, see *The Human Condition*, 33–34. Michel Foucault—influenced in part by Arendt's models, though questioning her value judgments—provides a similar genealogy of biopower in postclassical Europe but opposes it to the figure of the monarch rather than the *agora*. He describes the supersession of royal sovereignty by forms of social governmentality and, like Arendt, claims that systems designed to produce conformity across populations gradually displace agonistic interactions between privileged individuals. See especially *Society Must Be Defended, Lectures at the Collège de France 1975–76* (New York: Picador, 2003), 25–40. Agamben (who acknowledges Arendt's influence explicitly) is also insightful on the similarities and differences between classical and medieval forms of sovereign power (*Homo Sacer*, 91–94).

10. Jacques Derrida, *Specters of Marx*, trans. Peggy Kamuf (New York: Routledge, 2006), xix. Rayner suggests that the propensity of ghosts to produce temporal disruptions will be more marked in the space of the theater, since performances must navigate the mismatch between different time schemes. Alice Rayner, *Ghosts: Death's Double and the Phenomena of Theater* (Minneapolis: University of Minnesota Press, 2006), 1–32.

11. "Haunt, v.," definition 5b, *OED Online*.

12. "Haunt, v.," definitions 1–3.

13. Death as king is a standard motif of macabre art, represented by images of "The dark monarch's progress . . . a formal triumph *all'antica*: mounted in splendor, like the monarch of some Renaissance royal entry, King Death rides through the world on a magnificent parade chariot." Michael Neill, *Issues of Death: Mortality and Identity in English Renaissance Tragedy* (Oxford: Clarendon, 1997), 89, 88–101. See also Philippe Ariès, *The Hour of Our Death*, trans. Helen Weaver (New York: Knopf, 1981), 118–19.

14. Luis-Martínez, "Shakespeare's Historical Drama as *Trauerspiel*," 689.

15. *Macbeth* 5.5.24–26.

16. On the *danse macabre*, see Neill, *Issues of Death*, 51–88; Elina Gertsman, *The Dance of Death in the Middle Ages: Image, Text, Performance* (Turnhout: Brepols, 2010); Amy Appleford, *Learning to Die in London, 1380–1540* (Philadelphia: University of Pennsylvania Press, 2015), 83–97.

17. Luis-Martínez, "Shakespeare's Historical Drama as *Trauerspiel*," 689. On anamorphosis as a trope, see also Slavoj Žižek, *Looking Awry: An Introduction to Jacques Lacan through Popular Culture* (Cambridge, MA: MIT Press, 1991), 9–12.

18. Regina Schwarz, for instance, argues persuasively that some believers experienced the rejection of transubstantiation as a loss of Christ's immediate presence. See Regina Schwarz, *Sacramental Poetics: When God Left the World* (Stanford, CA: Stanford University Press, 2008).

19. On early modern traditions of *imitatio Christi* in England, see Nandra Perry, *Imitatio Christi: The Poetics of Piety in Early Modern England* (Notre Dame, IN: University of Notre Dame Press, 2014); and Adrian Streete, *Protestantism and Drama in Early Modern England* (Cambridge: Cambridge University Press, 2009).

20. Mark 8:34–35.

21. Romans 6:5.

22. Thomas á Kempis, *The Imitation of Christ*, ed. and trans. Joseph N. Tylenda (New York: Vintage, 1998).

23. Jacobus de Voragine, [*Legenda aurea sanctorum, sive, Lombardica historia*], trans. William Caxton (London: 1483), 347. On this passage, see Brad S. Gregory, *Salvation at Stake: Christian Martyrdom in Early Modern England* (Cambridge, MA: Harvard University Press, 1999), 51.

24. In G. R. Morgan, "A Critical Edition of Caxton's *The Art and Craft to Know Well to Die* and *Ars Moriendi* Together with the Antecedent Manuscript Material," PhD diss., Oxford University, 1972, 2:37.

25. Discussing the wealthy lay owners of manuscripts of *The Crafte*, Appleford suggests "a continuing command over material riches can offer almost as good a basis for mortification as its renunciation, providing the same, rare resources available to members of wealthy Carthusian houses—silence, solitude, freedom from worry over material necessities—while also requiring a focus on inner self-separation from the world made only more demanding by the absence of the institutional props available." Appleford, *Learning to Die*, 104.

26. Green records thirteen English translations and two paraphrases of á Kempis between 1500 and 1700. See Ian Green, *Print and Protestantism in Early Modern England* (Oxford: Oxford University Press, 2000), 303.

27. Rogers claims that "I haue left out nothing but what might be offensiue to the godlie. Yet is it neither for quantitie much, nor for number aboue foure sentences" in "A second Epistle concerning the translation and correction of this Booke" in *Of the imitation of Christ, three, both for wisedome, and godlines, most excellent bookes; made 170. yeeres since by one Thomas of Kempis, and for the worthines thereof oft since translated out of Latine into sundrie languages by diuers godlie and learned men: now newlie corrected, translated, and with most ample textes, and sentences of holie Scripture illustrated* (London: 1580), 10. For an account of Rogers and of other Protestant respondents to the *imitatio Christi* tradition, see Elizabeth K. Hudson, "English Protestants and the *Imitatio Christi*, 1580–1620," *Sixteenth Century Journal* 19 (1988): 541–58; Streete, *Protestantism and Drama*, 14–30; Perry, *Imitatio Christi*, 22–48.

28. Rogers, "The first Epistle of the Translator touching Christian imitation in general, to the faithful Imitators of our Sauior Christ in England," in *Of the imitation of Christ*, 3.

29. Rogers, "First Epistle," 6.
30. Rogers, "First Epistle," 6–7.
31. Henry of Hasselt was a kind of devout hunger artist notorious for public fasting. Roger's sources for his story is Johann Weyer, *Liber: Item, De Commentitiis Ieiuniis* (Basileae: Ex Officina Oporiniana, 1582), 127–28.
32. Rogers explains further by saying "Our Sauior Christ therefore in those things which he did as a God must religiouslie be worshipped; and folowed zelouslie in what he did as a man. He that loueth and hateth what Christ as a God, doth loue and detest, imitates Christ as much as man maie imitate God. He that doth that which Christ did as a man, doth folowe Christ as a Christian should" (First Epistle, 7).
33. John 10:18.
34. "The spirit of the Mediator showed how it was through no punishment of sin that He came to the death of the flesh, because He did not leave it against His will, but because He willed, when He willed, as He willed. For because He is so commingled [with the flesh] by the Word of God as to be one, He says: 'I have power to lay down my life, and I have power to take it again. No man takes it from me, but I lay down my life that I might take it again.' And, as the Gospel tells us, they who were present were most astonished at this, that after that [last] word, in which He set forth the figure of our sin, He immediately gave up His spirit." Augustine, *On the Trinity*, trans. Arthur West Haddan, in *A Select Library of the Nicene and Post-Nicene Fathers of the Christian Church*, vol. 3 (Edinburgh: T&T Clark, 1979), bk. 4, chap. 13.
35. 1 Corinthians 11:1.
36. Compare μιμηταί μου γίνεσθε, καθὼς κἀγὼ χριστοῦ. According to the *OED*, the verb "follow" was used between c. 1386 and 1675 to mean "To conform to in likeness, resemble, take after; imitate or copy." In this sense, it predates the word "imitate," which first appears in English around the 1530s. See "follow v., def 8b" and "imitate v," *OED Online*.
37. On More and Bilney, see J. A. Guy, *The Public Career of Sir Thomas More* (New Haven, CT: Yale University Press, 1980).
38. Thomas More, *The Confutation of Tyndale's Answer*, ed. Louis Schuster, Richard Marius, James Lusardi, and Richard Schoek, in *The Complete Works of Thomas More*, vols. 8–10 (New Haven, CT: Yale University Press, 1973).
39. See Guy, *The Public Career of Sir Thomas More*, 167–68.
40. Brian Cummings, *Mortal Thoughts: Religion, Secularity, and Identity in Shakespeare and Early Modern Culture* (Oxford: Oxford University Press, 2013), 136.
41. Roberto Esposito, *Communitas: The Origin and Destiny of Community*, trans. Timothy Campbell (Stanford, CA: Stanford University Press, 2010), 5.
42. Esposito, *Communitas*, 11.

43. Esposito, *Communitas*, 10.

44. Esposito, *Communitas*, 9.

45. For sacramental interpretations, see Kantorowicz, *The King's Two Bodies*, 35; Walter Pater, *Appreciations* (London: Macmillan, 1890), 205–6. For a reading of the scene in terms of political strategy, see Andrew Leggatt, *Shakespeare's Political Drama: The History Plays and the Roman Plays* (London: Routledge, 1988), 68. For a demonic reading, see Robert M. Schuler, "De-coronation and Demonic Meta-Ritual in *Richard II*," *Exemplaria* 17 (2005): 169–214.

46. Raphael Holinshed, *The Third Volume of Chronicles* (London: 1587), 503.

47. Holinshed, *Chronicles*, 503.

48. Holinshed, *Chronicles*, 505.

49. Maus similarly reads the play as a meditation on shifting relationships between humans and possessions. Katherine Eisaman Maus, *Being and Having in Shakespeare* (Oxford: Oxford University Press, 2013), 1–37.

50. Christopher Pye, *The Regal Phantasm* (London: Routledge, 1990), 82–105.

51. Marjorie Garber, *Shakespeare's Ghost Writers* (New York: Methuen, 1987), 20.

52. Since Richard is repeatedly condemned for placing the realm "in farm," we could read the social debts between Richard and his courtiers as personalized manifestations of a larger breakdown in the political and economic systems traditionally used to distribute resources between king and country.

53. Annabel Patterson, *Reading Holinshed's Chronicles* (Chicago: University of Chicago Press, 1994), 112–17.

54. On the early history of English parliaments, see J. R. Maddicott, *The Origins of the English Parliament, 924–1327* (Oxford: Oxford University Press, 2004), esp. 226–232.

55. G. L. Harriss, *King, Parliament, and Public Finance in Medieval England to 1369* (Oxford: Clarendon, 1975), 514.

56. *Modus Tenendi Parliamentum*, in *Parliamentary Texts of the Later Middle Ages*, ed. Nicholas Pronay and John Taylor (Oxford: Clarendon, 1980), 89–90.

57. Matthew Giancarlo, *Parliament and Literature in Late Medieval England* (Cambridge: Cambridge University Press, 2007), 51.

58. To get a sense of the problem, compare Pronay and Taylor, *Parliamentary Texts*, 22–31; with Kathryn Kerby-Fulton and Steven Justice, "Reformist Intellectual Culture in the English and Irish Civil Service: The *Modus Tenendi Parliamentum* and Its Literary Relations," *Traditio* 53 (1998): 149–202.

59. Giancarlo, *Parliament and Literature*, 34–46.

60. On the limitations of parliamentary representation in the Elizabethan and Jacobean eras, see Oliver Arnold, *The Third Citizen: Shakespeare's Theater and the Early Modern House of Commons* (Baltimore, MD: Johns Hopkins University Press, 2007), 47–75.

61. See Pronay and Taylor, *Parliamentary Texts*, 56–57.

62. Richard experiences the desertion of the Welsh in physiological terms. When Aumerle notes his pallor, Richard replies: "But now the blood of twenty thousand men/Did triumph in my face, and they are fled;/And, till so much blood thither come again,/Have I not reason to look pale and dead?" (3.2.71–74). King and soldiers are united in a body politic by the exchange of blood. However, this body appears constitutionally anemic; there is not enough blood to go around, and the threat of death (signified alternatively by the lack of blood and by the excess of blood) is always present. The notional exchanges of mutual favors that bound Richard to his courtiers, along with the unceasing demands that threaten to consume the courtly economy with guilt, are recast in far more material terms as literal obligations that bind subjects to deal or experience death for their king under a sovereignty of blood.

63. Berger, *Imaginary Audition*, 64–67. Compare *Doctor Faustus*, "O soul, be changed into little water drops/And fall into the ocean, ne'er to be found!" (5.2.110–11); "Was this the face that launch'd a thousand ships/And burnt the topless towers of Ilium?" (5.1.90–91).

64. Phyllis Rackin, *Stages of History: Shakespeare's English Chronicles* (Ithaca, NY: Cornell University Press, 1990), 94.

65. Lister Matheson traces the parallels between Richard and Becket in "English Chronicle Contexts for Shakespeare's Death of Richard II," in *From Page to Performance: Essays in Early English Drama*, ed. John Alford (East Lansing: Michigan State University Press, 1995), 211–12. I am grateful to Stephen Campbell for drawing my attention to similarities between Richard II and Henry VI (especially after the Reformation put an end to Henry's progress toward sanctification). For a recent survey of critical assessments of parallels between Richard and Elizabeth, see Jason Scott-Warren, "Was Elizabeth I Richard II? The Authenticity of Lambarde's 'Conversation,'" *Review of English Studies* (2012).

66. The precise relationship between the Essex rebellion and Shakespeare's play is uncertain. For a balanced assessment of the possibilities, see Scott-Warren, "Was Elizabeth I Richard II?"

67. Thomas Hobbes, *Leviathan*, ed. Richard Tuck (Cambridge: Cambridge University Press, 1991), 120–21.

68. See Patrick Colinson, "*De Republica Anglorum*: Or, History with the Politics Put Back," in *Elizabethan Essays* (London: Hambledon, 1994), 1–29.

69. Compare Genesis 4:11: "Now therefore thou art cursed from the earth, which hath opened her mouth to receive thy brother's blood from thy hand."

70. For example, Bede says, "Some understand . . . the killing of Abel as the passion of the Lord and Savior"; Origen asks us to "suppose that the verse 'The voice of your brother's blood is crying to me from the ground' is said as well for each of the martyrs, the voice of whose blood cries to God from the ground." Bede, *Homilies on the Gospels* 1.14; Origen, *Exhortation to Martyrdom* 50; both quoted and translated in Andrew Louth, ed., *Genesis 1–11*, Ancient Christian Commentary on Scripture (Downers Grove, IL: InterVarsity, 2001), 106–8.

71. Drew Daniel, "Joy of the Worm: Suicidal Slapstick in *Antony and Cleopatra*," unpublished manuscript, 15. I am grateful to Drew for sharing this with me.

72. For discussion of post-Reformation reception of Mary in England, see Regina Buccola and Lisa Hopkins, eds., *Marian Moments in Early Modern British Drama* (London: Routledge, 2007).

73. On the Reformation's effect on notions of national and transnational identity, see Jeffrey Knapp, *Shakespeare's Tribe: Church, Nation, and Theater in Renaissance England* (Chicago: University of Chicago Press, 2002); Christopher Highley, *Catholics Writing the Nation in Early Modern Britain and Ireland* (Oxford: Oxford University Press, 2008), esp. 54–79.

4. DYING COMMUNALLY: *VOLPONE* AND HOW TO GET RICH QUICK

1. The most important literary sources for the con are Horace's *Satires* 2.5, Lucian's *Dialogues of the Dead*, and Petronius's *Satyricon*. For an account of them, see Ben Jonson, *Volpone, or the Fox*, in *The Cambridge Edition of the Works of Ben Jonson*, ed. Richard Dutton (Cambridge: Cambridge University Press, 2012), 3:13. All subsequent citations of the play and other works by Jonson will be from this edition.

2. For discussions of the significance of avarice in *Volpone*, see Kathleen Eisaman Maus, "Idol and Gift in *Volpone*," *English Literary Renaissance* 35 (2005): 429–53; Oliver Hennessey, "Jonson's Joyless Economy: Theorizing Motivation and Pleasure in *Volpone*," *English Literary Renaissance* 38 (2008): 83–105.

3. In this, *Volpone* stands in pointed contrast to *The Merchant of Venice*.

4. Roberto Esposito, *Communitas: The Origin and Destiny of Community*, trans. Timothy Campbell (Stanford, CA: Stanford University Press, 2010); Roberto Esposito, *Bíos*, trans. Timothy Campbell (Minneapolis: University of Minnesota Press, 2008).

5. Jonas Barish, *The Anti-Theatrical Prejudice* (London: University of California Press, 1981), 132–54. See also Alexander Leggatt, "The Suicide of

Volpone," *University of Toronto Quarterly* 39 (1969): 19–32; Thomas M.
Greene, "Ben Jonson and the Centered Self," *Studies in English Literature* 10
(1970): 325–48; Mathew R. Martin, *Between Theater and Philosophy* (Newark:
University of Delaware Press, 2001), 23–38; Gregory Chaplin, "'Divided
amongst Themselves': Collaboration and Anxiety in Jonson's *Volpone*," *ELH*
69, no. 1 (2002): 57–81; Joseph Loewenstein, *Ben Jonson and Possessive Authorship* (Cambridge: Cambridge University Press, 2002); James P. Bednarz,
"Jonson's Literary Theatre: *Volpone* in Performance and Print (1606–1607),"
in *Volpone: A Critical Guide*, ed. Matthew Steggle (New York: Continuum:
2011), 83–104.

    6. Robert Cawdry, *A Table Alphabeticall* (London: 1609), I5v.

    7. Romans 6:23.

    8. Romans 6:5.

    9. *"Boni bene moriantur quamvis sit mors malum* [good men die a good
death although death is an evil thing]." Augustine, *The City of God against the
Pagans*, ed. and trans. Philip Levine, Loeb Classical Library 414 (Cambridge,
MA: Harvard University Press, 1998), XIII.5.

    10. Augustine, *Confessions*, ed. and trans. William Watts, Loeb Classical
Library 27 (Cambridge, MA: Harvard University Press, 1997), X.6.

    11. John Donne, *Devotions upon Emergent Occasions*, ed. Elizabeth Savage
(Salzburg: Institut für Englische Sprache, 1975), 2:123.

    12. Donne, *Devotions*, 2:130.

    13. Eamon Duffy, *The Stripping of the Altars: Traditional Religion in Eng-
land c. 1400–c. 1580* (New Haven, CT: Yale University Press, 1992), 317. For
alternative accounts of Renaissance death culture placing different emphases
on the transition from Catholicism to Protestantism, see Philippe Ariès, *The
Hour of Our Death*, trans. Helen Weaver (New York: Knopf, 1981), esp. 299–
301; Ralph Houlbrooke, *Death, Religion, and the Family in England* (Oxford:
Oxford University Press, 2000).

    14. Thomas Becon, *The Sycke Mans Salve* (London: 1561), 8. Though
The Sycke Mans Salve does have some distinctively Puritan features (most
notable in its strong condemnation of Catholic deathbed practices), the
communal deathbed it imagines is broadly consonant with that of *ars
moriendi* texts from different confessions and sects. For accounts of textual
history and spiritual orientation, see Mary Catherine O'Connor, *The Art of
Dying Well: The Development of the* Ars Moriendi (Columbia University
Press: New York, 1942), 195–96; Nancy Lee Beaty, *The Craft of Dying: A
Study of the Literary Tradition of the* Ars Moriendi *in England* (New Haven,
CT: Yale University Press, 1970), 108–156. The tract is mentioned in *Epicene*, 4.4.98–9; and *Eastward Ho*, 5.2.42–3 (see notes 25 and 27 in this
chapter).

    15. Becon, *The Sycke Mans Salve*, 539–40.

16. For example, William Perkins states that "housholders must set their families in order before they die" and gives advice derived from scripture on the proper distribution of property in *A Salve for a Sicke Man: or, a Treatise Containing the Nature, Differences and Kindes of Death* (London, 1595), 83; Christopher Sutton's *Disce Mori: Learne to Die* (London, 1600) includes a chapter on "How the sicke shoulde dispose of worldly goods and possessions." For a discussion of religious attitudes to will-making and the link between wills and the deathbed, see Lloyd Bonfield, *Devising, Dying, and Dispute* (Burlington, VT: Ashgate, 2012), 22–25.

17. Becon, *The Sycke Mans Salve*, 138–39.

18. Valuable modern histories of social and legal understanding of wills in early modern England include John Addy, *Death, Money, and the Vultures* (London: Routledge, 1992); Houlbrooke, *Death, Religion, and the Family in England*; Bonfield, *Devising, Dying, and Dispute*. Henry Swinburne, *A Brief Treatise of Testaments and Last Wills* (New York: Garland, 1978), is a useful account of testamentary law first published in 1590 and intended for a lay audience.

19. For example, in *Shelley's Case*, one of the first prominent cases to deal with perpetuities, the dispute centered on a settlement intended to ensure that property devolved to a male child likely to be born after the death of the landowner rather than to the female line. See Edward Coke, J. H Thomas, and John Farquhar Fraser, *The Reports of Sir Edward Coke, Knt.: In Thirteen Parts* (Union, NJ: Lawbook Exchange, 2003), 1 Co. Rep. 93a.

20. Becon, *The Sycke Mans Salve*, 140.

21. For a summary of early modern trends in the law of family settlements, see J. H. Baker, *An Introduction to English Legal History*, 4th ed. (London: Butterworths, 2002).

22. 10 Co. Rep. x. Speaking about the same case, Coke further describes perpetuities as "a monstrous brood carved out of mere invention, and never known to the ancient sages of the law . . . At whose solemn funeral I was present, and accompanied the dead to the grave, but mourned not."

23. This, in essence, is the argument of Maine, who sees the development of Roman testamentary law as exemplifying a universal historical shift from status to contract. Henry Sumner Maine, *Ancient Law: Its Connection with the Early History of Society and Its Relation to Modern Ideas* (New York: Charles Scribner, 1864).

24. 1 Co. Rep. 93b.

25. Ben Jonson, *Epicene*, ed. David Bevington, in *The Cambridge Edition of the Works of Ben Jonson* (Cambridge: Cambridge University Press, 2012), 3:4.4.80–84.

26. Jonson, *Epicene*, 4.4.98–9.

27. Ben Jonson, *Eastward Ho*, ed. Suzanne Gossett and W. David Kay, in *The Cambridge Edition of the Works of Ben Jonson* (Cambridge: Cambridge

University Press, 2012), 2:5.2.42–3. Admittedly, the collaborative authorship of *Eastward Ho* makes it impossible to be certain whether Jonson was directly responsible for this line.

28. Dennis Kezar, *Guilty Creatures: Renaissance Poetry and the Ethics of Authorship* (Oxford: Oxford University Press, 2001), 153–4.

29. Critics who have discussed the Venetian setting of the play and its relation to contemporary London include Jonathan Goldberg, *James I and the Politics of Literature* (Baltimore, MD: Johns Hopkins University Press, 1983), 72–80; Julie Sanders, *Ben Jonson's Theatrical Republics* (London: Macmillan, 1998), 34–46; Jonathan Gil Harris, *Sick Economies: Drama, Mercantilism, and Disease in Shakespeare's England* (Philadelphia: University of Pennsylvania Press, 2004).

30. Chaplin, "'Divided amongst Themselves,'" illuminates the differences between the two characters and what tensions within their partnership suggest about Jonson's attitudes to (especially authorial) collaboration more generally.

31. Adolf Berger, *Encyclopedic Dictionary of Roman Law* (Philadelphia: American Philosophical Society, 1953), 721.

32. Harold Skulsky discusses the pervasiveness of the cannibalism motif within the play in "Cannibals vs. Demons in *Volpone*," *Studies in English Literature* 29 (1989): 291–308.

33. For discussions of the trio in terms of monstrosity and the grotesque, see Harry Levin, "Jonson's Metempsychosis," *Philological Quarterly* 22 (1943): 231–39; Jonas Barish, "The Double Plot in *Volpone*," *Modern Philology* 51 (1953): 81–92; A. K. Nardo, "The Transmigration of Folly: *Volpone's* Innocent Grotesques," *English Studies* 58 (1977): 105–9.

34. Notably, Mosca excludes himself from this narrative of paternity, anticipating that the strategies Volpone uses to avoid obligations to the grotesques will not work on him.

35. Dutton in the *Cambridge Edition of the Works* suggests that "bauble" carries the meaning of penis here.

36. The grotesques in their opposition to conventional community and inheritance bear some resemblance to the queer in Lee Edelman, *No Future: Queer Theory and the Death Drive* (Durham, NC: Duke University Press, 2004). However, where Edelman aligns the queer with the death drive against the false promise of immortality embedded in reproductive futurity, Volpone sees death in the reproductive impulse and immortality in its refusal.

37. Maus, "Idol and Gift in *Volpone*," 438.

38. In this, she departs from Mauss, who sees gift giving paradigmatically as a collective experience. Marcel Mauss, *The Gift: The Form and Reason for Exchange in Archaic Societies*, trans. W. D. Halls (London: Routledge, 1990).

39. See Esposito, *Communitas*, 10–11. For an example of a seventeenth-century thinker focusing on the inevitable inadequacy of responses to Christ's sacrifice, see John Donne, "Deaths Duell," in *The Major Works*, ed. John Carey (Oxford: Oxford University Press, 1990), 401–17.

40. Jean-Luc Nancy, *The Inoperative Community*, ed. and trans. Peter Connor (Minneapolis: University of Minnesota Press, 1991).

41. "Immanence, communal fusion, contains no other logic than that of the suicide of the community that is governed by it." Nancy, *The Inoperative Community*, 12.

42. Esposito, *Communitas*, 5.

43. Esposito, *Communitas*, 7.

44. Esposito, *Communitas*, 13.

45. "The category of immunization is so important that it can be taken as the explicative key of the entire modern paradigm. . . . The modern individual, who assigns to every service its specific price, can no longer bear the gratitude that the gift demands." Esposito, *Communitas*, 12.

46. In particular, see Leggatt, "The Suicide of Volpone"; Greene, "Ben Jonson and the Centered Self"; and Kezar, *Guilty Creatures*. Barish (*The Anti-Theatrical Prejudice*, 154) is more willing than some of his followers to admit nuance in Jonson's relationship to the theater, seeing "an uneasy synthesis between a formal antitheatricalism, which condemns the arts of show and illusion on the one hand, and a subversive hankering after them on the other."

47. C. B. Macpherson develops the notion of possessive individualism in *The Political Theory of Possessive Individualism: Hobbes to Locke* (Oxford: Oxford University Press, 1962), 1–4. Macpherson sees its origin in the later seventeenth century. However, for suggestions that similar ideas can be found in earlier thought, see Richard Tuck, *Natural Rights Theories: Their Origin and Development* (Cambridge: Cambridge University Press, 1979); Laura Brace, *The Idea of Property in Seventeenth-Century England* (Manchester: Manchester University Press, 1998).

48. Barish, *The Anti-Theatrical Prejudice*, 132–54.

49. In particular, his behavior evokes Esposito's (*Bios*, 63–69) reading of Lockean property ownership as an immunitarian strategy.

50. Various critics have noted how Volpone loses control as he moves further from home. Sanders, drawing on Jean-Christophe Agnew, suggests that "the act of crossing the threshold of his own front door and into the Venetian community . . . threatened the integrity of any individual, and Volpone as an oligarch in disguise, as Scoto of Mantua, certainly compromises himself in this fashion." Julie Sanders, *Ben Jonson's Theatrical Republics* (London: Macmillan, 1998), 43. Baker and Harp note that Volpone's "immoral agency" fades and his vulnerability increases as he moves further from the

bedroom. Christopher Baker and Richard Harp, "Jonson's *Volpone* and Dante," *Comparative Drama* 39 (2005): 55–74.

51. Greene ("Ben Jonson and the Centered Self," 339) and Baker and Harp ("Jonson's *Volpone* and Dante," 66) discuss his fate in terms of Dantean *contrapasso*.

52. As many commentators have noted, Jonson is concerned with verisimilitude in the court scenes, and the names of the institutions are derived directly from Gasparo Contarini's *The Commonwealth and Government of Venice*, trans. Lewes Lewkenor (London, 1599). See Dutton in *The Cambridge Edition of the Works*, 3:15–16. Romano suggests that power shifted in Venetian society during the Renaissance from vertically organized, locally defined communities to citywide institutions and class identities. See Dennis Romano, *Patricians and* Populani (Baltimore, MD: Johns Hopkins University Press, 1987), 152–58. Though Jonson's knowledge of Venice is disputed, the play does seem to mirror actual, historical change in the city.

53. J. G. A. Pocock suggests this is the reason for Contarini's obsessive detailing of procedure in *The Machiavellian Moment: Florentine Political Thought and the Atlantic Republican Tradition* (Princeton, NJ: Princeton University Press, 2003), 324–25. Jonathan Goldberg also discusses Pocock's claims about Contarini in relation to *Volpone* in *James I and the Politics of Literature: Jonson, Shakespeare, Donne, and Their Contemporaries* (Baltimore, MD: Johns Hopkins University Press, 1983), 76.

54. Contarini, *The Commonwealth and Government of Venice*, 189.

55. Archivio di Stato, Venice, *Provveditori alla Sanità*, Reg. 2, folio 31r, Februrary 22, 1521, m.v., quoted in Richard Palmer, "'Ad una Sancta Perfettione': Health Care and Poor Relief in the Republic of Venice in the Era of the Counter-Reformation," in *Health Care and Poor Relief in Counter-Reformation Europe*, ed. Ole Peter Grell, Andrew Cunningham, and Jon Arrizabalaga (London: Routledge, 1999), 85–98. Also see Palmer for a wider discussion of Venetian treatment of public health.

56. Dutton, in *The Cambridge Edition of the Works*, suggests Jonson may have been influenced by Thomas Garzoni's *L'hospidale de' pazzi incurabili* (1586), which was translated into English in 1600 as *The Hospital of Incurable Fools* (5.12.120n).

57. William Ingram, *The Business of Playing: The Beginnings of the Adult Professional Theater in Elizabethan London* (Ithaca, NY: Cornell University Press, 1992), 132–33.

58. "Rather than being superimposed or juxtaposed in an external form that subjects one to the domination of the other, in the immunitary paradigm, *bios* and *nomos*, life and politics, emerge as the two constituent elements of a single, indivisible whole that assumes meaning from their interrelation." Esposito, *Bios*, 45.

59. "Mortification, n.," 1, 2, 3; "mortify, v.," 1, 6; *OED Online*. This is also discussed by Dutton, in *The Cambridge Edition of the Works*, 5.12.125n.

60. Volpone's wordplay evokes Augustine's discussion of how the peculiarity of the word *mortuus* reflects the impossibility of grasping death. The adjective *mortuus "quasi ut declinetur quod declinari non potest, pro participio praeteriti temporis ponitur nomen. Convenienter itaque factum est ut, quem ad modum id quod significant non potest agendo, ita ipsum verbum non posset loquendo declinari* [is employed in place of a past participle as if to make a tense where none can be. The result of this is, appropriately enough, that the verb itself can no more be declined by us in speech than can the act that it denotes in reality]." *City of God* XIII.11.

61. "[Each singularity] is not enclosed in a form—although its whole being touches against its singular limit—but it is what it is, singular being (singularity of being), only through its extension, through the areality that above all extroverts it in its very being—whatever the degree or the desire of its 'egoism'—and that makes it exist only by *exposing it to an outside*. This outside is in its turn nothing other than the exposition of another areality of another singularity—the same other." Nancy, *The Inoperative Community*, 29.

62. This is not to deny significant differences between Volpone's position and the ecstatic participation of the community imagined by Nancy. For one thing, Volpone may well be attempting to retain a greater sense of himself as a subject than Nancy would allow for. For another, Volpone's motivations, at least up to this point, raise questions about Nancy's implicit assumption that the inoperative community is of the left.

63. Ben Jonson, *Sejanus, His Fall*, ed. Tom Cain in *The Cambridge Edition of the Works of Ben Jonson* (Cambridge: Cambridge University Press, 2012), 2:5.790.

64. Ben Jonson, *Sejanus*, 5.804.

65. Aristotle, *Poetics*, trans. Richard Janko (Indianapolis, IN: Hackett, 1987), 49b25.

66. Richard Halpern, *Eclipse of Action: Tragedy and Political Economy* (Chicago: University of Chicago Press, 2017), 2–3.

67. Stanley Fish, "Author-Readers: Jonson's Community of the Same," *Representations* 7 (1984): 26–58.

68. See Loewenstein, *Ben Jonson and Possessive Authorship*, for a sophisticated account of the different and changing ways in which Jonson uses textual apparatus and revision to refigure plays for readers and to assert possessive authorship.

69. This terminology is from Robert Weimann, *Shakespeare and the Popular Tradition in the Theater: Studies in the Social Dimensions of Dramatic Form*

and Function (Baltimore, MD: Johns Hopkins University Press, 1987). See also Robert Weimann and Douglas Bruster, *Prologues to Shakespeare's Theater: Performance and Liminality in Early Modern Drama* (London: Routledge, 2004), for an account of the liminal qualities of prologues that in many ways is transferable to epilogues, an account that has influenced my reading.

70. In saying this, I distinguish my reading from that of Jonathan Goldberg (*James I and the Politics of Literature*, 80), who is inclined to place more emphasis on the fact of Volpone's persistence as confirming his escape from the laws.

EPILOGUE: AFTERLIFE

1. Philippe Ariès, *The Hour of Our Death*, trans. Helen Weaver (New York: Knopf, 1981), 611–14. For a more recent example of the same line of reasoning, see Carlo Leget, "Retrieving the *Ars Moriendi* Tradition," *Medicine, Healthcare, and Philosophy* 10 (2007): 313–19.

2. "I can't breathe" were Eric Garner's last words. See Oliver Laughland, Jessica Glenza, Steven Thrasher, and Paul Lewis, "'We Can't Breathe': Eric Garner's Last Words Become Protestors' Rallying Cry," *Guardian*, December 4, 2014.

3. William Perkins, *A Salve for a Sicke Man, or a Treatise Containing the Nature, Differences and Kindes of Death* (London, 1595), 61.

4. Although I lack the space to discuss them here, non-Western cultures of mortality (a subject Ariès ignores) also suggest alternative approaches to death. For instance, Lock argues that widespread resistance to organ transplants in Japan demonstrates that "the majority of Japanese live and work with ontologies of death that differ from those of North Americans." Margaret Lock, *Twice Dead: Organ Transplants and the Reinvention of Death* (Berkeley: University of California Press, 2012), 11.

5. Paul Kalanithi, *When Breath Becomes Air* (New York: Random House, 2016).

6. The Catholic Bishop's Conference of England and Wales, *The Art of Dying Well*, http://www.artofdyingwell.org.

7. "Death Positive," Caitlin Doughty, *The Order of the Good Death*, http://www.orderofthegooddeath.com/death-positive.

8. On the legal position of seventeenth-century testatrices, see Lucinda Becker, *Death and the Early Modern Englishwoman* (Burlington, VT: Ashgate, 2003), 151–66.

9. Ferdinand admits that he "had a hope/Had she continued widow, to have gained/An infinite mass of treasure by her death." John Webster, *The Duchess of Malfi and Other Plays*, ed. René Weis (Oxford: Oxford University Press, 2009), 4.2.275–77. Subsequent references will be given parenthetically.

10. Although the primary connotation of "mummy" here is undoubtedly human flesh used for medicinal purposes, the *OED* records "mammy" as a word for "mother" as early as 1523, and "mum" in 1595. "Mammy, n.," definition 1a; "mum, n.², " definition a, *OED Online.*

11. For instance, Adelman reads Shakespeare's maternal grotesques through a psychoanalytic lens as projections of the male child's desire to separate himself from the mother. Janet Adelman, *Suffocating Mothers: Fantasies of Maternal Origin in Shakespeare's Plays*, Hamlet *to* The Tempest (New York: Routledge, 1992), 77.

12. John Donne, "Deaths Duell," in *The Major Works*, ed. John Carey (Oxford: Oxford University Press, 1990), 403.

13. Donne, "Deaths Duell," 408.

14. Donna Haraway, "The Biopolitics of Postmodern Bodies: Constructions of Self in Immune System Discourse," reprinted in *Biopolitics: A Reader*, ed. Timothy Campbell and Adam Sitze (Durham, NC: Duke University Press, 2013), 282–83.

15. Roberto Esposito, *Immunitas: The Protection and Negation of Life*, trans. Zakiya Hanafi (Cambridge: Polity, 2011), 170–71.

16. Thomas Goad, "Approbation," to Elizabeth Jocelin, *The Mother's Legacie, to her Unborn Childe* (London: 624), A9v. Further references will be given parenthetically.

17. Precisely how dangerous is disputed by historians. Analyzing the records of three early modern Somerset parishes, Willmott Dobbie estimates somewhere between 24.4 and 29.4 maternal deaths for every thousand baptisms. B. M. Willmott Dobbie, "An Attempt to Estimate the True Rate of Maternal Mortality, Sixteenth to Eighteenth Centuries," *Medical History* 26 (1982): 79–90. However, more recently, Allison has claimed six East Anglian parishes experienced only around 7.5 deaths for every thousand birth events between 1539 and 1619 Julia Allison, "Maternal Mortality in Six East Anglian Parishes, 1539–1619," *Local Population Studies* 94, no. 1 (2015): 11–27.

18. Lucinda M. Becker, *Death and the Early Modern Englishwoman* (Burlington, VT: Ashgate, 2003), 34–35; Ralph Houlbrooke, *Death, Religion, and the Family in England* (Oxford: Oxford University Press, 2000), 68.

19. Wendy Wall, "Isabella Whitney and the Female Legacy," *ELH* 58, no. 1 (1991): 45.

20. Teresa Feroli, "Infelix Simulacrum: The Rewriting of Loss in Elizabeth Jocelin's *The Mothers Legacie*," *ELH* 61, no. 1 (1994): 97.

21. See Ian Watt, *The Rise of the Novel: Studies in Defoe, Richardson, and Fielding* (Berkeley: University of California Press, 1957), 217–19.

22. Nancy Armstrong, *Desire and Domestic Fiction: A Political History of the Novel* (Oxford: Oxford University Press, 1987), esp. 108–34.

23. See Margaret Anne Doody, *A Natural Passion: A Study of the Novels of Samuel Richardson* (Oxford: Clarendon, 1974), 151–87; Laura Baudot, "'Spare Thou My Rosebud:' Interiority and Baroque Death in Richardson's *Clarissa*," *Literary Imagination* 7, no. 2 (2015): 153–79.

24. Samuel Richardson, *Clarissa* (London: Penguin, 1985), 1002. Subsequent references will be given parenthetically.

25. Baudot, "'Spare Thou My Rosebud,'" 158–59.

26. Wendy Beth Hyman persuasively argues that intellectual iconoclasm of the sort Lovelace displays is a constitutive rather than a contingent feature of early modern *carpe diem* writing. See her *Impossible Desire and the Limits of Knowledge in Renaissance Poetry* (Oxford: Oxford University Press, 2019).

27. Sandra Macpherson, *Harm's Way: Tragic Responsibility and the Novel Form* (Baltimore, MD: Johns Hopkins University Press, 2010), 63.

28. Stephanie Insley Hershinow, "Clarissa's Conjectural History: The Novel and the Novice," *The Eighteenth Century* 56, no. 3 (2015): 308–9.

29. Again, the novel draws attention to this lacuna. Confronted with John Harlowe's query, "if you have any reason to think yourself with child by this villain," Clarissa responds, "a little, a very little time, will better answer than I can" (1192–93). Yet her plans for her funeral refuse her mourners the sort of access to her body that could supply the answer.

30. Jonathan Kramnick, *Actions and Objects from Hobbes to Richardson* (Stanford, CA: Stanford University Press, 2010), 296–298n.

31. Terry Castle, *Clarissa's Ciphers: Meaning and Disruption in Richardson's* Clarissa (Ithaca, NY: Cornell University Press, 1982), 32–37.

32. Jolene Zigarovich, "Courting Death: Necrophilia in Samuel Richardson's *Clarissa*," *Studies in the Novel* 32, no. 2 (2000): 112–28.

33. Ann Louise Kibbie, "The Estate, the Corpse, and the Letter: Posthumous Possession in *Clarissa*," *ELH* 74, no. 1 (2007): 117–43.

34. Kramnick, *Actions and Objects*, 219–30.

35. David Bowie, "Lazarus," video (ISO and Columbia, 2015).

36. Simon Critchley, *On Bowie* (London: Serpent's Tail, 2016), 180.

37. Ryan Dombal, "David Bowie: *Blackstar*," *Pitchfork*, January 7, 2015, http://pitchfork.com/reviews/albums/21332-blackstar.

38. Tony Visconti, January 11, 2016, https://www.facebook.com/tony.visconti1/posts/10208522003550232.

39. Chris Roberts, "Time May Change Me: David Bowie, *Blackstar*, and Mortality," *The Quietus*, January 14, 2016, http://thequietus.com/articles/19533-david-bowie-blackstar-lyrics-death.

40. Visconti, quoted in Brian Hiatt, "The Final Years," *Rolling Stone*, February 11, 2016. Other sources suggest Bowie learned his cancer had

returned during the filming of "Lazarus." See *David Bowie: The Last Five Years*, dir. Francis Whately (BBC, 2017), TV.

41. Paul Morely is notably more cautious, saying only that Bowie "must have considered it as a serious possibility" that *Blackstar* "would be taken once he died as a goodbye." Paul Morely, *The Age of Bowie* (New York: Gallery, 2016), 37–38.

42. Critchley, *On Bowie*, 180, 177–78.

43. For a discussion of Bowie's manipulation of notions of surface and authenticity through personae and interviews, see Bethany Usher and Stephanie Fremaux, "Turn Myself to Face Me: David Bowie in the 1990s and Discovery of Authentic Self," in *David Bowie: Critical Perspectives*, ed. Eoin Devereux, Aileen Dillane, and Martin J. Power (New York: Routledge, 2015), 56–81.

44. Quoted in Kathryn Johnson, "David Bowie Is," in *David Bowie: Critical Perspectives*, ed. Eoin Devereux, Aileen Dillane, and Martin J. Power (New York: Routledge, 2015), 1.

45. For readings of Bowie in terms of the simulacrum, see Usher and Fremaux, "Turn Myself to Face Me"; and Tiffany Naiman, "Art's Filthy Lesson," in *David Bowie: Critical Perspectives*, ed. Eoin Devereux, Aileen Dillane, and Martin J. Power (New York: Routledge, 2015), 178–95.

46. Izaak Walton, *The Life of John Donne* (London: 1658), 112–13.

47. Ramie Targoff, *John Donne: Body and Soul* (Chicago: University of Chicago Press, 2008), 181.

48. Helen Gardner, "Dean Donne's Monument in St. Paul's," in *Evidence in Literary Scholarship: Essays in Honor of James Marshall Osborn* (Oxford: Clarendon, 1979), 29–44.

49. In the days after the singer's death, a Welsh medic wrote a widely shared post on a *British Medical Journal* blog, which discussed his therapeutic use of Bowie's music and biography in counseling terminal patients. See Mark Taubert, "A Thank You Letter to David Bowie from a Palliative Care Doctor," *BMJ Supportive and Palliative Care Blog*, January 15, 2016, http://blogs.bmj.com/spcare/2016/01/15/a-thank-you-letter-to-david-bowie-from-a-palliative-care-doctor.

INDEX

I. Outside (Bowie), 161

abdication, 28, 61–62, 74, 81, 103, 106, 111–12
Abel, 113, 116
"Act to Restrain the Abuses of Players," 33
actors: and death, 3, 76, 79, 82–84, 122, 134–35; and political representation, 110
Acts and Monuments (Foxe), 18, 22, 41, 126
Agamben, Giorgio; on bare life, 20, 66–67, 85, 90, 176n53; on *forma vitae*, 20–21, 48–49; on Kantorowicz, 57; on modernity, 176n54; on parody, 32, 35–36, 180n29
Anatomy of Abuses (Stubbes), 34–35
Anderson, Thomas P., 79, 82–83
antitheatricality, 33, 35, 52, 133–34
Antony and Cleopatra (Shakespeare), 117–18, 143
Appleford, Amy, 13, 97, 172n18, 192n25
Arendt, Hannah, 19, 90–91, 190n6; on origin of modernity, 176n54
Ariès, Philippe, 28, 147, 159
Aristotle, 143
Armstrong, Nancy, 155
Art of Dying Well, The (website), 148
artes moriendi (arts of dying), 8–19, *11*, 21–22, 24–26, 37–38, 42, 48, 51–52, 55, 64, 75–76, 123–25, 140, 144, 148, 155–56, 159, 162–64, 167–68; gendering of, 148, 159; and the imitation of Christ 14–15, 97; and phenomenology, 15–17; and Stoicism, 12–14; and Ben Jonson, 126–27; and Protestantism, 8–9, 37
Atheist's Tragedy, The (Tourneur), 14
Augustine, on Christ's death, 99; on Christian community, 122; on evil, 32; on death, 183n61, 202n60; on Lucretia, 5

Baker, Christopher, 201n50
Bakhtin, Mikhail, 35–36, 180n29, 182n48
Barish, Jonah, 121, 133–34, 200n46
Barthes, Roland, 161
Baudot, Laura, 157
Baudrillard, Jean, 161
Bayless, Marta, 34
Beard, Thomas, 41
beauty, 45–46
Becket, Thomas (saint), 18, 113
Bede, 196n70
Benjamin, Walter, 2, 84
Berger, Harry, 112
Bersani, Leo, 27
betrayal, 105–7, 110–11
Bevington, David, 38
Biathanatos (Donne), 13
Bible. *See individual books*
Bilney, Thomas, 100–1
Black Lives Matter, 148
Blackstar (Bowie), 160–62, 167, 206n41
blasphemy, 35, 51; in *Doctor Faustus*, 42–44, 47, 52
Blau, Herbert, 3
blood, 44, 49, 51–52, 66–68, 71–72, 76–77, 107, 115–16, 183–184n2, 195n62
Bodin, Jean, 56
body, 48–49, 76, 78, 83–84, 100, 129, 132, 134–35, 139–41, 158–59, 162, 165, 183n62; of Christ, 12, 14, 95–96, 102, 106, 122, 187n35; gendered as female, 150–52; of the sovereign, 57, 65–67, 74, 89, 104, 115, 195n62. *See also* corpse
Bolingbroke, Henry (King Henry IV), 103–4
Borlase, Edmond, 185n17
Bowie, David, 159–62, *160*, 167–68; and *ars moriendi*, 167; and Donne, 167; and *memento mori*, 167; personae of, 161; reviews of, 160–61. *See also individual works*

Bray, Alan, 55, 86, 186n24
burial, 5, 118, 150–51, 153, 164

Cahill, Patricia, 20
Cain, 113, 116
Calvin, John, 32, 41, 178n4
Campana, Joseph, 24, 185n11
carpe diem, 157
Castle, Terry, 158
Catholicism, 9, 22, 37, 97–98; and saints 17–18
charity, 29–40, 123–24, 130, 143–44
Charles I (King), 56
Cheney, Patrick, 79
Christ: body of, 12, 14, 95–96, 102, 106, 122; imitation of, 7, 14–15, 18, 27–28, 88–89, 95–103, 113, 131; as a model for kingship, 88, 107; Passion of, 95–96, 99, 105–6, 113, 117
Chronicles of England, Scotland and Ireland (Holinshed), 24, 69, 103–4, 107
Clarissa (Richardson), 29, 155–59, 164
coffins, 79–80, 84, 157–58
Coke, Edward, 125–26, 198n22
Collison, Patrick, 114
comedy, 38, 41, 117–18, 122, 142–43
community, 28, 121, 128–33; Christian conceptions of, 12, 21–22, 122–24, 129, 157; Esposito's understanding of, 21–22, 101–2, 132–33; and literature, 141–44
Conflict of Conscience, The (Woodes), 26, 32, 41–42, parody in, 41–42, reprobation in, 41
Confutation of Tyndale's Answer, The (More), 100
Contarini, Gasparo, 139, 201n52
I Corinthians, 99
corpse, 75–79, 82–83, 94–95, 115–16, 142, 151, 158, 162, 183n60
coverture, 148–49, 153
Cowell, John, 58
Craft and Knowledge for to Dye Well, The, 8
Crewe, Jonathan, 186n24
Critchley, Simon, 160–61
crown, the: and the body politic, 57; as a corporation, 56–57; disherison of, 59, 187n27; as perpetual minor, 57–58. *See also* sovereignty
Cummings, Brian, 100
Curratt, John, 100–1

Daniel, Drew, 117
danse macabre, 93–95, *94*, 143
de Grazia, Margreta, 59, 172n17
death: Augustine's understanding of 183n61, 202n60; and community, 132–33; as a king, 92–93, 191n13; medicalization of, 148; non-Western attitudes to, 203n4; phenomenology of, 15–17; and sovereignty, 59–61, 67, 71, 76–77, 81–82, 84–85; secularization of, 148. *See also artes moriendi*
Death Positive Movement, 148
"Deaths Duell" (Donne), 150–51, 154, 162, 200n39
demise: Heidegger's concept of, 15, 174n41; Plowden's concept of, 64, 69, 74, 78, 80, 85, 103–4, 113
Derrida, Jacques, 91
Dessen, Alan, 80
devotio moderna, 96
Devotions on Emergent Occasions (Donne), 122–23
DiGangi, Mario, 61
Digby, John, 185n17
digital media, 148
Doctor Faustus (Marlowe), 19, 31–33, 42–53; and antitheatricality, 52; and *ars moriendi*, 48, 50–52; beauty in, 45–46; blasphemy in, 42–44, 47, 52; blood in, 44, 51–52; deed of gift in, 49, 51–52; differences between A and B texts, 42, 177n1; hell in, 49; and homiletic tragedy, 53; lack of divine presence in, 31–32, 43; *memento mori* in, 46; parody in, 42–47, 49, 52–53; predestination in, 179n7; salvation in, 43–44; time in, 49–50
doctrine of coverture, 148–49
Dombal, Ryan, 160–61
Donne, John: and *ars moriendi*, 163–64; on charity, 123; on community, 122–23; and *memento mori*, 163–64; portrait of, 162–64, *163*, 167; on pregnancy, 150–51, 154; preparations for death of, 162–64, 167. *See also individual works*
Doughty, Caitlin, 148
dreams, 75–76
Droushout, Martin, 162–64
Duchess of Malfi, The (Webster), 149–50, 189n61
dynasty, 59. *See also* succession

Eastward Ho (Jonson), 126–28, 156

Edelman, Lee, 27, 58, 186n25, 188n50, 199n36

Edward II (Marlowe), 23–24, 27, 54–56, 59–86, 118; abdication in, 61–62, 81; and *ars moriendi*, 64, 75; blood in, 66, 72, 77; coffin in, 79–80, 84; crown in, 56, 60, 79; demise in, 69, 74, 78, 80, 85; dreams in, 75–76; execution in, 67, 70, 78–79, 81–83; funeral in, 79–84; hearse in, 77, 79–80, 82–83, 85; marriage in, 55, 61, 81–82; martyrdom in, 71–75; maternity in, 81–82; perpetuity in, 54–55, 60, 73, 76, 79, 84; regicide in, 60, 63–64, 67–70, 73–77, 85; republicanism in, 79; sleep in, 73–76; sodomy in, 24, 55, 60–61, 65, 69–70, 76; sovereign mortality in, 27–28, 56, 59–61, 63, 67–68, 71, 76–77, 81–82, 84–85; sovereignty in, 63, 65–66, 69, 71, 74, 76–77, 79, 82–84, 86; stage directions in, 24, 69, 77, 80; stage props in, 69, 80, 83–84; succession in, 60–64, 69–70, 77, 79, 81; suicide in, 68; and theater, 76, 79–80, 82–86; and the theory of the king's two bodies, 65–66, 78; and tragedy, 71–72

effigy, 79, 82–84

Elizabeth I (Queen), 56, 59

Enough Is as Good as a Feast (Wager) 26, 32–33, 35, 38–41; parody in, 40–41; reprobation in, 39–41; will-making in, 39–40

Epicene (Jonson), 126–28

Erasmus, Saint, 17

Esposito, Roberto, 107; on biopolitics, 140; on community, 20–22, 101–2, 132, 141; on immunity, 132, 140–41, 152–53; on the *munus*, 21, 101, 121, 132–33; on pregnancy, 152–53

Essex Rebellion, The, 113

Eucharist, the, 96, 129

Every Man in His Humour (Jonson), 34

Everyman, 38

exception, the, 23

execution, 23; in *Edward II*, 67, 70, 78–79, 81–83; in *Richard II*, 106; in *Sejanus, His Fall*, 142

Faerie Queene (Spenser), 24, 187n35

Feroli, Teresa, 153–54

Filmer, Robert, 59

Fish, Stanley, 144

Fletcher, Angus, 181n33

Foucault, Michel, 19–20; on biopolitics, 175n50, 183n2, 191n9; on modernity, 176n54

Foxe, John, 18, 22, 41

Franciscans, 21, 48–49

fraud, 121, 128, 133–37

free will, 32–33, 37, 178n2

Freud, Sigmund, 2, 171n1

funerals, 79–80, 84, 118, 156–57

Garber, Marjorie, 68, 106

Gardner, Helen, 162–63

ghosts, 2–4, 91–92, 113, 116, 119, 188n50

Giancarlo, Matthew, 108–9

gift giving, 105, 131–32

Goad, Thomas, 153

Goldberg, Jonathan, 61, 81, 186n24, 203n70

Golden Legend, The (Jacobus de Voragine), 24, 97, 177n63

Grady, Hugh, 171n1

Greenblatt, Stephen, 22, 111

Greenes Groats-Worth of Wit, 126

Hadfield, Andrew, 69–70

Hales, Sir James, 172n14

Halpern, Richard, 56, 143

Hamlet (Shakespeare), 2–8, 73, 81, 91

Hammill, Graham, 51

Haraway, Donna, 151–52

Harp, Richard, 201n50

Harriss, G. L. 108

hearse, 77, 79–80, 82–83, 85, 189n62

Heidegger, Martin: on death, 15–17; on demise, 174n41

Henry V (Shakespeare), 113

Henry VI (King), 113

Henry VII (King), 59

Hershinow, Stephanie, 157

HIV/AIDS, 164–65

Hobbes, Thomas, 67, 113

Holbein, Hans, 94

homiletic tragedy, 38, 51, 53, 142

hospitals, 138–40

humanism: and notions of parody, 34; and the reception of Stoicism, 13

Hyman, Wendy Beth, 205n26

Imitatio Christi, (Kempis), 96–97

immortality, 130

immunization: in *Clarissa*, 157; in *Volpone*, 132, 135, 140–41, 143
incurabili, 138–40, 143
Ingram, William, 139
inheritance. *See* wills
Interpreter, The (Cowell), 58, 185nn15,16
Irwin, Terrance, 174n36

Jewel, John, 18
Jocelin, Elizabeth, 153
John's Gospel 99
Jonson, Ben: antitheatricality of, 121, 200n46; and *ars moriendi*, 126–27; and authorship, 202n68; on comedy, 142; and satire, 127–28. *See also individual works*
Judas, 28, 100, 105–7, 110–13, 116
Julius Caesar (Shakespeare), 14

Kalanithi, Paul, 148
Kantorowicz, Ernst: on Christological models of kingship, 88; on perpetuity, 57–58; on theory of the king's two bodies, 57–60, 78
Kempis, Thomas á, 96–97
Kezar, Dennis, 127, 173n, 176n62
Kibbie, Ann Louise, 158–59
Knight of the Burning Pestle, The (Beaumont), 122
Kottman, Paul, 20
Kramnick, Jonathan, 158–59
Kuzner, James, 24

Lake, Peter, 9
"Lazarus" (Bowie), 159–60, 162, 167
Levinas, Emmanuel, 15–17
libertinism, 156–57
Livy, 5
Loraux, Nicole, 3
Lowenstein, Joseph, 202n68
Lucian; *Dialogues of the Dead*, 46, 182n57
Lucretia, 5
Luis-Martínez, Zenón, 93, 95
Lunney, Ruth, 42
Lupset, Thomas, 13
Lupton, Julia, 23, 171n1, 185n11
Luther, Martin, 32, 181n39; on free will, 178n4

Macbeth (Shakespeare), 73, 93
Macpherson, C. B., 200n47
Macpherson, Sandra, 157
Mark's Gospel 7, 10–11, 96

Marlowe, Christopher: as depicted in the Baines note, 35; and Protestantism, 51; on tragedy, 52. *See also individual works*
marriage, 4, 55–56, 81–82, 149, 187n25
martyrdom, 18–19, 22–24, 27, 99–101; in *Edward II*, 71–75; in *Richard II*, 88, 115
Mary, 117–18, 166
Mary Portington's Case, 125
maternity, 81–82, 117, 149, 150, 153–54, 204n17
Matthew's Gospel, 130
Maus, Katherine Eisaman, 59, 131–32
Mauss, Marcel, 131
Mbembe, Achille, 175n52
Measure for Measure (Shakespeare), 122
medicalization, 148
memento mori, 3, 46, 94–95, 150, 163–65, 167–68, 182–83n57
Merchant of Venice, The (Shakespeare), 129
Merchant, W. Moelwyn, 63
Midsummer Night's Dream, A (Shakespeare), 93, 122
Miracles of Henry VI, The, 17
modernity, 8, 19, 132, 136, 143, 147, 176n54
Modus Tenendi Parliamentum, 108–9
More, Thomas, 100–1
Mothers Legacie, The (Jocelin), 29, 153–55
mourning, 2–4, 8
murder, 64, 67, 70–78. *See also* regicide

Nancy, Jean-Luc, 132–33, 141, 202n62
negative theology, 180n28; parody as a, 32
Neill, Michael, 12–13, 49

O'Connor, Mary Catherine, 173n19
Orgel, Stephen, 69
Origen, 196n70
Othello (Shakespeare), 129

palliative care, 206n49
Parker, John, 45, 182n53
Parliament, 89, 103–11, 114; historical development of, 107–9
parody, 32–36; Agamben on, 36; Bakhtin on, 35; in *Doctor Faustus*, 42–47, 49, 52–53; and homiletic tragedy, 40–42; Scaliger on, 34
Parris, Benjamin, 73
Passion, The. *See* Christ
paternity, 8, 60, 62, 78–79, 81, 87, 129, 154
patriarchy, 5, 59–60, 81, 87, 149, 152

Patterson, Annabel, 108
Paul (Apostle), 12, 95; on community, 122; on imitation of Christ, 96, 99; on the Passion, 101–2
Perkins, William, 9–12, 14, 148
perpetuity (aspect of sovereignty), 56–60; in *Edward II*, 54–55, 60, 73, 76, 79, 84. *For testamentary clause see* wills
Perry, Curtis, 186n24, 187n26
Petrarch, 13
Phelan, Peggy, 3
Philippians, 12
Pilate, 28, 100, 107, 113
Plato, 35–36
Plowden, Edmund: *Commentaries*, 57, 64; on dynasty, 186n19; and *Edward II*, 78; *Treatise of Succession*, 186n19
Pocock, J. G. A., 201n53
Poole, Kristen, 173n26
possessive individualism, 134, 136, 147, 149
prayer, 9, 11–12, 37, 41, 111, 153
predestination, 33, 37–38; in the A-text of *Doctor Faustus*, 177n1; different varieties of, 181n42; in *Enough Is as Good as a Feast*, 39–40
pregnancy, 149–55
Protestantism, 18, 22, 32–33, 37, 41; and *ars moriendi*, 9, 37; and the imitation of Christ, 97–99; and Marlowe, 51; and the rise of the novel, 155; and saints, 18, 115–16
Psalms, 63
Pseudo-Dionysius the Aeropagite, 180n28
Pye, Christopher, 105, 111
Pythagoras; idea of metempsychosis, 48, 130

rape, 155–58
Rayner, Alice, 3, 191n10
Rede, Edward, 100–1
regicide: in *Edward II*, 54–56, 60, 63–64, 67–70, 73–77, 85; in *Richard II*, 90, 114–16. *See also* murder
Reinhardt, Kenneth, 171n1
Reinis, Austra, 173n18
reprobation, 39–41
republicanism, 79, 113–14, 184n5
Revenge of Bussy D'Ambois (Chapman), 14
Richard II (King), 103–4
Richard II (Shakespeare), 87–95, 102–19, 195n62; abdication in, 103, 106, 111–12; betrayal in, 105–7, 110–11; blood in, 115–16; demise in, 113; ghosts in, 91–92,

113, 116, 119; imitation of Christ in, 88–89, 106–7, 110–14; martyrdom in, 88, 115; Parliament in, 89, 105–11, 114; regicide in, 90–91, 114–16; saints in, 115–16; sovereignty in, 88–90, 92, 107
Richardson, Samuel, 155–56, 159
Roach, Joseph, 3
Roberts, Chris, 161
Rogers, Thomas, on translation of *Imitatio Christi*, 97–98, 115–16, 192n27, 193n32
Rose, Margaret, 34
Rules and Exercises of Holy Dying, The (Taylor), 155–56, 159
Rutkoski, Marie, 188n46

sacrament, the. *See* Eucharist
saints, 22; Catholic cults of, 17–18, 115; Lupton's concept of a citizen-saint, 23–24; Protestant condemnation of Catholic, 18, 115–16
salvation, 43–44
Salve for a Sicke Man, A (Perkins), 9–12, 14, 148
Sanders, Julie, 200n50
Santner, Eric, 20
satire, 127–28
Scaliger, J. C., 8, 34
Scarry, Elaine, 9, 173n25
Schmitt, Carl, 177n65
Schneider, Rebecca, 3
Schoenfeldt, Michael, 187n35
Schwarz, Regina, 191n18
secularization, 2, 46, 84, 136, 148
Sejanus, His Fall (Jonson), 142–43
Seneca, 12–13, 131
Shakespeare, William, 24. *See also individual works*
Shelley's Case, 126, 198n19
sickness, 10–11, 14, 37, 57, 123–24, 135, 139–40, 148, 165–66
skulls, 2, 46–47, 93–95, 162, 167
sleep, 73–76
Smith, Adam, 143
Snow, Edward A., 43
sodomy, 24, 55, 60–61, 69–70, 76
soul, 10, 31, 44–45, 47–51, 115–16, 130, 183n61
sovereignty, 27–28, 56–61, 63, 65–68, 76–77, 79, 81–86, 87–92, 104, 107, 117; as Christological, 88, 107; and death, 27–28, 56, 59–61, 63, 67, 76–77, 81–82, 84–85, 92; and sleep, 73–74

Spanish Tragedy, The (Kyd), 14
Spiera, Francesco, 41
Stachniewski, John, 44
stage props, 69, 80, 83–84
Stoicism, 12–14, 174n36
Stubbes, Philip, 34–36
Stymeist, David, 65
succession, 56; in Edward II, 60–64, 69–70, 77, 79, 81
suicide, 4–5, 68, 99, 117, 68; and Christianity, 5, 13; and Stoicism, 13–14, 174n36
Sycke Mans Salve, The (Becon), 39, 123–25, 133, 156, 197n14

Targoff, Ramie, 162
Taylor, Carman, 174n41
Taylor, Jeremy, 155–56, 159
theory of the king's two bodies, 57–60
Thomson, Leslie, 80
"Tis Pity She Was a Whore" (Bowie), 167
torture, 54, 79
Tractatus Artis Bene Moriendi, 8, 10, 13, 97, 148
tragedy, 2, 38, 42, 52, 71–72, 122, 143
transi tombs, 94–95

Venice, 128, 139–40, 201n52
Visconti, Tony, 161
Volpone (Jonson), 28, 114, 120–22, 128–47, 149–50; and antitheatricality, 121, 133–34; *ars moriendi* in, 138; charity in, 130; as comedy, 142–43; community in, 28, 121, 128–31, 133, 135–38, 141–44, 146–47; law court in, 137–40; fraud in, 121, 128, 133–37; gift-giving in, 130–32; hospitals in, 138–40; immortality in, 130; immunization in, 132, 135, 140–41, 143; institutions in, 138–39, 145; and theatrical performance, 121, 133–34, 144–45; wills in, 129–30

Wager, William, 32–33, 38–41, 51
Wall, Wendy, 153
Walton, Izaak, 162–64
Watson, Robert N., 173n32
Watt, Ian, 155
Webster, John, 82, 149
Weimann, Robert, 145
Wilke, Hannah, 165–68, *166*
wills, 126, 129–30; as charitable, 124–25; and perpetuities, 125, 198n22; as religious documents, 39, 153; of women, 149–50, 153, 158
Wilson, Luke, 172n14
winding sheets, 150, 153–54, 162–64
Wojnarowicz, David, 164–68, *165*
Woodes, Nathaniel, 41–42, 53

Zigarovich, Jolene, 158
Zimmerman, Susan, 83, 171n1

ABOUT THE AUTHOR

Maggie Vinter is Assistant Professor of English at Case Western Reserve University.